# THE PRESS GANG

# The Press Gang
*Naval impressment and its opponents in Georgian Britain*

Nicholas Rogers

continuum

Continuum UK, The Tower Building, 11 York Road, London SE1 7NX
Continuum US, 80 Maiden Lane, Suite 704, New York, NY 10038

*www.continuumbooks.com*

Copyright © Nicholas Rogers 2007

All rights reserved. No part of this publication may be reproduced or transmitted in any form or by any means, electronic or mechanical, including photocopying, recording or any information storage or retrieval system, without prior permission from the publishers.

First published 2007

British Library Cataloguing-in-Publication Data
A catalogue record for this book is available from the British Library.

ISBN 978 1 85285 568 0 (hbk)
ISBN 978 1 84714 468 3 (pbk)

Typeset by Pindar New Zealand (Egan Reid), Auckland, New Zealand
Printed and bound in Great Britain by Biddles Ltd, Kings Lynn, Norfolk

# Contents

| | | |
|---|---|---|
| | Illustrations | vii |
| | Acknowledgements | ix |
| 1 | Introduction | 1 |
| 2 | Impressment and the Law | 17 |
| 3 | Resisting the Press Gang: Trends, Patterns, Dynamics | 37 |
| 4 | Spotlight on Two Ports: Bristol and Liverpool | 59 |
| 5 | Manning the Navy in the Mid-century Atlantic | 81 |
| 6 | The Navy and the Nation 1793–1820 | 103 |
| | Epilogue | 127 |
| | Notes | 139 |
| | Index | 165 |

## *Illustrations*

### *Figures*

| | | |
|---|---|---|
| 1 | Affrays 1739–1748 | 43 |
| 2 | Affrays 1755–1762 | 43 |
| 3 | Affrays 1776–1782 | 44 |
| 4 | Affrays 1793–1801 | 44 |
| 5 | Women opposing the press gang, 1779 | 51 |
| 6 | Chelsea pensioners reading the Waterloo dispatch | 102 |

### *Table*

| | | |
|---|---|---|
| 1 | The geography of impressment affrays, 1739–1805 | 55 |

## *Acknowledgements*

In writing this book I have incurred many debts. The Faculty of Arts at York University awarded me a leave fellowship to begin this project a decade ago, and the Social Science and Humanities Research Council of Canada provided me with the initial funding. Subsequently fellowships at the Huntington Library, California and at the Humanities Research Center at the Australian National University, Canberra, in 2001 gave me the opportunity to discuss and hone my ideas on the subject of naval impressment. I would particularly like to thank the directors of research there at that time, Roy Ritchie and Iain McCalman, for their hospitality and for making my time at those sun-blessed locations so pleasant. In the greyer climes of London, where much of the archival research was done, I benefitted from the fact that my sister, Sally Powell, and her husband, Iain Coleman, offered a warm welcome, good cheer and free accommodation. Perhaps the free accommodation delayed the completion of this book, but I would like to attribute its long gestation to the fact that the potential documentary material at the National Archives was vast; as far as the Admiralty records go, almost an historical 'black-hole'. I also discovered a cache of historical evidence in the Caribbean naval stations and associated Colonial Office records that took me on other tacks, the fruits of which I hope to publish in the near future.

Although the Admiralty records formed the backbone of this study, I also consulted relevant archival collections at the Huntington Library in San Marino, California, and at the William L. Clements Library at the University of Michigan, Ann Arbor. Closer to home, the Mills Library at McMaster University, the Stauffer Library at Queen's University and the Robarts Library at the University of Toronto gave me access to important pamphlet and newspaper collections. While much of the pamphlet literature is now available electronically, this is still not true of the newspapers, a critical source for this study, and I am fortunate that the golden horseshoe of southern Ontario has one of the best collections of eighteenth-century newspapers in North America. I thank all the librarians and archivists for their help, particularly the librarians at Robarts Microtext, who have always handled my enquiries with unfailing courtesy and efficiency.

An earlier version of Chapter 2 appeared as a chapter in Norma Landau (ed.), *Law, Crime and English Society 1660–1830* (Cambridge: Cambridge University Press, 2002). Parts of Chapter 5 and 6 draw on essays I wrote in Felicity A.

Nussbaum (ed.), *The Global Eighteenth Century* (Baltimore and London: The Johns Hopkins University Press, 2003) and in Mark Philp (ed.), *Resisting Napoleon: The British Response to the Threat of Invasion 1797–1815* (Aldershot: Ashgate, 2006). I thank the publishers for permission to excerpt from these essays. I also thank the National Portrait Gallery, London, and the Victoria and Albert Image Library for my two illustrations, namely James Gillray, *The Library of the Subject* (1777) and David Wilkie, *The Chelsea Pensioners Reading the Gazette of the Battle of Waterloo* (1822), the last of which is a reproduction of the painting in the Wellington Collection, Apsley House, London.

On a more personal note, I should like to acknowledge the help of a number of then graduate students who helped me with my research, namely Jennine Hurl-Eamon, Adele Perry, Stephen Moore and Catherine Thompson. Other historians have thoughtfully pushed references my way. They include Donna Andrew, John Beattie, Clare Brant, Jeff Chamberlain, James Epstein, Susan Foote, Douglas Hay, Joanna Innes, Andrea McKenzie, Jeanette Neeson, Steve Poole, Tom Malcomson and David A. Wilson. Daniel Baugh deserves a special mention for encouraging me with this project and for handing over some of his own notes on mid-century impressment and naval policy. John Bohstedt generously sent me his own file of anti-recruitment riots for the late eighteenth century, which offered some good leads into other material as well as adding to my own roster of anti-impressment affrays. Dorothy Thompson brought to my attention Elizabeth Gaskell's novel, *Sylvia's Lovers*, which became central to my epilogue. To all of them I am greatly indebted.

Aspects of this book were presented to audiences in Britain, North America and Australia. They include conferences at Oxford, the University of the West of England, York University, Toronto, St Mary's University, Halifax, Nova Scotia, and the Pacific Coast branch of the Conference of British Studies. Talks were also given to seminars at the Institute of Historical Research, London, the University of Warwick, the University of Tacoma, Puget Sound, the Toronto legal history group, Griffith University, Brisbane, and the Humanities Research Center, ANU, Canberra. I thank the audiences for their constructive criticism and feedback.

Two of my departmental colleagues, Jeanette Neeson and Douglas Hay, read over the last draft and saved me from some egregious errors and well as prompting me to clarify aspects of the argument. Another York colleague, Brenda McComb, passed her critical eye over the epilogue. I thank the three of them for helping to polish the final version. At Continuum, Ben Hayes and Slav Todorov have been efficient and helpful in bringing this book to press.

I was born and bred in Bristol and knew about press-gangs from an early age. One of my relatives by marriage, Peter Simpkins, was a pilot on the river Avon. My grandfather, Gilbert Thomas, spent many hours at Avonmouth as a representative of the National Union of Seamen. On my paternal side, some of my distant relatives hailed from Clutton, then part of the North Somerset coalfield, in the eighteenth century a seamen's sanctuary from the Bristol press-gangs. Not all history books are about roots, but in a small, oblique way this one is.

*In memory of my grandfather, Gilbert Thomas,* MBE, *who joined the merchant navy as a lad, later came ashore to work for the National Union of Seamen, and finished his public life as the sheriff of Bristol in 1968.*

1

## *Introduction*

Mary Jones is said to have cursed the justices when the sentence came down.[1] An attractive Irish woman, she had been accused of stealing four pieces of worked muslin from a draper's shop in Ludgate Hill. In her defence she claimed she had always been a very honest woman, but the impressment of her husband had driven her and her two small children to near starvation. Only a teenager, and confronted with the seizure of her family's furniture and goods to repay the small debts of her husband, she was thrown out of her lodgings and forced to beg in the streets.[2] Eventually she became desperate, and with Ann Styles, a lodger from the same house in Angel Alley in the Strand, she conspired to steal to make ends meet. From the trial at the Old Bailey it appears that their plan was clumsily executed. Styles attempted to keep the assistant busy while Jones snuck 'the remnants of worked muslin' under her cloak. Whether it was the 52 yards cited in the indictment or the twelve yards noted in the press, it was an easily detectable crime.[3] At her trial on 11 September 1771, after a month in Newgate prison, Mary Jones was sentenced to death for shoplifting. Her accomplice was acquitted. On her way to Tyburn she suckled her youngest child. According to one later account, she continued to do so until the hangman placed the noose around her neck.

There were no protests against her hanging at Tyburn, at least not according to the newspapers. Nor were there efforts by the two sheriffs of the day, John Wilkes and Frederick Bull, to intervene on her behalf; despite the fact that both of them had been vocal in their opposition to press warrants, even to the point of questioning their legality. What struck the newspapers and the predominantly middling constituency of the City of London was the fact that the two new sheriffs did their job of taking malefactors to Tyburn without military support.[4] The presence of troops at some public executions had brought the law into disrepute as well as setting ominous precedents for a liberty-loving City that 130 years earlier had shut its gates to Charles I. Mary Jones' case was subsumed in this larger discussion about the role of the military at public executions, one that recalled the military turnout at the execution of several Spitalfields weavers a year earlier in Bethnal Green.

As it turned out, Mary Jones was not forgotten. In a debate on the bill for providing the dockyards with better security some six years later, Sir William

Meredith expressed some dismay at the willingness of the Commons to add yet another capital offence to the statute book in its reactive efforts to stamp out a perceived evil, in this case the threat of arson that had dramatically surfaced with the discovery and apprehension of John the Painter. Harsh sanguinary laws often implicated the wrong people, he maintained, citing Mary Jones' trial and execution under the Shoplifting Act. In Meredith's eyes, Jones had deserved mercy, given the predicament she faced, namely the loss of the family's principal wage-earner to the navy during the Falkland Islands crisis of 1770–71. But parliament and the courts had too easily deferred to the interests of bankers, silversmiths and other affluent shopkeepers who claimed that shoplifting had reached epidemic proportions. Despite the mitigating circumstances, despite the good word of the parish authorities on her behalf, Mary Jones was made an example. 'The state bereaved the woman of her husband, and the children of a father', Meredith declared; 'the law deprived the woman of her life, and the children of their remaining parent. Take all the circumstances together, I do not believe that a fouler murder was ever committed against law than the murder of this woman by law.'[5]

Sir William's remarks might be dismissed as the frothy rhetoric of politicians. Many of the complaints about naval impressment and the Bloody Code have been so described. Yet the Mary Jones story continued to haunt the public consciousness. In the wake of the naval mutiny of 1797, when there were further complaints about the iniquities of impressment in the so-called land of freedom, the story surfaced once more, this time in Newcastle upon Tyne.[6] In this account, which might well have been embroidered over time, Mary gave birth to her second child after the impressment of her husband. It was to clothe the babe, rather than to fence the linen, that she stole from the Ludgate shop. In this version Mary stole in a state of temporary derangement, a fact that made her sentence seem harsher. Even so, the main theme of the narrative remained the same. It was naval impressment, the forcible recruitment of seaworthy people into the navy, that put Mary and her children at risk and pushed her to commit a fatal theft. Impressment destroyed families; it was a social and political evil that the state shamelessly upheld in the interests of Britain's defence and overseas policies.

Mary Jones' tale may have been dramatically tragic, but it was not particularly exceptional in the eighteenth century. In the parish examinations of St Martin in the Fields, for instance, there are stories of impressment throwing families on the parish. In the final months of 1776, when the navy scoured the streets of London looking for eligible men, Tony Tearney, a lamp lighter, was taken up by the press gang, leaving his partner, Sarah Morris, unable to provide for their two children aged three and one.[7] Eighteen months later, Elizabeth Leigh, a 38-year-old woman who lodged in Marygold Court, found herself destitute with two small children when her husband, an unemployed gold and silver lace weaver who had been forced to make candles for a living, was pressed into the service.[8] These are examples taken from a predominantly artisan parish along the Strand, not one known for its seafaring lodging houses, which were concentrated along both banks of the Thames to the east of Tower Bridge. There, and in other seafaring communities, impressment routinely left its mark. In 1797 Sir Frederick Eden remarked on the impact of impressment upon poverty levels in North and South Shields. A year earlier, in the first mendicity report of the metropolis for which information about destitution was systematically gathered, many beggars who sought relief from the Mendicity Society proved to be married women who were the casualties of military service.[9] No doubt some of their husbands joined up out of necessity, or even to evade family responsibilities, but others were likely coerced into the service at a time when the Admiralty was desperate for men. In that year there were several serious confrontations between Londoners and the press gangs, two of them culminating in the deaths of impressed men.[10]

None of this evidence – of people physically opposing naval impressment or feeling its pinch – features very prominently in the naval histories of the period. With a few exceptions, the focus is determinedly on the manpower problem, of the difficulties the navy faced in recruiting its crews and the strategies it employed for doing so. These are important questions, but viewed from a purely administrative angle, they foreclose a comprehensive treatment of naval impressment. The preoccupations of naval historians tend to focus on their lordships at the Admiralty, or the commissioners of the Navy Board, or, in the tradition of Jack Aubrey, upon naval commanders on the high seas. Impressment inevitably intrudes on the decisions of all these gentlemen, but it does so rather impressionistically. We get conflicting opinions about the incidence of naval impressment, and usually only fleeting glimpses of the opposition to it. Who actually opposed impressments, and in what manner, are not questions that are systematically addressed, at least over the long term. Nor is the question of whether impressment was as large a social and political grievance as some of its more vocal opponents claimed. In their accounts of the rise of British sea power, especially those that reach their apotheosis in the figure of Nelson, naval historians find the issue of impressment something of an embarrassment. Indeed, they largely evade the question of how the perceived reluctance to join the navy can be reconciled with the more triumphal version of British naval power with its emphasis on king, country and the formation of stronger national identities. These are the sorts of questions that are addressed here.

Impressment is an odd word. It has an antique aura. To impress means essentially to stamp or to make one's seal. In the military context it meant to register or to enrol a recruit. Throughout the eighteenth century it was continually used in this sense, for both the army and the navy – although it also carried with it an element of coercion. For while one Latin root is suggested by the word *imprestare*, meaning to advance money for a service, the other, *pressare*, meant to weigh down, afflict, or oppress.[11] 'What was pressing', asked the Duke of Richmond in the Lords debate on manning the navy in 1779, 'but a compulsory mode of obliging persons to take up arms, to become either soldiers or sailors.'[12] Whether it was the recruiting sergeant plying the needy or gullible with drink and enticing them to take the king's shilling, or the naval lieutenant scouring the streets and quayside pubs for seamen, impressment often entailed a high degree of coercion. In the case of the navy, this was particularly so, for a soldier's enlistment was officially supposed to be confirmed as voluntary before a justice of the peace, whereas no such recourse was open to a sailor once he had been entered by a press officer as a fit recruit for the navy.[13] In the labour-intensive era of sail, the Royal Navy simply could not recruit enough volunteers to man its fleets. It had their regulating officers and their gangs seek out the unwilling as well as the willing. This was especially the case on shore, for the regulating officers of the ports were responsible for entering volunteers as well as pressed men, and even for taking in seemingly disreputable characters handed over by the civil authorities.

What proportion of naval crews were actually coerced men? There is no easy answer to this question. The most obvious source for tracking pressed men is the muster books of the individual ships, for these encompass those impressed both afloat and ashore. Yet the muster books are notoriously uneven in quality as an historical source. Principally designed to record to the pay of seamen, muster books are helpful in tracking deaths, desertions, transfers and discharges, as well as the money docked for clothes and medicine. But they are not always very helpful in tracking the modes of entry into the service. Men transferred from one ship to another are simply listed by their previous boat, and it would be a Herculean task to track them to their original point of entry. Consequently boats with high turnovers provide very imperfect evidence of the proportion of pressed men on crews, and these constitute the largest portion in wartime. In N.A.M. Rodger's selection of five ships in the Seven Years' War, 15 per cent of the crews were pressed, 55.6 per cent volunteered, but nearly 30 per cent were turned over.[14] What the original means of entry was for those turned over is impossible to say. The problem is amplified in a larger sample, this time of men recruited for the Leeward Islands station during the wars at the end of the century.[15] Of a cohort of over 7400 men, the original means of entry are unknown for over half, either because they were turned over (22 per cent) or because they were simply not stated (29 per cent). Only 7 per cent of the men are recorded as being impressed and 39 per cent as being volunteers, but with such a large number of unknowns the figures are meaningless as an index of impressments.

Muster books are generally poor indicators of the proportion of men who were impressed into the navy. They may be helpful in limited contexts, where the recording is good and the unknowns are few. Daniel Baugh noted that the percentage of impressed men on Admiral Vernon's squadron of 1739 was 17 per cent; but this was only for nine ships at the beginning of a war when a hard winter likely induced many to volunteer. N.A.M. Rodger has offered further figures for twelve ships commissioned at Plymouth during the 1770s, where the percentage of press men is only 6 per cent. By contrast, Michael Lewis calculated that 50 per cent of a representative crew of the Napoleonic era was impressed, excluding those men brought in under the Quota Acts and foreigners, which in his opinion raised the 'coercive' quotient to 75 per cent.[16] Most historians would consider this claim extravagant, but in the current state of research most would also hesitate to venture any strong generalizations.

Muster books prove something of a dead end when it comes to calculating the proportion of men pressed into the navy. Figures from impressments on shore are arguably better but they are also partial, in that the navy also impressed at sea from home-coming vessels. Regrettably, the Admiralty and Navy Board never managed to come up with reliable figures that combined both of these operations. Nonetheless, we do have some accurate snapshots of onshore recruitment. In the first three years of the Seven Years' War, for example, it appears that 45 per cent of the men recruited ashore were impressed. A few years later, in an eighteen-month period during 1759–60, the figures for the headquarters of the press gang at Hull, the rendezvous as it was known, reveal that 63 per cent of all recruits were impressed men.[17] Returns for Liverpool and Newcastle in the American war offer percentages of 85 and 66; for Seaford and Newhaven, 42. A larger sample, for nearly 16,000 men recruited in England and Ireland in 1780–1, claimed that over 44 per cent were impressed. A survey conducted by the Admiralty for 32 British ports in the period 1803–05, London and Ireland excluded, reveals that over 48 per cent of some 11,600 recruits were impressed into the navy.[18] Certainly the proportion of pressed men varied according to the local labour supply, the size of bounties for volunteers, and the disposition and success of the regulating officers to track down reluctant recruits. How the dynamics of this worked out will be explored for Bristol and Liverpool in Chapter 4. But clearly these figures suggest that impressing on shore was substantial. Often 40 per cent or more of all those who were entered by the press gangs ashore were coerced into the navy.

These figures are significant when we place them in the context of the larger market for seafarers in eighteenth-century Britain. Britain was at war approximately one in every two years from 1690–1815, and within the timeframe of this book, 1739–1815, just under two in every three. At the turn of the eighteenth century the government had attempted to create a register of seamen to ensure that the navy could mobilize seamen quickly, but this never proved successful. Despite various recommendations on this theme throughout the century, a naval reserve never materialized, largely because legislators feared a standing navy of some sort would be either too expensive or politically too vexatious.[19] The result was that the Admiralty stuck to a time-honoured policy of seize, hire and discharge, relying on the merchant marine as a nursery for seamen. The Navigation Acts provided the basic framework for this strategy, since British and colonial seamen had to constitute 75 per cent of all crews and, with the expansion of British commerce and coastal traffic, the merchant marine grew faster than the general population which itself grew substantially as the century progressed. Yet the demand for men in the royal navy proved enormous. It grew from around 23,000 borne – that is, registered on the ships' books – at the beginning of the War of Jenkins' Ear, to 85,000 at the peak of the Seven Years' War, to over 100,000 in the American war, to roughly 145,000 at the end of the Napoleonic wars (1815). This is a six-fold increase in the space of roughly 75 years, and it is sustained even if we look at the number of seamen who were actually mustered.[20] The merchant marine, by contrast, grew more slowly. At roughly 36,000 on the eve of the Seven Years' War (1756) and just over 52,000 in 1792, it simply could not accommodate the manning imperatives of the navy, even with a relaxation of the foreign quotas allowed on British ships.[21] The emergent colonial marine, perhaps 10,000 strong by 1760, did little to alleviate the problem, as I shall explain in Chapter 5. Taking into account the peacetime naval establishment, which stood at about 17,300 in 1755 and 25,100 in 1792, the wartime demand for seamen outstripped supply by roughly two to one. The problem was intensified by the fact that pay in the merchant marine was always higher than in the navy and increased dramatically during wartime, making the mariner very reluctant to switch sectors. Efforts to place a ceiling on merchant wages failed, and consequently wartime wages were two, even three times as high as those offered by the navy.[22] Large bounties from the navy, with top-ups from local communities, might have at times lowered the differentials, but seamen also assessed the working conditions aboard ship in deciding in which service they would work. At times of war shore leave in the Royal Navy was very infrequent with crews being regularly turned over to other ships when their own needed repairs or re-servicing. In the merchant marine the average voyage lasted a matter of months, on average 9–10 months; even on a wartime privateer, a single voyage lasted only six months. By contrast, seamen could find themselves working for the Royal Navy for years on end, isolated from their friends and families on shore. Moreover, life on a man-of-war with the complement of several hundred men was a lot more hierarchical than on a merchant boat, even from that of a large privateering crew. And discipline was generally tougher. The consequence was that the symbiotic relationship between maritime commerce and naval power – one that worked reasonably well during the wars of William III and Queen Anne when naval excursions at sea were short – became increasingly problematic as Britain's naval commitment increased, both in terms of the number of vessels deployed and the duration of the operations.[23]

The result was that the Royal Navy could not rely on market forces to man its crews. Even with bounties, it had to rely on coercion. Impressing on the seas was a long-standing practice in the navy and continued to be so, but with the big wars of the eighteenth century impressing on shore became increasingly important. In the early years of the century impressment had largely been a southern problem. Its centre of operations was London, the Downs and the south-coast ports of Portsmouth and Plymouth. As late as 1740 the Admiralty's activities remained concentrated in this region, although press warrants were also issued in Bristol, Liverpool, Newcastle, Hull and Yarmouth.[24] During the Seven Years' War, however, the impress service, as it later became known, expanded dramatically to meet the government's demand for seamen, drawing roughly a quarter of its men from the northern ports.[25] Regulating captains, hitherto confined to London, were posted in many provincial ports as well as a few inland towns. By 1780, the impress service was employing 30 captains, 105 lieutenants, 215 petty officers and over 1200 men to recruit in Britain and Ireland. It was also employing over 1200 officers and men on the tenders that transported recruits to places like Plymouth, Portsmouth and the Nore where they would be assigned berths on vessels of war.[26] These amphibian initiatives were prompted by the desire to co-ordinate the recruiting drives of the navy in a more systematic fashion: to tap a broader section of the merchant marine; to enlist more landsmen, who sometimes constituted roughly 30 per cent of all recruits who entered at the rendezvous; to take up sailors who had moved inland to evade the press gangs; and to recapture stragglers and deserters.[27]

The civil authorities were encouraged to collaborate in this enterprise so that the local labour demands could be more satisfactorily coordinated with the imperatives of national defence and imperial expansion. Press warrants were sent to over 60 English towns during the opening mobilization of the Seven Years' War and to over 70 during the American.[28] The bait for such participation was to offer exemptions, or 'protections' as they were known in the eighteenth century, to a specified number of seafarers in order to reconcile the needs of commerce with the needs of the state. Statutory exemptions from impressment had been given to sea apprentices and Greenland harpooners in the early years of the century, and a quota system had been arranged for the Thames watermen and the colliers of the Tyne and Wear.[29] These exemptions were reaffirmed in 1740 and more liberal concessions were allowed the whaling industry.[30] Equally important, the Admiralty and other government departments issued protections to a broader range of seafaring and portside men: to crews of ships bound abroad; to coasters and fishing vessels; to watermen, lightermen, bargemen, pilots and some harbour workers. These departmental protections were discretionary; they could be withdrawn if manning shortages became too severe. But between 1740 and 1757 the number of protections rose threefold or more, from 14,800 to approximately

50,000, taking in a sizeable proportion of the merchant marine as well as many riverside trades. Protections were even offered to Newcastle broad-glass workers, Bermondsey anchorsmiths, London orange porters and to several employees of a biscuit manufacturer in Limehouse.[31]

Why, you may ask, did these men require protections from the press?

The answer is because naval impressment did not simply encompass seamen, despite statements to the contrary.[32] From 1740 it implicated anyone between the ages of 18 and 55 who 'used the sea'.[33] In fact, press warrants from the 1750s routinely talked of seamen, seafaring men and 'such persons whose Occupations and Callings are to work in vessels and Boats upon rivers'.[34] The Admiralty, moreover, had an increasingly capacious view of who it could take in and, following the watermen precedent, that could mean pretty much anyone who had some aptitude with small craft on a river. Consequently in 1776 lightermen from Bere Alston in Cornwall, who carried limestone up and down the river Tamar, found themselves the object of press-gang raids. They were 'dragged out of their craft like dogs', one newspaper reported, 'leaving their families in great distress'.[35] The same was potentially true of Boston bargemen, Medway oystermen, the tacksmen of the river Tay – many of whom were really farmers – and Tyneside wherrymen or foymen; even carters like James Bowie, who hauled coals from the keels and confessed that 'he had never been to sea although he had laboured in the river'.[36] On that pretext the Admiralty decided to keep him, as it did John Rose, a quarryman employed in gathering coals at the wharfside for a Tyneside limeworks.[37]

The target population for impressment was therefore quite large. In an age of by-employments, when tin miners doubled as pilchard fishermen and small Scottish farmers took to their boats in the fishing season, impressment potentially took in a sizeable proportion of portside populations and fishing villages. On the south Devonshire coast Admiral MacBride reported there were hundreds of 'Southams, a sort of half Farmer half Sailor' who were impressible, although he despaired of getting them.[38] In Bristol and Liverpool, two of the principal provincial ports in the eighteenth century, the adult male population threatened by impressment was probably a quarter or more, which helps to explain why the subject inflamed the passions of those cities. In Newcastle, where keelmen as well as colliers were vulnerable, the proportion of men actually taken up by the gangs during the American war was in excess of 10 per cent, by no means an insignificant number.

Impressment was an intrusion into the lives of ordinary citizens. William Lovett remembered it well from his early days in Newlyn during the Napoleonic wars. 'The cry that "the press gang was coming"', he recalled, 'was sufficient to cause all the young and eligible men of the town to flock up to the hills and away to the country as far as possible, and to hide themselves in all manner of places till the danger was supposed to be over.' In this Cornish fishing village, just south-west of Penzance, the Light Horse were sometimes stationed on the roads to prevent men escaping the clutches of the gangs. 'Then might the soldiers be seen, with drawn cutlasses, riding down the poor fishermen, often through the fields of standing corn where they had sought to hide themselves.'[39]

Impressment did not simply occur in seafaring haunts, whether quayside pubs or lodgings. In London, for example, where there are over 130 reported incidents of clashes with the press gang, the main sites of conflict were predictably in the well-established seafaring quarters such as Whitechapel, Ratcliff Highway, Wapping, Shadwell, Limehouse, Poplar and across the river in Southwark and Bermondsey. Yet a third of the confrontations took place in the City, along the Strand, in Covent Garden, Drury Lane, and St Giles, in Oxford Market and Haymarket. These were areas within easy walking distance of the maritime parishes, from which seamen might disappear when a hot press was expected – that is, when the gangs would ignore all but statutory protections in a sweep of the river and the streets. Press gangs would venture there to pick up stragglers, some of whom might have been recognizable only by their gait or language. They would also collar men with riverside occupations, for among those taken in the mid-century decades was a tanner in Bermondsey, a servant to a lighterman and a carpenter who served his apprenticeship on Bankside.[40] Down-at-heel artisans might also be a quarry, especially if they had taken a youthful adventure in the navy, or had been forced to sign up because of some personal misfortune.

We have strong corroborative evidence for this from the testimony of witnesses at the Old Bailey. In the trials defendants sometimes used the press gangs as some sort of alibi. Accused of stealing some shoes from a shop off Lincoln's Inn Fields, Bartholomew Quickly said he ran out of the shop because he thought 'the Press-Gang was come'. Found guilty of stealing some sugar, raisins, barley, pepper and rice from a lighter on the Thames, John Flat claimed he was aboard the vessel hiding from the gang.[41] Similarly, a lad accused of stealing lead claimed he was hiding from the press gang behind a stack of chimneys.[42] We might find these rather lame explanations, and generally so too did the juries; yet the fact they were consistently advanced as a defence suggests they did have an aura of plausibility about them. Press gangs were wide ranging in their searches; they were often abusive and intrusive. In 1757 the Lord Mayor was called to intervene in a case in which a 50-year-old footman was yanked from the house of a well-to-do merchant in Savage Gardens simply because he had once been to sea. According to the merchant, the raid took place at 11 pm, when he was already in bed. He was awakened to the cry of 'Murder' and 'much affrighted', he continued, 'on which he got up and came down stairs and found a press gang in my house … who had seized the footman.'[43]

Incidents like this gave press gangs a bad reputation among householders, as did the casual violence they dished out to ordinary folk on the street.[44] Some able-bodied men without sea service were afraid of walking the streets when the press gangs were searching for men, if only because the definition of who could be impressed was interpreted very liberally by the gangs, who were happy to pick up able-bodied men on the slightest pretext. In the parish examinations of St Clement Danes and St Martin in the Fields there are examples of lamplighters, brass founders, tailors, tavern servants and even an ex-farmer being pressed, all of them with families.[45]

What also increased the potential intrusiveness of impressment was the fact that vagrants or people without any visible livelihood could be forced into the navy. Picking up the wandering poor was an old practice, with precedents in the Tudor and Stuart eras, but it was not until the first decade of the eighteenth century that the practice was given explicit statutory endorsement.[46] 'I take it for granted that those who are of least use at home are the fittest to be employed in the service of their country abroad', wrote one author. 'Sturdy beggars' would make good cannon fodder, along with pickpockets, barrowmen, chimney sweeps and market people, all who are a 'dead weight upon the community'. It freed the nation, claimed another, 'of idle and reprobate Vermin by converting them into a Body of the most industrious People, and even, becoming the very nerves of our State'.[47]

By the mid-century wars, bridewells and streets were routinely scoured for potential recruits. Despite the fact that some thought the impressment of beggars was a 'Species of Tyranny', magistrates seldom hesitated about using the navy as a dumping ground for its undesirables.[48] In late 1776, for example, the rookeries of St Giles were raided for potential recruits, and magistrates delivered hundreds to the rendezvous. Just how many vagrants made their way into the navy is a debatable point, and much disputed by historians who want to keep the navy's image respectable.[49] Yet we do have some figures. In the years 1803–5, the magistrates from 32 ports in England and Wales turned in over 800 eligible men to the regulating officers, some 8 per cent of the total recruited. A fair proportion of these must have been men of no visible means.[50] In Newcastle during the American war, the proportion of recruits turned in by the magistrates was noticeably lower, only 2 per cent of the total regulated by the press-gang captain. Still, the fluctuations in male and female property offenders suggest that war removed many men perceived to be undesirable or unemployable from city streets.[51] In emergencies, the impressment of the roving poor was certainly an important stop-gap measure in the overall strategy of recruitment. In the manning crisis of 1759 the constables of Newcastle packed the jails with potential recruits, although the regulating officer, Edward Wheeler, discharged many of them as unsuitable for the service. In 1787, when Britain geared up for a potential war with France on account of its likely intervention in Dutch politics, the round-up of vagrants in London as part of the pre-war mobilization was said to have made a 'visible change in the streets'.[52] As a result of a 1795 statute (35 George III c. 34), magistrates turned over stragglers to the navy. Eight were sent from Shrewsbury to the *Three Friends* tender in Liverpool; Captain John Cheshyre negotiated with magistrates in Manchester about bringing in more, while the 23-year-old son of a respectable farmer, deep in his cups over a sweetheart of whom his father did not approve, was picked up by the watch in Clapham and sent aboard the tender at the Tower as a 'fit man for a seaman'. It took a writ of habeas corpus from his father and some legal pressure to get him discharged.[53]

The impressment of vagrants into the navy underscored the elite's intolerance of work-shy habits and idleness, at least among those who were poor enough to have to work for a living. The impressment of seamen was a different and contradictory matter. Seamen were forced into the navy because of their skills, not because they lacked or refused to use them. They were made bondsmen to the state to preserve other people's freedom and independence. Unlike any other class of men in the eighteenth century, the crown required their services as liege subjects of the realm to man Britain's wooden walls in wartime. This early form of selective conscription was moreover a life-long commitment. Once in the navy, a man could be recalled to duty at any point before the age of 55. Granville Sharp, who amassed a file on press-gang abuses, even cited a case where the navy attempted to impress a 76-year-old sailor in Leith on the grounds that in Scotland the 55-year limit did not apply if the man was deemed fit enough to serve.[54] The navy would have got away with it had the man's family not appealed to the Edinburgh Court of Session to have him released from the Nore.

This case was untypical, but the records show that the navy was not simply interested in impressing young men. Muster books reveal that pressed men had roughly the same age profile as able seamen, only there were arguably more over 40. Over half (54 per cent) were in their twenties, 20 per cent were in their thirties, but 14 per cent were 40 or more.[55] Given the demographic peculiarities of wage-earners in the eighteenth century, many of these men were likely married, over 50 per cent of them being 25 years of age or more. Defenders of impressment sometimes insinuated that seamen were a reckless bunch of rovers without strong familial ties. Charles Butler bluntly asserted that impressment saved seamen from 'idleness, intemperance, and bad company'. He dismissed the notion that sailors craved domestic comfort as sheer sentimentality.[56] Yet judging from the persistence of the domestic theme in impressment narratives few would have agreed with him. The ballads of the era are full of stories of wives and lovers being separated by impressment, and even of anxious or malicious parents using the press gang to get rid of undesirable suitors for their daughters.[57]

Some of the older tars had settled into jobs on shore when the press gang came looking for them. Writing from the *Culloden* in 1804, Admiral Collingwood noted that he had a nurseryman from Ryton aboard his ship. 'It is a great pity that they should press such a man because when he was young he went to sea for a short time. They have broken up his good business at home, distressed his family and sent him here where he is of little or no service.'[58] A similar fate nearly befell John Nicol, who also suffered from a press-gang search. He returned to Edinburgh after 25 years of service in the navy, married one of his cousins at the age of 46, and set up shop as a cooper on Castle Hill. He thought he was 'once more my own master' but with the outbreak of war in 1793 the press gang pursued him. 'My wife was like a distracted woman', he recalled, 'and gave me no rest until I sold off my stock in trade and the greater part of my furniture and retired into the country.'[59] For the next eleven years he eked out a living in Cousland doing farm work and quarrying, returning to Edinburgh when he was too old for the navy and unable to prosper in the coopering business.

The restrictions on seamen, on their liberty, their marketability, on their chance to pursue a different trade, fuelled hostility towards impressment. Seamen resented the fact they were denied their rights as free-born Britons, that they were subject to the prerogative powers of the crown when those powers were thought to be in abeyance. James Oglethorpe, who collected eye-witness accounts of press-gang activities, recaptured these sentiments in the words of an impressed man taken down in the hold of a press tender on the Thames. 'Why was I shut in here?' exclaimed the sailor. 'I that am born to be free; are not I and the greatest Duke in England equally free born? If I have done nothing, who has the power to confine me? Where is the liberty of an Englishman?'[60] This theme, the constitutionality of impressment and the legal challenges to it, is addressed in the next chapter.

Seamen were also angry that they were deprived of the opportunity to bargain their labour in a society that increasingly proclaimed the benefits of the free market. The fact that naval impressment increased, at a time when the older forms of wage regulation under the Statute of Artificers were falling into desuetude, must have reinforced the servile status of the seamen. Aside from Scottish miners and until 1772 visiting slaves, seamen were the most servile labour force in Britain. At least indentured servants served a specified term, however slavishly they were treated. In fact, the actual process of impressment was often symptomatic of their servile status. Seamen were more or less treated as criminals upon capture, dumped in dark holds to await shipment to the Nore or some other recruiting station. William Robinson recalled how he was ordered down to the hold of the rendezvous 'with my companions in wretchedness, and the rats running over us in numbers'. On their transfer to the tender he remembered being guarded by marines with loaded muskets and fixed bayonets, 'as though we had been culprits of the first degree, or capital convicts'. For the next day and a half, as they sailed down to the Nore, the impressed were huddled together in another hold with no room to sit or stand apart. 'We were in a pitiable plight', he remembered, for some were 'sea-sick, some retching, others were smoking, whilst many were so overcome with the stench that they fainted for want of air.' When the hatches were removed and 'day-light broke in upon us', he continued, 'a wretched appearance we cut, for scarcely any of us were free from filth and vermin'.[61]

Historians have sometimes suggested that impressment was not a significant social problem. N.A.M. Rodger has claimed that it was largely a 'humdrum affair calling for little if any violence', and that impressed men quickly acclimatized themselves to the realities of naval life.[62] This interpretation is very debatable. It rests on dubious inferences from the incidence of desertion, where it is claimed that pressed men deserted in proportionately fewer numbers than volunteers. Unfortunately there are too many imponderables about why men jumped ship and too many difficulties in isolating impressed men from others. In the sample offered by Rodger,[63] there are 594 unknowns (27 per cent) and 637 men (29 per cent) who were turned over; in other words, for 56 per cent of all deserters we do not know whether they were volunteers or impressed men, vitiating the conclusions he wishes to advance.

Rodger's benevolent view of impressment is incomplete in that it tends to focus upon the press gang's activities towards the end of wars, when it spent its time tracking down deserters in what was a revolving-door operation designed simply to sustain the existing levels of recruitment. Yet the most confrontational phase of a press gang's activities occurred at the beginning of the wars, as the state was remobilizing, or when the navy faced serious manpower shortages that had to be resolved quickly. These conclusions, derived from a survey of over 600 press-gang affrays in the period 1739–1805, are set out in Chapter 3. That survey also assesses the geographical reach of the gangs over time, the participation of portside communities in supporting protests against the gangs and the incidence of violence that was involved.

Unlike other forms of collective protest, press-gang affrays were extremely violent, for threatened seamen were quite prepared to use knives, cutlasses, pokers, shovels and broken glass to defend themselves. Cuts, bruises and fractures were commonplace in these affrays, and sometimes gangers and their prey lost eyes, ears and even parts of their noses. In the 65 years to 1805, a quarter of all affrays involved serious injuries or fatalities, so the suggestion that 'there was a holiday element in being sent pressing either by sea or by land', that 'it was a welcome relaxation from the unvarying round of shipboard life and offered the prospect of rambling about on shore',[64] strains credibility to put it mildly. This might have been the case at Godalming, where a bunch of ex-farm labourers escorted volunteers and deserters to Portsmouth. Their main complaint seems to have been that they were 'tired' by the tramp in winter.[65] But the placidity of press-gang life does not hold for many places. Even sleepy Appledore, a town of 2000 inhabitants at the bar of the Taw and Torridge rivers, caused problems for the press gangs. Early in 1804 the lieutenant and midshipmen recruiting there were assaulted and one impressed man was rescued from the gang.[66] In the eleven months that lieutenant Jones and his gang of two midshipman and six men were stationed at Appledore, Barnstaple and Bideford, he only brought in 67 impressed men at a phenomenal cost of over £1000. Part of the reason for this poor performance was that the local miners served notice that they would not tolerate mass impressment, and with no tender to whisk men away, Jones and his gang faced the wrath of the pits if they became overly energetic in their duties. 'The whole of the Impress Service on this part of the Coast', mourned one vice-admiral, 'wants regulation.'[67]

What was true of these Devonshire backwaters was triply so for major ports. As I will show in Chapter 4, press-gang business could be physically dangerous and mentally fatiguing. Gangers were sometimes so badly beaten up that they were incapacitated from doing their duty. Officers suffered the indignity of scaling the roofs of houses to avoid raging mobs below. Some had breakdowns as well as bruises. Press-gang officers were divided about whether it was better to recruit local men into the gangs, or total strangers. Bristol tended to opt for the former, on the grounds that local men would better know the haunts of resident seamen, but this exposed them and their families to local ostracism and reprisals. Liverpool opted for the latter, knowing how hostile the local populace was to the presence of the gangs. That meant that press gangers operated in both strange and hostile territory where the balance of numbers could be decisively against them. A typical press gang in large ports at the end of the century consisted of a captain, two lieutenants, four midshipmen and twenty men, some of whom had to attend to the press men in the lock-up while others were on patrol. It is not surprising that they suffered considerable wear and tear at the hands of mobs and large privateering crews of five to 50 times their size.

The last two chapters of this book move out from impressment to address other issues that have recently preoccupied historians. Chapter 5 explains why the navy found it difficult to impress in colonial waters, and examines the legal and physical opposition it faced in doing so. It argues that in situations where the depletion of crews was dire through death and desertion, the Royal Navy recruited prisoners of war as a stop-gap measure. By and large it resisted employing large numbers of slaves on board ship, although slaves were commonly used to careen boats, to carry baggage and generally to perform the heavy work that expeditionary forces required. In taking this line, the chapter takes issue with the expansive claims that have recently been made about the racially mixed crews of the Royal Navy. It also suggests that everyday racial divisions of labour and the conventions of naval prizes and privateering were too ingrained to facilitate the sorts of multi-ethnic alliances among servants, slaves and seamen that are said to characterize the 'revolutionary' Atlantic.[68]

The final chapter addresses the theme of the navy and the nation during the French wars at the turn of the century. It has been argued that these wars were critical events in the creation of a British national identity, especially in their ability to incorporate many men within the auspices of the armed forces, both regular and voluntary.[69] The chapter explains why the navy does not fit this scenario, despite all the ink that has been spilled on heralding the exploits of Nelson and his crews as a paradigmatic form of patriotism. Paradoxically, hostility to impressment intensified during this era of aggressive loyalist propaganda. Even during the invasion scares of 1803–5, when the pressure to identify with the plight of the nation was at its most intense, the seafarers' commitment to king and country was pragmatic and selective. Indeed, the willingness to join the naval volunteer force, the sea fencibles, proved to be an early form of draft-dodging, a means of avoiding service in the Royal Navy as much as a commitment to defend the coast. The reasons for this aversion to the service were long standing; many of them had been voiced in the naval mutinies of 1797, an event which not only terrified the ruling class but changed the whole climate of labour relations within the service. Attempts to re-incorporate the seamen within the panoply of the nation by applauding their bravery and their contributions to public service did something to narrow the distance that had opened up between officers and men in 1797, but ultimately it left a legacy of frustration and bitterness once the war was over. In the massive demobilizations at the end of the Napoleonic wars, seamen were left to fend for themselves. Their sacrifices never received their full public recognition, or, like Nelson, their full recompense. If the achievement of British naval supremacy was a national one that drew on the economic and social resources of Britain and Ireland, the contribution of the lower deck was sidelined in the interests of property and political economy. The strikes that followed the war illustrated this well.

2

## Impressment and the Law

In September 1744, the press gang of the *Royal Sovereign* was informed that a deserter was hiding in the Fountain tavern off Rag Fair, in the heart of the seafaring quarter of London's East End.[1] Led by the flamboyant and braggart Hamilton Montgomery, the ship's mate who sported a 'lac'd hat', the gang entered the pub and commandeered 'a man in a sailor's habit' who happened to be singing a sea shanty. A scuffle ensued in which the landlord, one Robert Wallis, was wounded and a ganger was pummelled to the ground by a group of local curriers who had come to the seaman's rescue. The seaman was eventually taken, but the gang swore revenge for the affray. They returned the following morning, threatening 'to have the landlord's blood, cut his Head off, chop him to pieces, & be the Death of him'. They ransacked the house while searching for Wallis, ran their cutlasses through the bedding in an attempt to find their quarry, and sword-whipped the local headborough who had attempted to raise a posse against them. When one of their men was arrested and taken to Clerkenwell prison, the press gang collected reinforcements and secured his rescue, admonishing the turnkey for 'taking in a King's man'. 'Damn your Blood, you rascall', they swore at the turnkey, 'if ever you take in another we will cut you all to pieces, and pull down your Gaol to the Ground.' Only the intervention of the Tower guard prevented an escalation of insult and violence, and it was only after a two-hour stand-off at another tavern that the gang finally surrendered to the civil authorities. Montgomery and his gang were charged with threatening the life of the landlord, with assaulting the headborough and rescuing a ganger from prison. At the Middlesex Quarter Sessions they were lucky to get away with the relatively small fines imposed upon them: 6s. 8d. apiece for the rescue; 2s. each on two counts of assault. Had the Admiralty not made discreet settlements out of court to both the landlord and headborough for the injuries and damages they had incurred, had the presiding justice not looked leniently on their transgressions, noting that the 'Admiralty needed their service at this time', they might well have felt the full rigour of the law.

Anyone familiar with the popular folklore of impressment would not find this episode unusual. The rough way in which press gangs recruited for the Royal Navy has long been commemorated in print and ballad, supplemented in the press by often harrowing accounts of the affrays that ensued. Yet the episode is also noteworthy for the light it sheds on the legal actions that civilians could take in curtailing the excesses of naval impressment. How the law was used in this manner, how it was deployed as a political strategy of containment as well as a means of evading impressment, is the subject of this chapter.

Historians have seldom looked at impressment in quite this way. Certainly they have addressed the legal status of impressment, even the degree to which press gangs operated within the law. But such inquiries have generally served as a prelude to the 'manning problem' of the Royal Navy, foreclosing rather than opening a discussion of how the law was mobilized in the controversies surrounding impressment.[2] In practice naval impressment was a very contentious issue in the eighteenth century, involving a good deal of give-and-take among the interested parties about what was 'legal' and what was 'just'. The troubled relationship between these two concepts has been usefully explored in the context of the popular struggles surrounding the rights of subsistence and customary perquisites in Georgian Britain. It applies equally to naval recruitment, where the legality of impressment was hedged by operational constraints and inconsistencies, and where the gulf between what was legal and what was popularly considered just was often very wide.

Opposition to naval impressment has sometimes been attributed to the self-interest of merchants or to the 'frothy talk' of 'hypocritical politicians'.[3] It struck deeper roots than such statements suggest. Levellers protested against impressment in the mid-seventeenth century. A remonstrance to the Commons in 1646 asked 'what difference there is between binding a man to an oar, as a galley-slave in Turkey or Algiers, and pressing of men to serve in your war'. The *Agreement of the People* the following year denounced impressment as a violation of English freedom; every 'man's conscience', it asserted, had 'to be satisfied in the justice of that cause wherein he hazards his own life or may destroy another's'.[4] Similar complaints were echoed in the eighteenth century in popular tracts such as *The Sailor's Advocate*, one that ran through seven editions in 50 years. Impressment was not only seen as a violation of the 'native liberty' of Englishmen,[5] it was contrary to Magna Carta. Clause 39 of the Great Charter declared that 'No free man [freeman] shall be arrested or [and] imprisoned or disseised or exiled or in any way victimised, neither will we attack him or send anyone to attack him, except by the lawful judgment of his peers or [and] by the law of the land'.[6] This principle was re-affirmed in a statute of Edward III, and also in the Petition of Right, or so it was claimed.[7] After the 1688 coup d'état, it was commonly believed that the prerogative powers on which impressment had been based had been irrevocably contained, if not nullifed. One owner of a Greenland whaler, angered by the forcible recruitment of several of his seamen during the off-season, told Captain Fergusson that impressment was contrary to the 'revolution['s] principal topick', that is, freedom from arbitrary government.

Should Fergusson 'persist in his tyrannie', he threatened, 'it will be necessary to complain to the house of Co'mons who its hopt will not suffer these Laws to be trampled upon'.[8] In this specific instance the owner was referring to the statutory exemptions for Greenlanders,[9] but behind this concession lay the larger issue of whether the impressment of seamen was contrary to the immanent spirit of liberty that animated English law and manifested itself on such momentous occasions as the 'Glorious' Revolution (1688).

The Whig version of history provided opponents of impressment with clear evidence of its anti-libertarian character; the campaign to abolish slavery provided them with rhetorical grist for the mill. If slavery was a blight upon British libertarian traditions, was not impressment, especially when those called upon to defend British freedoms by force of arms were denied the right of personal protection?[10] If slaveholders had no right to deport their slaves from Britain, as the Somersett case appeared to establish in 1772, could seamen be forcibly set afloat to do the king's business? Impressment was a 'badge of slavery' incompatible with a 'free people', argued the *General Evening Post*. Custom and usage were poor arguments in its favour.[11] 'People may talk of negro slavery and the whip', remarked a gunner a few years later, 'but let them look nearer home and see a poor sailor arrived from a long voyage exulting in the pleasure of being among his dearest friends and relations. Behold him just entering the door, when a press gang seizes him like a felon' and sends him off to a man-of-war, where, 'if he complains he is likely to be seized up and flogged with the cat'.[12] Harsh treatment, chains and vermin-ridden holds aboard tenders only added to the ignominies of the British sailor. The fact that impressed seamen were locked down in hatches aboard tenders and confined in cramped fever-ridden conditions for days on end was sometimes compared to the deplorable stacking of slaves during the middle passage.[13]

In view of the general hostility to the principle of impressment, it is not surprising that pro-government politicians trod warily in its defence. Confronting opposition outrage in 1740, Sir Robert Walpole admitted that impressment was unpopular and of dubious legality. Yet without a voluntary and workable register, he added, it was the state's sole safeguard for its defence. 'To assert the empire of the sea' and to protect 'our dominions of the greatest value', he went on, 'we must not only have ships, but sailors; sailors ready to obey our call and rush out on sudden expeditions'. Such imperatives should not be 'impeded by an ill-timed regard for the case of particular persons [sailors], or a popular affectation of tenderness for liberty'.[14]

Politicians were seldom as blunt as Walpole. They usually appealed to patriotic or imperial sentiments to assuage the opposition to impressment. They left it to the judges to clarify the law. The critical decision was rendered by the recorder of Bristol, Mr Sergeant Foster, at the Bristol assizes in August 1743. The case in question involved Alexander Broadfoot, a seamen of the merchant ship, the *Bremen Factor*, who had resisted impressment in the King Road by firing a blunderbuss at the press gang, killing one of its members on the spot. Foster was called upon to direct the jury as to whether Broadfoot should be found guilty of murder or manslaughter, a matter which essentially turned on the legality of the press warrant and the rights of resistance to unlawful impressment. But he also took the opportunity to expatiate broadly on the legality of impressment, recognizing its 'very great and national importance'.[15]

Foster argued that naval impressment took precedence over private rights in matters of national security; that it was 'a prerogative inherent in the Crown, grounded upon common-law, and recognized by many Acts of Parliament'. In defining impressment in this braided manner, Foster made it impossible for opponents to argue that impressment was an anachronistic royal prerogative incompatible with 'revolution principles'. The rights of naval impressment were not based on feudal law, which pertained principally to the military obligations of great tenants (the Cinque ports excepted). Rather they inhered in the bonds of allegiance which every subject owed the sovereign in 'cases of extreme necessity' such as invasion or insurrection. Foster admitted that it was unfortunate that these obligations of personal service now fell to one occupational class of men; but he did not think that such obligations were illegal because they had not been positively recognized in statute law, as some critics implied.[16] In Foster's view there was plenty of evidence of commissions to impress from the medieval era onwards. None of this practice was incompatible with statute law, nor with the Augustan Press Acts which quite explicitly set up privy searches for seamen.[17] Furthermore, the statutory exemptions from impressment, which had grown apace since 1700, tacitly acknowledged the right of the crown to impress seamen and those 'who used the sea'. The right to impress did not rest on these statutory regulations, Foster insisted, but upon a royal prerogative 'grounded in immemorial usage'.[18] The various acts which exempted certain classes of mariners from impressment served only to confirm the seeming symmetry of custom, prerogative and statute law.

Foster's judgment concerning the legal complexities of impressment was broadly endorsed by the King's Bench in 1776 in *Rex v. Tubbs*.[19] In seeking to determine whether John Tubbs, a City of London waterman, was exempt from the press, Lord Mansfield and his fellow judges all concurred that impressment was a vestigial prerogative power of the crown, founded on 'immemorial usage', recognized but not authorized by an Act of Parliament. This unanimity of judicial opinion made it extremely difficult, if not impossible, to challenge the general principle of impressment in the eighteenth century.

Opposition politicians within the City of London certainly tried. During the American war, anti-ministerial alderman, encouraged by reformers such as

Granville Sharp, hoped to exploit suits designed to protect City freemen from impressment into a general campaign against the practice.[20] But in all of these cases the Admiralty's lawyers proved adept at sidestepping general principles. All that the City could achieve from these suits was a recognition that their own constables were immune to impressment. The Admiralty refused to concede that freemen were exempt from the press, having been advised that freeholders (and logically freemen) were not exempt from impressment.[21] No judge was prepared to clarify the law further, despite the fact that voters had been exempted from certain Press Acts in the reign of Queen Anne.[22] Nor were the City's legal counsel keen to muster a general challenge to impressment. Although they were well-known reformers, lawyers John Glynn, John Dunning and Alexander Wedderburn basically endorsed Foster's judgment of 1743. Impressment was 'founded on that Universal Principle of Laws, that private interest must give way to public Safety, being well established by antient and continued Usage, [and] frequently recognised and regulated by the Legislature'.[23] Consequently they advised the City to concentrate upon procedural infractions to impressment. When the City adopted such a cautious line of reasoning in the case of John Millichip, a lighterman and member of the Needlemakers' Company impressed at Gravesend, the frustrations of the radicals became very evident. As one complained of the City's lawyers: 'They are always hanging on the privilege of exemption of Lord Mayor's watermen &c., which, in fact, is nothing at all to the public at large.'[24]

Nonetheless, there were a few points in the judgments surrounding impressment that opponents could exploit. Both Foster and Mansfield had emphasized that impressment could only be vindicated as a measure intended to protect the safety of the state.[25] In time of war there could hardly be any disagreement of what this meant, but it was not unusual for the Admiralty to issue press warrants prior to formal declarations of war: in effect, to put Britain on a war footing. Britain was on such a footing for over a year prior to the declaration of war with France in 1756, for example. Moreover, naval mobilizations were sometimes little more than modes of diplomatic bullying, designed to impress upon other nations the seriousness of British objectives. In its disputes with the declining imperial power of Spain, for instance, Britain issued press warrants to assert territorial claims over the Falkland Islands in 1770 and trading rights in Nootka Sound twenty years later. In 1787, Britain also mobilized its navy to prevent the French fleet from assisting the Patriots (the opponents of the Prince of Orange) in the Netherlands.[26] Britons might reasonably have been forgiven for wondering how an obscure island in the South Atlantic and vague territorial claims in the North Pacific impinged on the safety of the state, or whether the internal struggles of a neighbouring European power quite necessitated such a show of force. Newspapers and politicians publicly aired such views. One radical complained that seamen had to face press gangs 'merely because a minister of the country may perhaps from motives of corruption, or views of ambition, chuse to enter into a war, and by an unjust exercise of power, *force* these honest fellows to become the instruments either of his villainy, or his vengeance'.[27]

This line of argument was also pursued by Granville Sharp. He likened the laws of impressment to those of Ship Money, on the grounds that both were defended by the crown on the basis of necessity. He thought this a very dangerous argument, very much open to abuse, and hoped that the stain of arbitrary government associated with Charles I's period of non-parliamentary rule, at least in the eyes of Old Whigs, could tarnish the government's policy of impressment. Sharp aired these views in the *Public Ledger* under the *nom de plume* of Maynard. He was also aggressively hostile to the doctrine of necessity on principle, not just from historical precedent.[28] 'It is a Doctrine without bounds when once admitted, for it insensibly declines to every evil, like a High Road to Hell. It is better for a Nation even to risk its very existence in the World, trusting in God's Providence, than to set aside the administration of equal justice & righteousness in order to subsist by a manifest oppression of any particular part of the community.'

Understandably, resistance to impressment in these 'phoney wars' was often high – proportionate to the number of seamen borne, higher than in more serious engagements. Magistrates were correspondingly reluctant to back press warrants in their various jurisdictions, feeling that the navy's manning requirements might well be fulfilled by encouraging volunteers through generous bounties, or by sweeping the streets of vagrants, however defined. The City of London magistrates strenuously advocated this policy during the Falklands crisis of 1770–71. The Lord Mayor, Sir Thomas Sainsbury, did so again in 1787, suggesting to Lord Howe and to members of the Privy Council that press warrants were of questionable legality in the circumstances of this European conflict, which did not directly involve Britain or imperil its territories. The Privy Council did not take kindly to this intervention. Lord Chancellor Thurlow retorted that 'his Lordship might be a very good tradesman, but he was not a politician; that he (as Lord Chancellor) was to judge of the necessity, and as to the warrants, he pronounced them *legal*'.[29]

Magistrates thus found themselves unable to challenge the necessity of impressment, but they certainly were able to constrain its operation. Under a press warrant, the civil power was enjoined to assist the press gangs in their task. Indeed, it was customary for the regulating officers to seek an audience with mayors and magistrates to get their endorsement. From the Admiralty's point of view this was a politic course of action. The co-operation of magistrates was important in any disturbance that might flow from impressing seamen, especially in larger ports where the constables and beadles (not to mention posses) outnumbered the press gang on duty. Furthermore, mayors in larger ports often had intimate contact with shippers and merchants, and gentlemanly agreements with them over protections (that is, exemptions) from the press were likely to smooth the day-to-day operations of the regulating officer. No captain wished to be mired in litigious proceedings with merchants over the quotas of men who were protected from the press, either by statute or Admiralty licence.

Whether magistrates were obliged to back press warrants or not was a contentious issue. The Admiralty sought legal advice on just this question in 1757 because the regulating officer at Gravesend, Captain Howard Hutchinson, had been given the run-around by the mayor when he had asked for his assistance. The Admiralty's legal counsel advised that civil co-operation was customary but not essential to press-gang operations.[30] He also thought there was no law that expressly mandated a magistrate to back warrants, even though the language of the warrant 'required' the civil power to 'aid and assist'.[31] The Admiralty Solicitor agreed with this judgment, but some magistrates continued to believe that their consent was necessary. The Greenock JPs argued this in 1760, when Captain Gentil was besieged by an angry mob while searching for deserters in this Clydeside port. In their view his search was irregular, and they committed him to gaol for trespass and assault.[32] This legal uncertainty put regulating captains in a difficult position. Faced with an uncooperative mayor or JP, press captains would often appeal to the Admiralty to put pressure on him to comply, perhaps by advising him that Admiralty protections would be withdrawn, or that Admiralty convoys of merchant vessels would be hard to come by. This tactic normally brought mayors to their senses, although sometimes further threats were necessary. In 1755 the lords of the Admiralty had to threaten the mayor of King's Lynn with a general press of the town before he agreed to back warrants.[33]

Local magistrates sometimes dragged their feet in backing warrants, if only to placate merchants who wanted a little time to protect their most experienced or skilful seamen from the press. They sometimes did not provide press gangs with the necessary back-up authority of constables when the gangs searched houses for available seamen, for technically search warrants had to come from the civil power. Captain Knowler complained of this in 1756 when on duty at Yarmouth. 'I am on very good terms with the Mayor & Magistrates of this Corporation', he informed the Admiralty, 'who tell me they will give me all the assistance in their power to procure men for His Majesty's Service, but cannot prevail on them to permit a lock to be forc'd open, even if we are certain of men being concealed in the Room, by which means we have mish (missed) taking some seamen.'[34] This passive resistance was a predictable problem for press-gang officers in towns where there was a close association between magistrates and the merchant elite. Mayors and aldermen were unlikely to defy the Admiralty in a stridently confrontational way.

The only significant exception to this rule was the aldermen of the City of London. In the Wilkesite era of the 1770s, in particular, they refused to back press warrants and strove to make the City a press-free zone. Although some pro-ministerial aldermen agreed to back warrants, and although the City's legal counsel thought this a good idea, since it would allow magistrates an opportunity to regulate impressment in the city,[35] radical aldermen felt such an endorsement would undermine their political objections to the press. As far as they were concerned, press warrants were analogous to general warrants and as reprehensibly unconstitutional.[36] Whenever they sat as presiding magistrates at Guildhall, they ordered the constables and beadles to bring all impressed men before them, discharging on the slightest pretext. At the same time, gangs were officially discouraged from operating within the City precincts by the Court of Aldermen, an order enforced by the City marshal. When one gang defiantly paraded past the Council House with drums beating and fifes playing, the Lord Mayor committed its members to the Compter for disturbing the peace.[37]

This policy of legal prevarication reached a crisis in 1777, when three lieutenants were restrained from impressing men within the City. Two of them were later charged with assault for continuing to press men in Lime Street ward. When their captain, James Kirke, expostulated with the Lord Mayor about the City's lack of co-operation with the war effort, he was told that the navy's mode of impressment was considered by the Court of Aldermen to be 'insupportable in law'.[38] On precisely what grounds Captain Kirke was unable to determine. The Lord Mayor, Sir Thomas Hallifax, refused to be pinned down and declined to render a written statement of the aldermen's decision without consulting the Recorder. Eventually the lieutenants were discharged because the two men who had been originally impressed in Lime Street failed to appear in court.[39]

The City's opposition to impressment was fuelled by radical ideology and pro-American sentiment. If its politicians failed to challenge the constitutionality of impressment, their vigilance against the gangs did have some basis in law. As the City's counsel had recognized, process was critical. Justice Foster may have defended the legality of impressment in *Rex v. Broadfoot*, but he also presided over a case in which a press warrant had been improperly executed. Warrants had to be properly dated and endorsed by the regulating officer on duty, who had to be present when boats were boarded or pubs entered in the search for eligible seamen. In 1798, the impressment of five apprentices from a collier in Shields harbour was considered legally dubious because the lieutenant in charge had supervised the search from the shore.[40] Lawyers representing clients who resisted impressment were quick to pick up on these matters, even to the point of demanding evidence that the signatures of the Lords of the Admiralty on the press warrant were authentic.[41] If there was an irregularity, then it was commonly thought that resistance to impressment was legitimate. Neither Sergeant Foster nor any other judge actually said this, but this was how their judgments were frequently represented in the newspapers.[42]

Magistrates, too, wanted evidence that due process had been observed. In 1778, Alderman John Sawbridge upbraided the press gang that had attempted to arrest James Blake, a grocer's assistant on Ludgate Hill, because it had not shown its warrant at the point of arrest, even though the warrant was in order and had been backed by the Lord Mayor.[43] Nine years later, magistrates in Edinburgh and Leith imprisoned the press gangs because no regulating officer led them in a massive round-up of seamen and shipwrights.[44] Ordinary citizens could also be assertive in demanding that press officers show their warrant to impress, not only because they wanted due process to be observed by gangs who sometimes had a reputation for lawlessness, but also because men were not above impersonating gangs to exploit the unwary.[45] In the summer of 1790, for example, when a disturbance broke out over the impressment of a man near Whitehall, several bystanders insisted upon the lieutenant 'showing his authority'. When he failed to deliver, he was chased through the streets and only escaped the fury of the mob through the intervention of some soldiers in St James's Park.[46]

Executing proper warrants was simply the first legal step that press gangs had to observe. They also had to be careful not to use undue force in securing men for the navy. Judges sometimes took a very dim view of gangs firing in pursuit of recruits. In 1742, the gang of HMS *Russell* fired at several seamen who were escaping from an outward bound Jamaicaman in Bristol's King Road, shattering the knee of one seafarer. In presiding over this case at the Bristol assizes, Justice Denison observed 'that although a regard was due to the King's Ships, yet that great care ought to be taken by the officers in the execution of their Duty, so as to not injure the rest of the King's subjects ... he knew of no Authority that a man of war's crew had of firing balls upon mariners belonging to merchant ships in order to oblige them to bring to, and that there was no evidence to prove the assertion'.[47] He therefore instructed the jury to disregard much of the testimony for the defendants, one Lieutenant Roots and William Ferrier, with the result that the jury awarded 120 guineas to the injured man.

Trials like this one made officers leery of firing across the bows of merchant ships to force them to heave to, unless there was clear evidence that putative recruits aboard the vessel openly resisted impressment, either by ignoring the signals to be searched or by verbal acts of defiance. Admiralty solicitors were scrupulous in collecting such evidence, especially in situations where resisting seamen had been killed and coroners' inquests had indicted officers for murder. Understandably, regulating captains sometimes went out of their way to placate local inhabitants in situations where the violence of the gangs had been fatal. In the summer of 1777, for example, the press tender in the River Avon fired on several men from the *Friendship* who had gone ashore for the purpose of obtaining a pilot from Pill, killing one seaman and wounding two others. Captain Hamilton had their wounds dressed by a surgeon at the Admiralty's expense and arranged for the burial of the dead man at a nearby parish. He was 'apprehensive of a tumult', he told the Admiralty, if 'the body had been brought to Bristol'.[48] He also helped organize a coroner's inquest aboard another tender, sensing that his co-operation might improve the chances of the master of the tender charged with murder.[49] Meanwhile, the Admiralty collected evidence that the *Friendship*'s crew had exchanged hostile words with the press tender further down the estuary, bolstering the argument that the gang had genuinely believed the men were evading impressment rather than seeking help to navigate the vessel to port.

Like those afloat, impressments ashore also had to be executed with restraint and due process. As a clerical justice from South Shields declared in 1803, the press gangs had 'no authority for dragging Men from their Houses in a forcible manner'.[50] Nor were they supposed to kidnap sailors from the benches and booths of quayside pubs, even though a 'hot press' left little time for formalities. They were supposed to inform landlords of their intention to search his/her house and if requested show their warrants. Moreover, they could not simply break down the doors of houses where seamen were harboured. Where rooms were locked, they had to obtain search warrants and have them executed by officers of the peace. Such regulations were known to publicans, who sometimes exploited their infraction in court. In 1755 former seaman and publican James Shambrooke successfully resisted a search of his house by insisting on such formalities. The local justice, George Rooke, irritated by Shambrooke's knowledge of the law, conspired with the gang to take up his son and brother in revenge, detaining them aboard a man of war for five days. But Shambrooke retaliated by successfully suing the constable and press officer for trespass, assault and false imprisonment.[51]

JPs may have bridled at the way in which ordinary citizens used the law against the press gang, but there were occasions when they followed suit. In 1779, Captain Alms, angered by the way in which the fishermen of Brighton were using protections to evade the press, ordered a general raid on the village with the help of a troop of soldiers from Lewes. When it was known that the village was about to receive a visit from the press gang, the inhabitants locked their doors and refused to co-operate with the search. So, too, did the resident magistrate, Mr Warden. He was requested to be present 'to force open the Doors of such Houses I should think proper to search', Alms reported. 'But to my great Disappointment, he flatly refus'd to grant me that Order, or even send the Constables with me, Unless I would give upon Oath that there was Men secreted in any particular House. This I could not do, And therefore in Course of staying Ten Hours, I was under the Necessity of quitting the Town without being able to get only one Man.'[52] His only consolation was that he was able to round up a gang of smugglers during the raid.

Captain Alms approached the legal technicalities of impressing seamen with a certain equanimity. Others let their exasperation get the better of them.

Regulating captains were not necessarily superannuated officers anxious for a quiet time. They were often young men on the make, ready to cut a figure in the navy and anxious to assume command of a ship.[53] As gentlemen they sometimes had a low tolerance of petty officers and officious landlords, not to mention fishermen who knew the law. When one oysterman refused to take some sick men to hospital without a ticket of leave, the captain called him a 'saucy son of a bitch' and clapped him in irons. 'You should have kept a better tongue in your head', the captain is alleged to have told him.[54] Naval officers were sometimes outraged if their own gentility was called into question. When one customs officer from Sheerness had the temerity to consider his commission equivalent to that of a naval captain, he was threatened with a flogging and forcibly detained aboard a man of war for over five months.[55]

Naval honour could be brittle; naval ambition careless of legal niceties. Admiralty solicitors were routinely confronted with lieutenants who denied constables their authority, denounced them as 'scurvy' fellows, or bucked the proprieties of search-and-entering because they suspected landlords were hiding deserters. In 1744, a lieutenant ordered his men to break down a 'Hundred doors', if necessary, while searching for deserters in a Bermondsey pub. When the landlord remonstrated with him, he hit him so hard that he coughed blood for days.[56] A similar incident occurred at Greenhithe, Kent, in 1803. On this occasion the landlord told the lieutenant he could search no further than the tap-room, having only a 'common press warrant' in his possession. The lieutenant replied 'he would go where he pleased, and his men should follow him, and break open every door in the house if he thought proper'. He promptly drew his sword and knocked the landlord down, whereupon the gang moved in and 'beat him dreadfully about the head with the butt end of their pistols'.[57] No Admiralty solicitor was about to condone this behaviour, nor the assault upon a landlord's wife, who thought the officer more of an 'Irish bog-trotting fellow' than a gentlemen because he had tried to silence her by thrusting his cane in her mouth.[58] If they were sued, such officers were advised to settle out of court or suffer the consequences.

The Admiralty would not, however, leave regulating officers and their press gangs at the total mercy of the civilian courts. It had no wish to encourage resistance to impressment or undermine naval morale by refusing to defend its men. It recognized that suits against the press gang could be vexatious, the culmination perhaps of deteriorating relations between the gang and port-side communities. It also knew that it was sometimes difficult to determine who was responsible for the many tavern brawls and street affrays that accompanied impressment. Consequently the Admiralty was routinely involved in defending or funding the legal suits of regulating officers and their men, even where their legal culpability was contestable. In 1787 the Admiralty took up the case of a lieutenant who had become embroiled with a militant publican and his cronies, even though the Admiralty's counsel thought that the lieutenant's visit to this house, a rendezvous for volunteers, to be 'improper' and likely provocative.[59] Seven years later, the Admiralty agreed to pay the legal costs of Captain Thomas Affleck, who had refused to release James Townsend on the grounds that he was a sea apprentice of less than two years' standing. In fact Affleck had defied a writ of habeas corpus to produce Townsend, shipping him off to the East Indies instead.[60] Although the Admiralty Solicitor admonished Affleck for flouting the jurisdiction of the courts, and warned him that any future help would be dependent upon his compliance with the law, he likely sympathized with the captain's complaint that the so-called apprentice had exploited the law to evade service.

The Admiralty would finance the suits of its officers where their opponents were suspected of manipulating the law, or where they appeared vexatiously litigious or aggressively hostile to impressment.[61] It would also try to protect its men from humiliating public punishments. In 1770 it was reported that a lieutenant who had falsely impressed an officer of the Lord Mayor had been pilloried, fined £500 and sentenced to imprisonment for seven years, but there is no evidence that this was more than wishful thinking on the part of City radicals.[62] In fact, in cases where press gangs were likely to bear the brunt of local anger, they were frequently removed to another jurisdiction.[63] In 1762 the Admiralty Solicitor was distressed that he had been unable to prevent a case involving Lieutenant Runsiman from being tried in the local courts. According to the depositions, Runsiman had impressed a local hero, a young sailor named Benjamin Bell who had been wounded at Quiberon Bay and had subsequently been exempted from the press. Bell, however, spent his spare time alerting other sailors of the gang's approach, and Runsiman thought he would teach him a lesson by detaining him on the tender until he could find a substitute, taking him up when he was without his protection on his person. In a strict sense, Runsiman operated within the law; but the locals in King's Lynn thought his actions vindictive and successfully charged Runsiman and two gangers for assaulting Bell's father in the course of their dealings with the young man. The lieutenant and his men were fined 1s. each and spent two weeks in gaol, impairing the impress service in the process. The Admiralty solicitor, Samuel Sedden, had hoped that the JPs would have allowed the Admiralty time to remove the case to King's Bench. He regretted that they had been unable to avoid the 'disgrace of an immediate commitment'.[64]

The most sensitive cases where local passions might influence the law were clearly those where gangers had killed someone. If the death occurred as the result of a tavern brawl outside the line of duty, gangers could expect no help from the Admiralty.[65] If it occurred in the course of an impressment affray, especially where a coroner's inquest had indicted a gangsman for murder, then the

Admiralty would organize a defence and muster evidence. Often it would try to remove the case to another jurisdiction, hoping thereby to insulate seamen from popular judgment. If the incident occurred in any place definable as the high seas, this would mean the High Court of Admiralty. In 1795, in a case involving the death of a fishermen resisting impressment in Poole Harbour, the Admiralty removed the case to the Old Bailey on the grounds that Brownsea Castle was outside the shire jurisdiction, much to the consternation of the corporation, which attempted to re-indict the officers at the Dorchester assizes.[66]

More frequently, cases were removed from the assizes to the Court of King's Bench to be considered as special verdicts. This happened to fifteen gangsmen prosecuted for the murder of an Ipswich publican, and to a midshipman who had attempted to recruit men from a fishing smack off the Devonshire coast and had fired at its master out of frustration.[67] In both instances the judges upheld the Admiralty's defence that the men had acted in the course of duty, reducing the charge to manslaughter. Where a ganger was successfully convicted for murder at a county assize, and this was rare, the Admiralty Solicitor moved quickly to obtain a respite of the sentence until his majesty's pleasure was known.[68] No government wanted gangsmen hanging from the gallows. That would be extremely damaging to naval morale and to the legitimacy of impressment. But no government wanted the press gangs to think they were above the law either.

Thus far I have argued that while impressment remained an unpopular method of naval recruitment in the eighteenth century, it proved extremely difficult, if not impossible, to challenge its legality. What opponents could do was to ensure that impressment was executed with due process: to check that press warrants were properly executed and to invigilate the operations of the press gangs whose search for men had to take into account the laws respecting the property and privacy of individuals and the jurisdictions of civil officers. On this terrain, there were opportunities for curbing the excesses of the gangs, and indeed for holding them at arm's length. Precisely who was able to avail himself of this regulatory space is something we must now examine; it has some bearing upon the larger historical question of who was able to use the law in the eighteenth century, and how successfully.

Most of the litigants who crop up in the papers of the Admiralty solicitor were men of property: merchants, shipowners, masters demanding the return of runaway apprentices, publicans seeking damages that accrued from tavern brawls, or perhaps demanding the release of a seaman-debtor to the civil authorities. These were middling people with enough credit or personalty and enough time to bring an action against the impress service. Seamen as mates, masters or apprentices were often the subject of litigation but rarely the litigants themselves. There were, of course, exceptions. John Alexander, the owner of an oysterboat on the Medway, successfully sued the captain who confined him in irons for refusing to take sick prisoners to Rochester without proper authorization.[69] George Duncan, a seamen-turned-smuggler who had sailed on several West Indian voyages, had enough money to hire an attorney to obtain his release from the service on the somewhat improbable grounds that he was a Middlesex freeholder.[70] Another exception to the rule was John Nicholson, a Greenlander who was working in the coal trade during the off-season who was impressed in November 1793 and carried aboard HMS *Eurydice*.[71] He threatened to sue the Admiralty for the losses incurred by his confinement of over one year. These included £40 wages for his next Greenland voyage and £17 for his release and costs. Nicholson had an attorney write to the Admiralty demanding his release, emphasizing the 'serious inconvenience' his detention had been to such 'a poor Man'. The Admiralty solicitor took the threat of prosecution seriously and, recognizing that Nicholson's impressment was contrary to statute, advised the captain and lieutenant of the *Eurydice* to settle out of court 'as no Defence could be made for them'.

Nicholson's was a clear-cut case of unlawful detainment and it is probable that an attorney would find it in his interest to pursue it with a good prospect of being paid. Not all cases would have been so simple, and a local attorney must have sometimes wondered whether the cost of a lawsuit, which could easily amount to £20 or 5–6 months' wartime wages for an able seaman,[72] was enough of an incentive. Unless seamen had powerful friends in port, litigation through the courts was usually something of a luxury. The best most seafarers could hope for was to exploit the law to evade impressment, not to confront it directly.

The prospects for evading impressment by manipulating its legal regulations were not bad. In order to reconcile the imperatives of trade with those of war, the Admiralty routinely came to some arrangement with local portside employers about the number of men who could be kept (anachronistically) in 'reserved occupations'. The number of protections that the Admiralty and Navy Office issued in 1757 amounted to about 17,250; together with those seafaring occupations protected by statute (10,761) and by other maritime agencies (nearly 20,000), the total number of seafarers annually exempted from impressment approached 50,000.[73] Whatever the economic benefits that accrued from this concession – and the Admiralty made a tidy sum in protection fees – it opened the door to the eighteenth-century equivalent of 'draft-dodging'. As early as 1734 Admiral Norris was told that 'there was not three seamen in Deal but what were protected, and that as soon as a man can but get three half-crowns or ten shillings to give to any freeman of Sandwich, he gets … a protection'.[74] This sort of practice so troubled the navy that after 1740 it insisted that protections carry an exact description of its holder; including height, hair-colouring, tattoos and facial scars. This curbed the trade in protections, but it certainly did not eliminate it. Captain Alms protested that the liberal distribution of exemptions among the Brighton fishermen made it difficult for him to know who was liable to be pressed, a 'game' the fisherfolk had played 'for two years past'. Similarly, Captain Patrick Baird complained that a master carpenter in King's Lynn had only used half of his sixteen protections, ensuring 'that room is left to foist on … any person they wish to protect'.[75] This sort of scam troubled the regulating officers, as did the prospect of protected sailors straggling along the quayside at the time of a hot press. In Liverpool the regulating captain attempted to ensure that the seamen and ship's carpenters who were protected remained near their dock during recruiting drives. Otherwise, he complained in 1777, the press gangs would never know who was a legitimate quarry, leaving themselves very vulnerable to altercations in the street and to mob intervention.[76]

The Admiralty could put the squeeze on portside communities who made a trade in protections by refusing to issue any under its own authority. When William Hurry's dockyard workers rioted against the press at the resumption of war against Napoleon in 1803, the regulating captain advised the Admiralty to withhold protections to the yard 'till their people behave properly'.[77] Even so, the Admiralty had to contend with those protections that were issued by other departments and, more importantly, with those that were guaranteed by statute. Foreigners were exempt from impressment. So too were the masters and first mates of shipping vessels and sea apprentices in the first three years of their indenture.[78] All of these concessions were open to abuse. Sailors sometimes impersonated foreigners, especially after American Independence, when seamen could plausibly claim they were citizens of the new republic. Others pretended, usually with their employer's connivance, that they were first mates or masters of ships. Captain John Bover of Newcastle complained that many Tyneside masters 'would swear a man was a mate to keep him out of the navy, tho' in reality he was not before; and by way of a *salvo* to their Conscience, have let him act as such for 3 or 4 days, and then turn him before the Mast again'.[79] What was true on Tyneside was also true further south. Captain Patrick Baird reported from King's Lynn that a local merchant and known enemy of the press gang had tricked him out of four seamen by producing fake evidence of their ratings. The one described as the master of the *Elizabeth*, he quipped, 'was never capable of any trust above a Cook'.[80]

The same strategy of evasion pertained to apprentices. In Anne's reign parliament had passed legislation designed to curb the abuse of sea apprenticeships by enacting that anyone who had prior experience of the sea could not then be bound to a master mariner.[81] The qualification was often ignored. Captain Napier believed that the Edinburgh shipmasters used 'every Stratagem' to keep their seamen at arm's length from the gangs, including the large-scale indenturing of their crews.[82] Lieutenant Scott revealed that on the Tyne and Wear, a shopkeeper named John Moreson provided false indentures on demand to any merchant who wanted them for his crews, thereby depriving the navy of 'many young men'.[83] Not that all of the so-called apprentices were necessarily young. Captain Thomas Affleck's disgruntlement with James Townsend was because he was too old and too worldly to merit exemption as an inexperienced apprentice. He thought that Townsend, a former chimney sweeper aged 28 or 29 years, was 'a great *rogue* & capable of almost *anything*'. There was 'every reason to think among his various employments', he advised the Admiralty, 'that he has been at sea at different times'.[84] The only trouble was that Affleck knew he couldn't prove it, as Townsend had been away from his Norfolk birthplace (South Repps) for years and now had 'connections & mates' who would swear anything. Consequently Affleck decided to send him aboard HMS *Stately*, beyond the reach of the law. It was illegal, but to the captain it was the rough justice Townsend deserved.

One of the ways in which seamen might avoid Townsend's fate was by having themselves sued for debt. No-one could order the arrest of a seaman in the Royal Navy for small debts, save conceivably in the Channel Islands, but under a 1758 statute a civil suit was possible if the debt was £20 or more.[85] The concession was sufficient to cause trouble to the navy. When Jonathan Kelly, a seafarer and publican in Liverpool, was impressed in August 1778 upon his return from a voyage, a local wholesale brewer sued him for a debt of £20-5-0d. and threatened the regulating officer with a suit if he was not released.[86] His case may well have been genuine, but in others it was dubiously so. James Dowell, a mate impressed in Newcastle while off duty, was immediately served with a debt of £20; but 'upon particular inquiries' the regulating officer discovered 'this had been done by the advice of some attorney or another, at the suit of his own Mother; & merely to screen him from the King's service'.[87] At Dover, writs for fictitious debts abounded, and when a notorious smuggler from Eyemouth was sued for debt upon his impressment, the regulating officer in the Firth of Forth feared the custom would soon spread further north. 'If such a precedent were once allowed', Captain Napier wrote to the Admiralty, 'every Man who is impressed would cause his friends [to] rear up debts against him and procure the judges warrant for taking him ashore'.[88] Napier was not alone in fearing that a flood of debt actions would undermine impressment. Captain Gordon complained of the same practice in Bristol, while at Plymouth it was discovered that the local publicans routinely made seamen take out bonds of £20 in order to secure their credit, a custom that placed the navy in this busy port at the virtual mercy of the crimp.[89] In fact the recovery of seamen's debt was a sufficiently grave problem for the Admiralty Solicitor to suggest a counter-strategy in 1777. Confronted with reports that bailiffs had been busily demanding the delivery of indebted sailors at the Nore, one of the other major stations of the navy, he wondered whether the Admiralty could claim that the Nore was 'upon the High sea' and therefore beyond civil jurisdiction. Perhaps 'a judicial determination' of this issue, he submitted to their lordships, would cut down the traffic in debtors and insulate the navy from the importunities of the civil courts.[90]

Admiralty officials were clearly worried that legal actions initiated in the civil courts would compromise its manning operations. While the Admiralty never openly defied the law, it certainly attempted to work it to its advantage. In some instances it shied away from testing the eligibility of impressment in the courts on the grounds that 'legal definitions would hamper rather than facilitate the service'. This was so on the question of whether keelmen were technically liable to impressment, a matter which had never been formally contested by Newcastle's hostmen, but one that could potentially disrupt Tyneside recruitment in a major way.[91] In other contexts, however, the Admiralty was not prepared to give any ground on matters that might widen the existing loopholes in the law. At various times in the eighteenth century, for example, discharged sailors had been allowed to set up in trade without fulfilling the normal apprenticeship requirements, a concession designed to minimize the social dislocations of demobilization in the aftermath of war.[92] Yet at the same time, men with adequate sea experience were legally bonded to the state until their fifties. Which law prevailed, statute or prerogative? In 1779 Admiralty counsel said the latter,[93] even though local regulating officers often gave some discretionary licence to sailors who had clearly settled into land-based trades. They would only insist on a strict reading of the law where dual occupations might seriously undermine the search for men. This was the case at Perth, where Alexander Wedderburn reported that it was 'common practice' for young men, who had served apprenticeships as weavers, shoemakers, or other trades, to go to sea, 'where they continue shorter or longer as they find it answer'.[94]

The degree to which regulating captains exercised their discretion was also dependent upon the overall manning imperatives of the navy. In periods when volunteers were flush, shore captains might turn a blind eye to minor infractions of the regulations governing impressment. In periods when the manning requirements of the Royal Navy assumed new levels of urgency, they were encouraged to be officious: to impress all apprentices who did not carry indentures; to follow up on debtors and try to re-impress them once they were discharged from gaol.[95] In the mid-1790s, when the government had to institute quota acts to tap the manpower of the nation, the Admiralty conducted a legal review of statutory protections to ensure that it had not been too liberal in its interpretation of them. It scrutinized the legal exemptions in the coal trade, for example,[96] and decided that the employment of juvenile workers under the system known as 'colting' was not a formal apprenticeship, making 'colts' vulnerable to impressment.[97] The Admiralty was also advised that those able bodied men impressed for being 'idle and disorderly' under the 1795 Vagrancy

Act could only be discharged for criminal, not civil, causes, making it impossible for them to be arrested for debt.[98] When this scrutiny failed to bring in enough men, the Admiralty would temporarily renounce its protections and institute a 'hot press' as it was called, taking up just about every seaman or riverside worker from the quayside. In the summer of 1779, when Britain faced the combined forces of America, France, Spain and Holland, the navy literally took up everyone: even those with statutory exemptions. Only after the manning crisis had passed did it seek a parliamentary indemnity for its actions.[99]

In the last analysis the Admiralty could be quite ruthless in the way it understood and applied the laws and regulations pertaining to impressment. On balance it had the power and resources to act first and ask questions afterwards. Potential plaintiffs had to have money and influence on their side if they were to stand a good chance of redress. And any action taken against arbitrary or illegal impressment had to be taken quickly; otherwise the press gang would whisk men away to the tenders and onto the men of war at the Nore or Spithead, where captains could make life difficult for those who came to petition them with writs of arrest or habeas corpus.[100] This necessarily placed poor men at a great disadvantage. Few seafaring families were in a position to mobilize a petition or suit against impressment lacking outside help, and much of this help emerged within a structure of employer or political paternalism. MPs of port constituencies would sometimes intervene on behalf of their seamen; or, as in the case of the Brighton fishermen, prominent patrons such as the Duke of Newcastle.[101] A more likely source of aid, however, was the ship-owner or master who wanted a particular apprentice or protected seaman before the mast and was prepared doggedly to pursue the Admiralty through the courts to get him. The Hurry family of Yarmouth – merchants, ship-owners, Dissenters, reformers – seems to have been noticeably litigious on this score.[102] But the more independent or surly the seaman, the less likely such protection would be offered. If such a seaman could not mobilize a few friends to have him arrested for debt – probably to cheapest way legally to evade the service – he would have to resist the gang in other ways. That included direct physical confrontation. With over 600 reported impressment affrays in the period 1740–1805, that would seem to be the more typical recourse of the beleaguered tar and other potential recruits.

What should we conclude, then, about the accessibility of the law in the eighteenth century from the experience of impressment? It is clear that one cannot regard seamen, or putative seamen, as legally illiterate subjects, simple victims of a recruiting system whose legal intricacies they did not understand. Edward Thurlow remarked in 1777, on the issue of whether freeholders were exempt from the law, that if the Admiralty ever conceded this exemption, sailors would readily exploit it. 'There is no knowing a Freeholder by sight', he noted, 'and if claiming that character, or even shewing deeds is sufficient, few sailors will be without it.'[103] Thurlow was in no doubt that seamen would work the system if they could, and we know that some became adept at evading impressment by exploiting the laws regarding debt, or volunteering for the militia or sea fencibles in order to exclude themselves; or by purchasing fake protections or having themselves 're-classified' as mates or masters.

We also know from the lengthier reports concerning impressment affrays, and from the often quite public confrontations between naval officers and the civil power, that seamen would have gleaned a rudimentary knowledge of the procedures that were designed to ensure that press gangs operated within the law and upheld the peace of the neighbourhood. Whether press warrants were properly endorsed, whether regulating captains sought the co-operation of the magistrates and constables in making thorough searches of quayside pubs and taverns, were not matters exclusive to middling shopkeepers and those above them. The critical issue is not whether seamen lacked the knowledge to use the law, but whether they had the money and social networks to use that knowledge in instances where they were improperly impressed. It is here that the notion of the law as an accessible use-right needs to be qualified. By and large seamen could only seek legal redress with the help of social superiors, and that usually meant some endorsement of or investment in the structures of patron–client relations through which the law was exercised. In the picaresque world of maritime labour, full of young men in their 20s who were impatient of the proprieties of rank and place, only a minority could avail themselves of the kinds of protection and aid that made legal redress a success.

# 3

# Resisting the Press Gang: Trends, Patterns, Dynamics

'*Pour faire de l'histoire*', wrote Georges Lefebvre, '*il faut compter*': 'to do history one must count'. Twenty-five years ago many social historians would have endorsed this position. In seeking to emancipate the common man (and later, woman) from the thrall of elitist political or administrative history, historians frequently looked to numbers as the answer. Many believed that history could be democratized by utilizing serial data, or data that could be reworked into a series. By this means one might uncover all manner of facts about the past that were usually ignored by political historians: the patterns of family living within households, for example, the rhythms of births, deaths and marriages, the height and nutrition of men, the social mobility of nineteenth-century societies, the composition of riotous crowds. Some prominent social historians saw the construction of such documentary series as nothing less than 'a revolution in the historical consciousness', displacing the 'thin' narratives of *histoire événementielle* (event history) from the summit of historical scholarship and forging new links between history and the social sciences. Emmanuel Le Roy Ladurie proclaimed that 'tomorrow's historian will have to be able to programme a computer in order to survive'.[1] In a special issue of *Daedalus* in 1971, François Furet argued that the future lay in processing the 'spaghetti junctions' of serial history. This was the route that would reveal the structural forces shaping society and the way in which common men and women, principally Mr and Mrs Average, negotiated them.

Times have changed. Cliometrics now thrives only in specific sub-disciplines of history. Quite ironically, some of its most vocal proponents have abandoned it for more fashionable lines of inquiry, such as micro-history and discourse analysis. The disenchantments with counting were many. From the beginning there were those who felt that cliometrics was little more than 'positivism armed with a computer';[2] an exercise in historical naiveté which posited that the 'facts', once counted, would computationally disclose their own meaning. When harnessed to a modernizing paradigm, serial history was accused of producing a homogeneous, packaged reconstruction of the past that marginalized popular agency and exalted the mass society of capitalist consumerism. More recently, quantitative history has been accused of being epistemologically bankrupt. Critics have argued that quantifiable data are too immersed in discursive fields to be translated into a more or less value free series of social facts from which valuable historical statistics might be obtained.

So why bother to count at all? My answer would be that the attempt to bring some typicality to events in the past does guard against heavy conclusions based on purely impressionistic evidence. In the words of Charles Tilly, it 'reduces the temptation to let a few spectacular and well-documented conflicts dominate interpretations of change'.[3] In the specific case of resistance to impressment, where J.R. Hutchinson's evidence has been accused of being overly dramatic, anecdotal and untypical, counting becomes essential. It allows us to re-open the question of how pervasive open, physical confrontations to the press gangs really were in the eighteenth century. At the present time there is little consensus on this issue. N.A.M. Rodger has suggested that while 'riots and fights ashore were commonplace', they were invariably 'led or instigated by deserters from the Navy'.[4] In other words, opposition to impressment was largely an in-service affair, from which ordinary people kept their distance. Whereas other historians have taken a more expansive view of the press gangs' presence, and of the disruptions they provoked,[5] Rodger disputes the bad image of the gangs, whose capacity to inflict harm was limited by their size and vulnerability to prosecution.

We have no reliable figures of press-gang affrays and of those implicated in them. This is not surprising. A series that would make this possible is extremely difficult to construct. The most accessible source for discovering impressment affrays is undoubtedly the newspaper, but newspapers were never straightforward windows to the world, least of all on matters of popular contention. Efforts to use them in this way over time, especially to tabulate the different actions within a single contention and the language that was used to advance claims to fairness, justice or retribution, are seriously flawed.[6] Newspapers varied considerably in size over the course of the eighteenth and early nineteenth century, responding to changes in the stamp and advertisement taxes and also to readership. This meant that printers were more selective in some decades about what news they might reasonably make public. Publishers and printers also had to be on guard against prosecutions for seditious libel and *ex-officio* information that could stymie their business. To complicate matters some forms of popular contention were conventionally covered more extensively than others. Protests against the local dearth of grain, for example, were more likely to find their way into print than labour disputes or seditious words, largely because the gentry, farmers and dealers who were the staple readers of many newspapers had a large stake in their resolution.

In the case of impressment affrays, much seems to have depended upon the political conjunctures of war and the politics of particular newspapers. The *Middlesex Journal*, for instance, was particularly attentive to the manning problems of the navy during the Falkland Islands crisis of 1770–1, because the issue of press warrants intersected with other matters pertaining to the liberties of the subject that were of acute interest to its predominantly Wilkesite constituency. Similarly, opposition newspapers vigorously reported confrontations over impressment in the summer of 1779, when Britain found itself at war with no fewer than four countries, simply because they wanted to emphasize the inadequacies and impotence of Lord North's ministry in its dealings with America. In contrast, newspapers seem to have been more guarded in their reportage of impressment in periods of political consensus and vigorous sabre-rattling, especially in the years 1757–59. This was also true of 1796–98 and 1803–5, when Britain's war with Napoleon assumed crisis proportions and the possibility of invasion seemed very real. In 1803, in particular, the newspapers tended to report only the most glaring struggles over impressment and ignored the depth of opposition to recruitment as the war with France was resumed.

Newspapers, then, cannot provide the basic data for a chronological series of anti-impressment affrays. Rather they are an important supplement to documents found in the vast Admiralty records in the National Archives. The most important of these is the Admiralty 1 series, the in-letters to the Lords of the Admiralty from its various officers. In the context of anti-impressment riots, the most critical single source is the letters of the Admiralty Solicitor, because he was responsible for advising the Admiralty on legal matters and setting in motion plans for defending naval officers, arranging for settlements out of court and prosecuting men and women who had infringed the law on matters pertaining to naval business. This source reveals evidence of the most factious and litigious affrays of the century. It can be usefully supplemented by the legal opinions of various lawyers solicited by the Admiralty, a source which sometimes offers some illuminating detail on particular affrays. Equally important are the in-letters of the regulating officers responsible for recruitment. One cannot guarantee that they reported every affray with which their gangs were involved. Had they done so, their own credibility as wartime recruiters might have been brought into question. But they did tend to report those that attracted public comment and those that were likely to affect the operations of impressment on a day-to-day basis, either because gang members were injured or vulnerable to prosecution, or because some local official – a mayor, a sheriff, a justice of the peace – was implicated. In effect, they tended to report those affrays that were likely to have a serious reverberatory effect on the logistics of impressment unless some counteraction by the government was not taken.

Taken together these sources offer a rough-and-ready guide to impressments affrays. I have used them to track the struggles of the period 1738–1805, from the War of Jenkins' Ear to the year of Trafalgar. From these, and from secondary sources, I have discovered 602 affrays and riots for this 67-year period, one which covers the five major wars of the Georgian era plus three significant mobilizations when Britain was poised for war without actually declaring one. This tally almost certainly omits the small affrays in pubs, streets and press tenders that regulating officers or their lieutenants and midshipmen never took the trouble to report: the taken-for-granted bruising and bullying in which press gangs engaged to bring reluctant seamen to the rendezvous. It certainly under-represents a good number of affrays that occurred at sea when men of war accosted home-coming merchantmen for their eligible seamen. But one can reasonably assume that the most contentious of all affrays are included in this survey. In this respect it is noteworthy that Admiralty and newspaper sources often complement one another, save in those periods of patriotic euphoria when the press avoided talking about incidents that might sully the war effort and muffle the war-whoop for King and Country.

Roughly 450,000 men were recruited into the navy during the period 1740–1815. In view of this, it could be argued that 602 affrays is an insignificant number, one for every 750 or so men enlisted. With this kind of ratio, recruitment appears to have been a success, despite the coercion involved. Such a statement contains a grain of truth: but it overlooks the fact that some of these affrays involved around 50 or even hundreds of people who could mount community-wide protests against the press gang. In 1741, for example, a Dublin crowd of '300 or more, all arm'd with Fire-Arms, Swords and Clubs', rescued impressed men from the town rendezvous. Five years later, a crowd of 200–300 men attacked the *Dispatch* sloop when it was on an impressment mission in Shoreham.[7] At the end of the century, a pregnant woman attempting to restrain the press gang from taking her husband drew a sympathetic crowd of 300.[8] A few years later, at the resumption of the French wars in 1803, 500 Irish haymakers defied a gang in Barking sent to impress them.[9] In earlier wars, especially those of the 1740s, this kind of detail is admittedly rare. Accounts in the press during those decades were generally less specific, referring simply to 'mobs' or 'riots' against the press gang, with little indication of the actual numbers involved. But these reports certainly suggest that press gangs often confronted large companies of seamen in their recruitment drives and they can be corroborated from Admiralty sources.

Those sources also reveal that seamen were not the only people involved in anti-impressment protests. When press gangs attempted to take up seamen who had settled into maritime trades, they frequently had to deal with fellow workers who were incensed by the intrusion of the navy into the lives of their workmates. Shipwrights, coopers, ropemakers, watermen and oyster dredgers, all of whom were vulnerable to impressment, certainly tangled with the gangs.[10] Keelmen on the River Tyne, who carried coals to the estuary of the river, even dragged a tender ashore on one occasion and told the captain and his men that if they persisted with impressing their members, they would be 'made sacrifices of'.[11] Few trades were as belligerent as this one, but quite a few urban or industrial workers were adept at swift collective interventions and were not averse to mounting rescue attempts. These included weavers, draymen, pitmen, tinners, stonemasons, ironworkers, butchers and even printers' devils.[12]

Taking on the press gang, moreover, was not exclusively a male pursuit. Women swarmed the recruiting officers when they arrived to impress and sometimes dissuaded men from entering the service. Captain Wheeler reported from Newcastle in 1755 that he might have recruited more men if the tender had been handy, especially volunteers who arrived in the evening, but they were 'teazed and baited out of it the next day by the women'.[13] Women also summoned neighbours to save their men from the press.[14] They verbally dressed down gangs, pelted them with chunks of coal or broken bottles, and even abetted the escape of men from the tenders.[15] At Bristol in 1759, one good-looking woman waylaid the sentinel on the tender in King's Road while her companion cut through the gratings to the hold to release twenty impressed men.[16]

Women were sometimes brazenly confrontational to the gangs. Hundreds attempted to rescue an impressed sailor outside the Clerkenwell sessions house in 1803.[17] In the North-East, several women were indicted for leading riots and assaulting press-gang officers. They included Elizabeth Johnston and Ann Raeburn, who were among the 'Multitude of Pilots and Women who threw a quantity of Stones and Brickbatts' at Lieutenant Mitchell when he attempted to impress at the fishertown end of South Shields in April 1803.[18] One woman, Hannah Snell, who helped rescue a man at Newington Butts, even swore she would drub any member of the gang who cared to take her on, provided she could don a pair of breeches to do so.[19] Hannah was an exceptional woman; and it may well be that her name was fictional, recalling a former Hannah Snell who had achieved some notoriety as a soldier during the 1740s. Certainly this incident offered a droll, colourful, if not transgressive, take on the resistance to impressment. Yet such episodes drove home the fact that protests against the press not only involved seamen; they encompassed other members of portside communities, male and female. In Poole the recruiting officer, James Chad, reported that 'the common people of this place hang all together which are numerous and would rescue the People that I might have in hold'.[20]

The tally of affrays also confirms that anti-impressment disturbances were not exceptional occurrences in Georgian Britain. Averaging fourteen a year in wartime, they compare favourably with the number of labour disputes that are reported to have taken a violent or intimidatory turn. According to newspaper accounts these numbered 383 for the period 1717–1800, rising conspicuously after 1760.[21] Certainly, they pale in comparison with the number of food riots that broke out in the eighteenth century, of which over 900 are known to have occurred in the period 1740–1801.[22] Yet there is little doubt that anti-impressment confrontations were a routine part of the repertoire of collective protest in the eighteenth century. They made regulating officers very wary of how they proceeded. Captain after captain was troubled by the physical resistance of seafarers and their supporters. In Cork Captain Bennett reported that the sailors travelled together in armed bodies and 'bid defiance to the press gangs'. He was troubled that they 'laugh at both the civil and military power'. At Whitehaven Captain Don found it almost impossible to impress men because the local colliers assembled 'at the least alarm' and easily rescued men from the tender in low tide. Rescuing men from the tender also haunted Captain Smith Child on Merseyside, and he feared for the lives of his men on shore'.[23] Child certainly overreacted to the tense situation in Liverpool, where mobs had ransacked two rendezvous in the preceding month. But the fearful tone of his message was not unprecedented for large ports where seamen and their allies could and did show some muscle in opposition to the recruiting drives of the gangs.

That muscle was particularly visible in the opening year of mobilization when the Royal Navy routinely needed to mobilize 25,000 seamen or more over and above its peacetime complement and was unable to do this through volunteers alone. In most wars the incidence of violent opposition to the press gang was highest in the opening year – even the first months of recruitment – once it was clear that there was a significant shortfall in the number of volunteers who came forward. In the Seven Years' War, for example, the number of affrays in the initial mobilization for war was 150 per cent larger than it was in the second year, 1756. It did not significantly rise again until 1759, when the government hoped to capitalize upon a series of victories on sea and land to force France to the negotiating table. In 1793, too, the opposition to impressment was highest in the opening year of the war, or, as in 1803, when the war was resumed after a brief interlude. In the War of Jenkins' Ear, recruitment began slowly, and violent resistance to the press gang was spread over the first four years as the numbers borne climbed towards the 40,000 mark. In the American war also, resistance to the press gang was spread over the first three or four years. In this instance, the British naval commitment to contain the recalcitrant colonies was already substantial before the actual proclamation of war in August 1775. Thereafter the government renewed its mobilization warily, troubled first of all by a series of strikes in the dockyards which impeded the supply of war-worthy ships, and then by the very vocal resistance of some pro-American corporations, who sought to challenge the legitimacy of impressment in the courts. As a result, naval mobilization did not pick up substantially until 1777, when over 45,000 seamen were put on the payroll. Predictably, this substantial increase in recruitment met with more resistance and a rise in the number of affrays between press gangs and portside populations.

The close link between press-gang affrays and recruitment is evident if one charts the rise in naval mobilization against the cumulating number of recorded

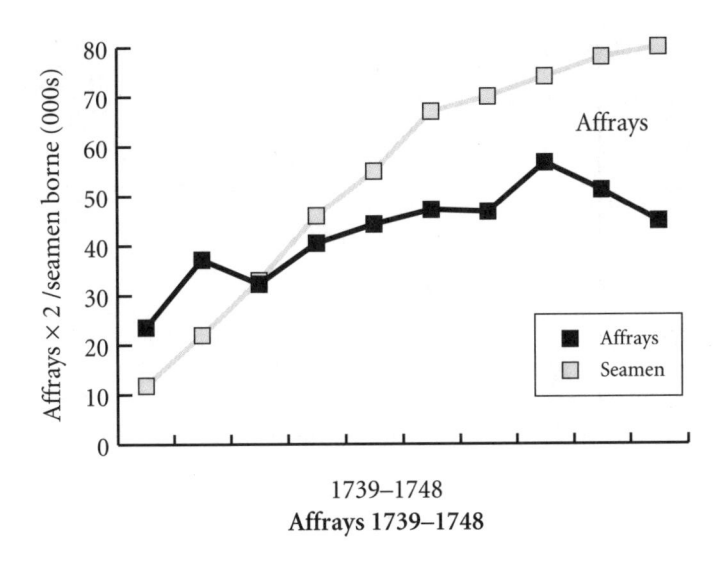

# RESISTING THE PRESS GANG: TRENDS, PATTERNS, DYNAMICS

**Affrays 1739–1748**

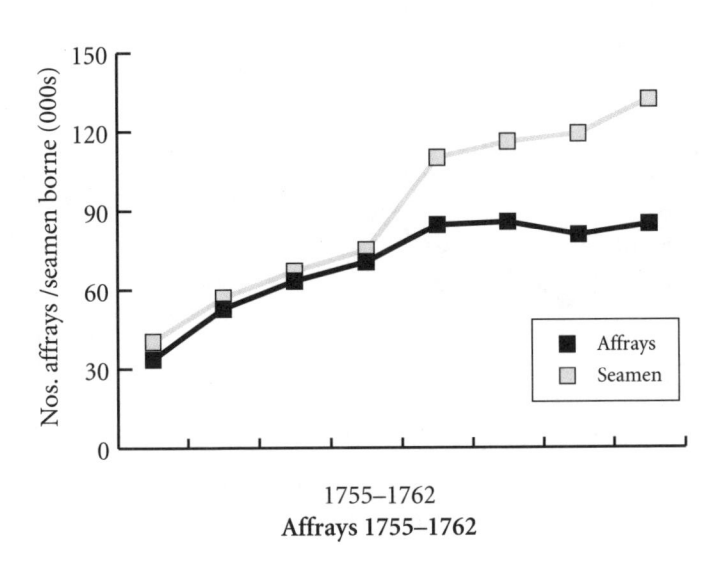

1739–1748

**Affrays 1755–1762**

1755–1762

**Affrays 1776–1782**

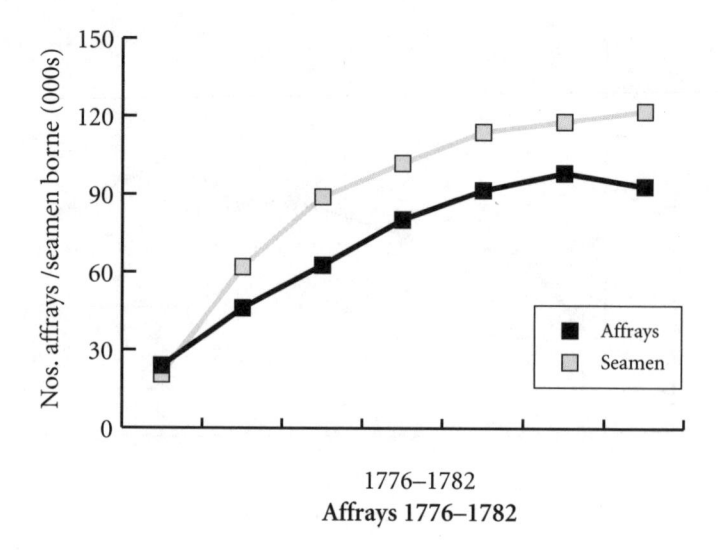

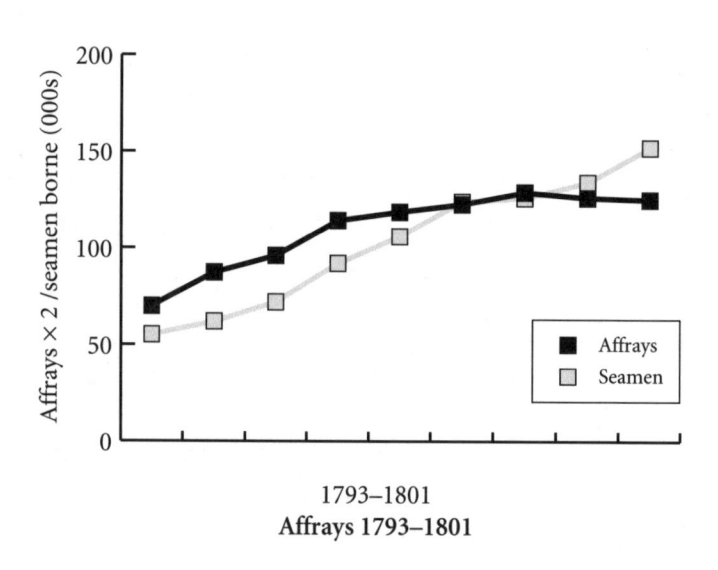

**Affrays 1793–1801**

confrontations. They tend to follow the same curve, reaching a plateau in the fourth year of war, when recruitment became largely a matter of tracking down deserters and returning them to the service. The graphs for the wars between 1739 and 1801 reveal this quite clearly. There are some variations. During the Seven Years' War, the protests against impressment shot up in 1759 when the government attempted to ratchet up recruitment. In the French war protests lagged slightly behind recruitment after the first year of opposition, only picking up in the years 1796–98, when the government strove to mobilize a wider section of the population under the Quota Acts. By contrast, the opposition to impressment followed a steeper curve than did recruitment during the American war, at least until 1780, when both began to plateau. This reflected the open resistance to the war against America in some civic communities and the reverberative effect this had on street protests.

If there is a link between the volume of affrays and the surges of recruitment, it is also worth emphasizing that there were some differences in the proportion of affrays to recruitment. In the wars of the 1740s and 1750s the number of affrays was higher than later in the century, if one takes into account the actual numbers entered into the navy. In the wars of 1739–48, the ratio was 1:526; in the Seven Years' War roughly the same, 1:572.[24] It is in the American and French wars that the incidence of affrays drops relative to recruitment. In 1775–82 the ratio is 1:759, and in 1793–1801, it is 1:1479, a significant decline relative to the number of men borne. This decline cannot be attributed to acclimatization: to the notion that after the early land forays in recruiting, seamen and their supporters begrudgingly accepted the reality of impressment ashore. It is rather, as I have hinted in the previous chapter, that resistance takes different forms.

If the decline thesis looks compelling, then the figures for 1803 should disabuse us of it. In that year anti-impressment protest was spectacularly disproportionate to the volume of men enlisted. In that year there were no less than 88 reported affrays against the press gang, more than during the Wars of Jenkins' Ear and the Austrian Succession (1738–48) combined, and also more than in the opening years of the war against revolutionary France (1793–1801).[25] These affrays not only involved the armed resistance of homeward bound vessels from places such as the East Indies; they also registered the anger of portside communities at the reopening of hostilities amid spiralling food prices and war weariness. In these confrontations, women were especially noticeable in their opposition to the gangs, haranguing press gangs, attacking rendezvous and attempting to rescue their husbands and others from the clutches of the navy. In April 1803, a 'mob of women' from South Shields attacked the press gang commanded by Lieutenant Mitchell that had attempted to reassert its authority in the port. A similar intervention took place in Greenock, where a mob of women pelted the gang that had impressed a man at the quayside. Even towns that had hitherto been peaceful centres of recruitment were caught up in the large-scale resistance to the impress service. In Carmarthen, for example, George Roach, the regulating officer, was totally taken by surprise when the town's women rang the tocsin against the press gang and helped release many impressed men from the guard room.[26]

1803 was an exceptional year of resistance to the press gangs and one that loyalists were reluctant to recognize, with the result that press-gang affrays were conspicuously underreported in the newspapers. Yet somewhat surprisingly, the mobilizations for the 'phoney wars' of the late eighteenth century incurred proportionately as much if not more opposition. In 1770 and again in 1790, when Britain geared up for war against Spain to defend far-off territories, opposition to impressment was greater than it was on other occasions when Britain was on war alert. In terms of the proportion of affrays to men borne, the ratio was 1:343 and 1:523 respectively. In the Falkland Islands crisis in particular, the number of protests was significantly higher than in most real war situations. On occasions such as this all manner of workmen and large heterogeneous crowds actively resisted the impressment of their mates and neighbours. In London, butchers, bricklayers, carpenters, coachmakers, journeymen and printers protested against impressment; in Norwich, woolcombers and weavers. In Greenock a crowd estimated to number four thousand, including many women, were 'much irritated' by the gang's sweep of the streets and its intrusive search of private houses for eligible men. According to one newspaper, the crowd assailed the press gang of the *Savage* sloop with stones and obliged it to take refuge in another boat by the pier.[27] Clearly wide sections of the community were angry that press warrants were issued when Britain's own safety was not directly involved. These protests suggest that sections of the populace were familiar with the legal complexities of impressment, particularly with the argument that its real legitimacy rested, if anywhere, upon the need to defend Britain's shores from outside invasion.

Opposition to impressment, then, appears to have followed the main trajectory of recruitment, billowing in volume on those occasions when Britain was mobilized for diplomatic engagements that seemingly had little to do with its own safety. But other questions need to be asked before we can assess the national significance of impressment affrays as a form of protest. For example, how violent were impressment affrays compared to other modes of collective resistance? And what was the geographical range of affrays over time?

Historians have frequently noted that physical confrontations involving violence against the person and severe wounding, if not homicide, were comparatively rare in eighteenth-century Britain. Rates of homicide declined over the century, as did random street violence and assault. Despite the disposition of English men and women to take to the streets and protest against all manner of social and political grievances, many historians have remarked that such spontaneous demonstrations seldom involved dramatic violence against perceived enemies. Food riots, for example, were sometimes only 'riots' in the most legalistic sense that twelve or more people threatened public order in the eyes of law officers. Quite often they involved intense negotiations between crowds and authority over the appropriate way to handle a food shortage, with crowds sometimes enacting the rituals of the open market in order to stress the legitimacy of their protests. That is to say, they rang bells to open the market and proclaimed a price as if they were officiating over the sale and distribution of bread in a quite formal manner. Sometimes there were extensive parleys with farmers or dealers who were thought to be withholding supplies. These confrontations certainly involved verbal abuse. One farmer returning from Thirsk market in 1800 recorded that 'a woman insulted me as I went through Sowerby saying I should have a halter provided for me against my return'. Another in Ipswich had to run a gauntlet of verbal abuse from women who formed a line on each side of the street. But seldom did rioters employ weapons other than their tongues.[28] Very unpopular dealers were sometimes set upon; they might be hazed or threatened with a hanging, although such intimidation rarely resulted in death.[29] Usually the rage of the crowd was directed at property, not people.

In the larger scenario of popular protest there were none the less some exceptions to this rule. Agrarian protest in Ireland often went beyond cattle houghing and arson. Whiteboy interventions against grasping landlords and their agents could be murderous. In Britain, confrontations between customs officers and smugglers also escalated into violent, bloody affrays. One customs officer from Folkstone reported in 1744, for example, that the struggle between the officers and several large gangs of smugglers could be compared to 'a frontier town in a state of war'.[30] Similarly, protests against impressment could be bloody. To be sure, crowds might demand to see a regulating officer's credentials and dispute the legitimacy of a specific recruitment – that is to say, they might test the laws pertaining to impressment. Wives might try to plead their husbands' case, and women in general could be as vociferously verbal against regulating officers as they were against profiteering millers or dealers. In Greenock, for example, a mob of women yelled insults at the gang as they attempted to impress a man at the quay and went on to smash the windows of the midshipman's house.[31]

Yet impressment disputes escalated into violent confrontations with alarming frequency. Sailors were not the kind of people who would duck a physical confrontation, and they frequently had the scars to show for it. They would not hesitate to use the knives or hangers (small swords) that they had on their person or any sharp objects within their reach. The Greenland whalers, in particular, earned a reputation for violent confrontations with the press gangs, sometimes warding them off with harpoons and flensing knives and defiantly ignoring them both afloat and ashore. In March 1755, for example, the press gang of

HMS *Chichester* was attacked by 'some hundreds of Men who came out of the Greenland Dock, who not only rescued the Men the Gang had Procured, but almost killed three of the press Gang by Cutts and Bruises in their Heads and some broken Ribbs'.[32] Forty years on, two Greenlandmen attacked the coxswain of the *Hound* sloop as he was coming out of a brothel in North Shields; 'for no other reason', the admiralty solicitor remarked, than he was 'frequently on the impress service'. The coxswain's head was found to be irreparably fractured, and great efforts were made to bring the culprits to justice in order to curb the unruly behaviour of the whalers in this northern port.[33]

Neighbourly sympathisers were not averse to joining in the melee either, using the tools of their trade or whatever accoutrements came to hand. A carpenter at Ratcliffe Cross in London stabbed a ganger with a chisel. Tanners attacked gangs with their knives, and a crowd from a pub in St Olave, Southwark, beat them with broomsticks, tongs and shovels. A Spitalfields tradesman even levelled a blunderbuss at a press gang that attempted to impress his son.[34] That casualties should ensue was hardly surprising.

By my calculations, about one in four (N = 150) impressment affrays ended in a death or serious injury. Of the 158 incidents reported – for some affrays resulted in wounds as well as death – five involved seamen who drowned while trying to escape the clutches of the press gang, and one involved a seamen who fell from the roof of a house while being pursued. Most injuries occurred in direct confrontation with the gangs. Very occasionally, those involved were innocent bystanders, or at least not people directly involved in the affray. In 1803 a press gang and troop of marines escorting some men to the tender at Rownham ferry in Bristol panicked when confronted by a mob and opened fire, killing one boy. Forty-three years earlier, a pilot's boy was shot on the Avon when the crew of the *Rising Sun* attempted to escape the clutches of the press gang by climbing down into the pilot's vessel.[35]

In most instances, however, it was the protagonists themselves who were injured in the affrays, with both sides sustaining broken bones, cuts and wounds from hurried pistol and musket shots. Newspapers reported men who had been cut in a 'horrendous manner'. In one struggle between a press gang and the watermen of Blackfriars Bridge, the lieutenant is said to have been 'almost killed' and one of his gang members severely wounded in the neck.[36] In another London confrontation, this time with the coachmakers, another lieutenant was so badly cut that 'scarce a human visage could be traced'.[37] Some of the injuries in these affrays predictably proved fatal or near-fatal. In 74 of these confrontations, that is approximately one in eight, someone died. In several instances impressed men were beaten to death. In 1747, for example, a Dutch sailor impressed on Tower Hill drew a knife on the gang and was pummelled into unconsciousness, dying the following day.[38] In an incident in the following war, one Anthony How was picked up at the Spread Eagle pub opposite St Thomas's hospital in London. He declared 'he had a great family, and had rather go anywhere, or do any thing, than go on board one of his Majesty's Ships'.[39] He drew a knife on one of the gang and 'Swore he would Stab the first Man than came near him'. He was hit over the head before he could stab anyone, so hard one witness reported that 'it sounded as if an Ox had been knock'd down'. The gang dragged him to a wherry where How begged the lieutenant to call in a surgeon. The surgeon did not think the blow had penetrated the skull, but by the time How was allowed to go home he was in a very rough state. His wife recalled that 'his face, Head & Cloaths were all bloody'. The 'Blood seem'd to come from the left side of his Head', she remembered. 'He was exceeding Ill, and Obliged to go to Bed as sone as he came home, and was very restless all Night.' How remained in bed for a few days until he thought himself able to work, but he found he 'could not stay at his Work and came directly home, went to Bed, & continued there till he went to St Thames's Hospital'. He became delirious in the hospital and had to be strapped down on the bed. He died six days later from what was probably a brain haemorrhage.

Most deaths from affrays were less protracted that this, the result of sword wounds or pistol shots fired at close range, or of press crews firing cannon balls across the bows of homecoming ships that refused to heave to, killing merchant seamen in the process. The most dangerous confrontations occurred in confined spaces where gangs grappled with potential recruits, or laid siege to sailors in pubs, houses or boats. Press gangs boarding homecoming vessels often had to face armed crews and troubling missiles. In 1742 the mate and midshipmen of the *Royal Sovereign*, accused of murdering a seaman in the act of impressment, were anxious to exhibit the crowbar and grindstone that had been thrown at the press boat.[40] In 1778, a crew in the Thames confronted the press gang with 'pistols and other weapons' and knocked two of the gangers into the water as they attempted to climb on board. The rest were 'treated so roughly', remarked the *General Advertiser*, that 'they were glad to take to their boat and steer off'.[41] Those gangs that did manage to get on board without any mishap sometimes had to deal with armed crew members clustered in the gangway, or hidden away in cabins, where they could only be forced to surrender by the threat of force. Some of these confrontations were inevitably bloody. William Spavens recalled that on boarding one privateer from New York in search of men, the gang 'discovered the men had taken close quarters', and so 'we scuttled their decks with axes, and fired down amongst them, while they kept firing up at us where they saw the light appear'.[42] One man was shot through the head and another through both his thighs in this encounter before sixteen sailors gave themselves up to the gang. In 1794 the *Aurora* frigate attempted to impress whalers from the *Sarah and Elizabeth*, but quickly discovered that the whalers had battened down the hatches and threatened armed resistance. In the attempt to ferret them out, one midshipman was shot in the chest and four whalers were killed, not to mention those that were wounded.[43]

The danger of violence was scarcely better ashore, on narrow quays or in ramshackle pubs. Straggling seamen were frequently armed and those that were not were quite willing to use anything that came to hand to fend off the gangs. In 1741, for example, a crowd of resisters from Southwark emerged from a public house armed with broomsticks, tongs and shovels and attacked the press gang.[44] A few years later, seamen and their comrades in Rosemary Lane beat off a gang with spits and pokers.[45] Those that were armed could do more damage. In an affray in a Shadwell pub, a lieutenant had his arm shot away by a blunderbuss. In a fight between some privateers and the press gang of the *Achilles* in a pub at Battlebridge, Surrey, swords were drawn and one of the privateers, Nathaniel Spenser, was left 'speechless, bleeding very much' from a cut on his head and from the left side of his body.[46] In 1776, an affray at the Rose and Crown in Back Lane Shadwell between jack tars and the press gang resulted in the death of the landlord and injuries to both midshipmen on duty. One of them lost several of his fingers.[47]

If press gangs sometimes had the advantage of weapons over unsuspecting tars, local sympathizers could inflict irreparable damage in the confined spaces of pubs with their nooks and crannies and narrow stairs. In 1778, a press gang broke into a Gloucestershire pub looking for recruits and attempted to ascend the stairs to search the bedrooms. The landlord's wife defended the stairs with a pick and spit, threatening to strike the first ganger who approached. One ganger paid no heed to these warnings and continued to climb the stairs brandishing a pistol. 'As he came near the Top of the Stairs', one newspaper reported, the women 'stuck the pick into him. He fell and dropt his Pistol upon the Stairs, which she instantly stept down and caught, and gave to her Husband, who stood behind her at the Top of the Stairs, and bid him defend himself. The five others, seeing their Comrade fall by the Hands of a Woman, were exasperated, and attempted to rush up Stairs; but the Woman still maintained her Ground, and as the Foremost advanced, she stuck the pick quite through his Temples. This Man's fate threw such a damp upon his Comrades that they instantly retreated.'[48]

In this instance it was clear who sustained the injury and who was the perpetrator. In some alehouse scuffles this was not so. In 1780 a case came before King's Bench in which a press gang had ventured into a pub in Bury St Edmunds in quest of men. It met with a hostile reception. One of the seamen drew a knife and 'swore he would stab the man who should prevent him from going to his wife'; another threatened the gang with a poker. A scuffle ensued, candles were blown out, and Thomas Nicholas, who had run among them telling the seamen to resist arrest, received a mortal wound from one of the press gang. The leader of this gang, Thomas Borthwick, and fifteen of his men were indicted for murder

*The LIBERTY of the SUBJECT.*

Women opposing the press gang, 1779

at the Suffolk assizes, but the case was removed to King's Bench prisoners where Justice Willes allowed the accused to be discharged on the grounds that 'there was no proof compleat enough for legal conviction that the murder was perpetrated by any of the gang'.[49] Some members of the public were upset with this verdict, not only because someone in the gang seemed culpable, but also because the gang had been irregularly commissioned to impress. But in the semi-darkness of small rooms and alcoves there was always some lingering doubt as to who struck the fatal blow.

Contemporary prints of impressment frequently portray the press gangs as overbearing villains, grappling with helpless men with tearful women looking on. The only possible exception is that of Gillray's famous print on the *Liberty of the Subject* in which women attempt to jostle gangers and assail them with mops and broomsticks. Even so, the tailor who is being impressed looks vulnerable, a victim of a contemptible episode of state-sanctioned violence. This conventional theme of vulnerability was echoed in the fictional literature of the day. In one minor novel Timothy Ginnadrake catches a glimpse of the 'unhappy men' boarding the tender at Tower wharf, describing them as little better than beasts being led 'to the slaughter house'. So great is his curiosity that he momentarily is taken up as well by a gang unconcerned about his eligibility.[50] In Smollett's

*Roderick Random*, the hero fends off one ruffianly ganger at the Tower only to be surrounded 'in a trice by ten or a dozen more' who laid him low by drawing their hangers and wounding him on the head and left cheek. Once aboard the tender, he recalled, he was 'pinioned like a malefactor' before being thrust down the hold 'among a parcel of miserable wretches, the sight of whom well nigh distracted me'.[51] The same trope of vulnerability before brutal ruffians occurs a little later in Thackeray's *Denis Duval*, where the hero is bludgeoned across the head by one of the gang and wakes up to find himself 'in a covered cart with a few more groaning wretches'.

As one might expect, this literature catered to a public troubled by press-gang violence and arbitrary arrest. It portrayed solitary men, or a line of sullen, defenceless men on their way to the tenders. What it ignored is the fact that press gangs of twelve, even twenty, seamen could easily be outnumbered on the quays and alleys of many ports, sometimes by as much as twenty to one when port-side communities were up in arms about their brutality. Thomas Gordon reported from Bristol that when they began to 'beat up' for volunteers in January 1759, 300 seamen came looking for them, 'threatning Death and Destruction of the officers, searching for them everywhere'. Nearly 50 years later, the regulating officer at Shields recalled that as they were returning from the tender, they 'were assaulted without any provocation whatever by a considerable mob of Men, Women, and Children' and forced to take refuge in a coopers' yard.[52] Examples such as these cast press-gang confrontations in a rather different light. It suggests that press gangs could quite easily be swarmed and rendered vulnerable to attack.

The figures on violence for the period 1738–1805 confirm this. They suggest that in about 10 per cent of all affrays ($N = 62$) it was the press gang members who were killed and wounded and not the other way around. Indeed, as a percentage of casualty-born confrontations, the press gang members were wounded in more than half of them (57.5 per cent). In cases where there was a fatality, it was a press ganger rather than a fugitive sailor and his supporters in roughly one in every three. This high quotient of violence helps to explain why there were occasions when regulating officers scarcely had a fit man in their gangs. Thomas Gordon, the officer in charge at Bristol, openly admitted this in 1759, at the height of the recruiting drive during the Seven Years' War.[53] In situations like this desertions from press gangs were not uncommon, especially when some of the gang members were actually pressed men themselves. In 1776 Lieutenant Katon reported that two of his Bristol gang, Andrew Hinds and Ben McCloskey, had taken off on a merchant ship bound for Jamaica at monthly rates of pay of 45 and 52 s. respectively.[54] Even where these sorts of financial inducements were absent, desertion could occur, especially from fever-ridden tenders where mutinies broke out with alarming frequency and where the prospect of policing men in fetid holds was both disagreeable and dangerous. On the *Thetis* tender which operated out of Liverpool, for example, there were constant fears that recruits would desert, especially when brisk westerlies forced the boat to shore on its way to Plymouth.[55] To complicate matters further, the commander of the vessel could not abide the lieutenant in charge of the gang, one Arthur Hayne, and this friction among the officers only intensified the gang's efforts to keep men in the hold free of fever, vermin and mutiny. In these circumstances it is not surprising to learn that five of seventeen gang members deserted in 1793–4, most of them being Liverpudlians or Irishmen well able to merge with the local population or find hideaways in sanctuaries like Parkgate.[56]

Pressing men was never free of violence, yet interestingly there is evidence to suggest that the frequency of violent affrays declined conspicuously at the turn of the century. In the wars of the mid-century the percentage of affrays where someone was wounded or killed was around 30 per cent. In the wars of the 1740s it was actually a little higher, 36 per cent of all affrays, and in the mobilizations of the period 1787–91, when Britain was concerned with the possibility of a French intervention in the Netherlands and with Spanish interference with British trade in Nootka Sound, it was as high as 43.5 per cent. During the 1790s, however, the number of heavy casualties dropped to 11 per cent of all reported affrays, and rose only slightly to 12.5 per cent after the Peace of Amiens. It is conceivable that this dramatic decline was partly the product of patriotic silence at the high level of violence in press-gang confrontations. In periods of high nationalist fervour, newspapers may have simply tried to avoid the issue, or perhaps they became increasingly insensitive to it. But it is more plausible to suggest that the decline reflected important changes in the pattern of resistance.

The changes were manifest in the North of England, now the principal theatre of recruiting conflict. Upon the initial mobilization in 1793, a threatening letter was thrown through the window of the rendezvous in Sunderland from the local 'saylors' informing the press gang that they 'had better take care of themselves, for if they do not we will take care of them and very soon'.[57] Within the next two months men were rescued from the gangs, and 'mobs of hundreds of seamen, soldiers and women' besieged the rendezvous, threatening the lives of the lieutenant and his gang.[58] Landing press gangs at South Shields were confronted with sailors and ship's carpenters waving 'Axes, Adzes and other weapons'. Crowds stoned the boat, and women, as visible at Shields as they were in Sunderland, thronged the marketplace and impeded impressments by throwing stones and brickbats. Vastly outnumbered and without much magisterial support, press-gang officers were humiliatingly run out of town. As Joseph Bulwer reported from North Shields, the sailors 'drove the Press Gang thro' the streets today with their Jackets turn'd, and their Hatts under their arms'.[59] According to the *Newcastle Courant*, the gang was told that if any of its members returned 'they should be torn Limb from Limb'.[60] Once the gang was gone, sailors attempted to take over the *Eleanor* tender moored in the harbour, only to be thwarted in that attempt by the crew. Some considered marching to Newcastle to mobilize the tars in that port.[61]

This resistance ran the gamut of the traditional repertoire of protest: threats, marches, raids, ritual humiliations. Turning jackets inside out was a standard motif of shaming rituals like the skimmington; sending threatening letters was a conventional form of intimidation, especially in circumstances where collective resources were weak or untried; and the physical mobbing of officers had long been part of plebeian crowd action. Women were more visible in these confrontations than formerly, but the participation of women in community-based protests was long-standing, especially in market interventions relating to food scarcity.

Yet there were some new elements in these anti-impressment demonstrations. To begin with the protests were more proactive than reactive. At the very beginning of recruitment on the Tyne, the sailors formed an association to protect themselves from the press 'by every legal means' until the government had increased their wages to allow them to support their families.[62] For two days they blockaded the lodgings of the regulating officer, Captain Rothe, in an attempt to pressure the government. They also circulated their resolutions to other ports. In this instance, the seamen appear to have consulted the Magna Carta club, one of several political societies spawned by a town that had become increasingly radical since the 1770s.[63] And they were canny enough to make contact with the striking keelmen on the Tyne, and quite possibly with some of the striking workers who worked in the Shields' shipyards.[64] In other words, seamen mobilized the local bases of support in pursuit of their claims. The extra foresight that these activities entailed probably meant, in the end, a lower level of incidental violence; although large confrontations, when they came, could still be casualty-ridden and bloody.

It remains to discuss the social geography of impressment affrays and the areas where opposition was most intense. The results are set out in the table on the opposite page.

It reveals that before the wars against Revolutionary France, London was always the principal centre of press-gang affrays. This was predictable in view of its status as the premier metropolitan port and the terminus for many long-haul vessels. None the less, over time London's predominance declined, from 46 per cent in the wars of Jenkins' Ear and the Austrian Succession (1738–48) to 14 per cent in the French wars at the turn of the century. Even so, London was always the principal recruiting ground during the phoney wars of 1770–71, 1789 and 1790–91, when the Admiralty ordered quick sweeps of the Thames and the quays around Wapping, and when London magistrates responded to the drive by impressing a larger number of stragglers from the streets. The result was that the resistance to impressment was strongest there during those mobilizations, despite the long-term decline in London's importance as a recruiting centre.

Table 1 The geography of impressment affrays, 1739–1805

|  | N | London % | SE | SW | NE | NW | Celtic | Unknown % |
|---|---|---|---|---|---|---|---|---|
| 1738–48 | 80 | 46 | 24 | 6 | 11 | 6 | 6 | 2 |
| 1755–62 | 132 | 22 | 8 | 20 | 10 | 22 | 16 | 1 |
| 1770–71 | 34 | 69 | 14 | 6 | 3 | 0 | 10 | 0 |
| 1776–82 | 122 | 30 | 8 | 18 | 12 | 18 | 9 | 4 |
| 1789–91 | 46 | 50 | 17 | 4 | 11 | 7 | 11 | 0 |
| 1793–01 | 76 | 11 | 23 | 9 | 35 | 3 | 19 | 1 |
| 1803–5 | 112 | 15 | 13 | 24 | 16 | 7 | 24 | 1 |
| Total N = | 602 | 173 | 83 | 93 | 82 | 71 | 89 | 11 |
| Total % |  | 29 | 14 | 15 | 14 | 12 | 15 | 2 |

The figures also reveal a wider geographical incidence of press-gang violence over time, which corresponds, one suspects, to the broader reach of the impress service. In the major wars the southern ports counted for roughly 30–37 per cent of all affrays, the distribution fluctuating between the south east and south west. The northern ports saw relatively few press-gang riots and serious affrays in the wars of the 1740s, but they too counted for 30 per cent or more of all affrays by the end of the century. Similarly, Scotland, Ireland and Wales rose in significance over time, and given the probable under-representation of Ireland, grew even faster as more Irish recruits filled British boats.

The geographic pattern of affrays thus reflects the Admiralty's growing sphere of operations on land, but it also suggests that the Admiralty met resistance in the expanding frontiers of recruitment: the south east in the 1740s; the south west in the 1750s; the north west during the American war, and the north east at the outset of the wars against Revolutionary France. None the less, one should not push these conclusions too far. The figures for the American war may well be skewed in favour of London, because it was here that opposition from local politicians was most obstinate and vocal, making it a favoured haunt for seamen on the run. The interest of the newspapers in forcible recruitment was also intense, so affrays in London during that period, as indeed during the Falkland Islands crisis of 1770–71, were more likely to be made public.

The figures in the table do not necessarily imply, of course, that London was the most vociferous opponent to impressment in the years 1739–1805, despite the fact that it singly accounted for more reported affrays than any other port. It would be important to measure the number of affrays against the actual number of men enlisted by the press gangs and perhaps take into account the actual size of the recruiting squads themselves. In the summer of 1779, for example, when Britain girded itself for a war on several fronts against four enemies, and found itself stretched to the limit, London provided 31.5 per cent of all new recruits to the navy and deployed just over 10 per cent of the impress service working onshore to do it.[65] If these figures were in any way typical, then London did not experience a high level of affrays (some 30 per cent of all reported during the American war) relative to the number of men enlisted. The really contentious port in this period would have been Liverpool, which recruited between 500–750 annually in the years 1777–9, using three tenders and a press gang ashore of sixteen men. Liverpool's intake was less than 5 per cent of the British recruitment on land, yet it chalked up about 18 per cent of all reported affrays.

Because it is difficult to get accurate figures of port recruitments to do these kinds of correlations, the number of affrays in themselves tell us little about the intensity or success of the opposition to impressment. It is quite conceivable, in fact, that a few dramatic interventions against the press gang could render it totally ineffectual. Such was the case at Whitby, where a concerted attack in February 1793 by a crowd of about 1000 people, including whalers and carpenters, wrecked the rendezvous and deterred others from establishing a permanent presence in the town.[66] When Richard Poulden, the regulating officer assigned to the port, attempted to impress Greenlanders in 1804 he found himself powerless to prevent their rescue. As he reported to the Admiralty Solicitor, when he attempted to put the impressed sailors into the boat, there was a 'sudden and general Shout (excited by the Populace on both sides of the river) from the whole of the crew, who armed themselves with their different weapons used in their trade & swore that not a man should be impressed. I then expostulated with the Harpooners. Line Managers and Boatsteerers (having only Lieut. Wallis & five men with me) on the illegality of their measures as they were unlawfully obstructing me in my duty ... they immediately took to the Boats, approved by loud huzzas from the shore, & rescued the men impressed.'[67]

Whitby was a virtual no-go area for the press gangs, a haven for straggling sailors who probably numbered over 1000 along the coast to Hull. Because of the town's opposition to the establishment of the rendezvous and the connivance of the only magistrate, it was virtually impossible for the Admiralty to recruit there. Similar circumstances obtained at Poole where the prevarication of magistrates and shipowners, not to mention the general hostility of the town, embroiled the regulating officer in harsh confrontations on the quays, law suits and complaints to the Admiralty about the rigour of the gangs.[68] This sort of opposition, so contingent upon the local context, cannot be quantified. Indeed, tracking resistance through affrays is always a tricky business, not only because some areas of the country were likely underrepresented in the lexicon of violence, but because it is often difficult to gauge the effect of persistent protests against the gangs. What is needed, and what is offered in the next chapter, is a zoom lens on particular ports, an assessment of how the opposition to impressment affected the recruitment drives of the navy over the long term.

Yet some conclusions can be established from this quantitative overview. Impressment affrays were not minor quayside incidents involving a few deserters. They involved whole communities, and often put residing magistrates in difficult positions, anxious as they were to retain the respect of their neighbours, yet obliged at the same time to support the government's seemingly endless quest for serviceable men. Moreover, quite apart from the discourse of liberty that resonated from the press – a discourse that highlighted the coercive aspects of national security for seafarers – many portside communities had direct experience of the gangs and the confrontations they provoked. As the geography of protest shows, every region of the country had a substantial number of affrays in at least one of the many wars of the century.

Over the course of the period 1739 to 1805, London accounted for 28.8 per cent of all reported affrays, while the south accounted for 29.2 per cent, the north 25.4 per cent and the Celtic fringe (including the Channel Islands) nearly 15 per cent. The latter might seem marginal, but in at least three wars the Celtic fringe accounted for a sixth of all affrays. During the Seven Years' War, Scotland was put in great ferment by the initial attempt to establish the country as a recruiting ground for the navy. Many magistrates resisted the call to co-operate with the Admiralty, and ultimately the navy had to make use of local patronage and the power of the heritors to make any headway. Later the Admiralty was confronted with a different set of problems. One was the protracted resistance to impressment of conventionally recalcitrant ports such as Greenock, where the seamen, caulkers, carpenters and riggers resolved 'to Stand by and support each other in case an Impress shou'd take place'.[69] On two occasions they burnt the small press boats in the public square, making the recruiting officer there, Captain Jaheel Brenton, doubt whether his gang would be able to handle them. If the recruiting returns of the port are any indication he could not, for he only managed to impress eight seamen out of a total of over 1000. Most of his recruits were landsmen (54 per cent) from the depressed areas of Glasgow.

What the Admiralty also encountered was the difficulty of extending the 'draft' to the Shetland islands, the Hebrides and the Channel Islands, none of whom were interested in being integrated into large state initiatives. Heritors in the Outer Hebrides, for example, couldn't deliver men in 1803, as the recruiting captains quickly discovered. They could only put pressure upon the local crofters by threatening to evict them from their plots if they failed to pay their annual rent, an economic predicament that gave the impress service some encouragement that the crofters would muster for the navy if the Greenland fishermen could not employ them.[70]

In the Shetland Islands Captain Fanshawe hoped the same predicament would prevail. He noted that a poor harvest and the absence of the Greenland boats had put many fishermen in dire straits, and he trusted that the heritors would be able to pressure them by insisting on a prompt payment of their rents. But the landowners knew that their rents could only be paid by summer fishing. They were not forthcoming with their help, especially when the press gang wrecked some warehouses and fishing boats in frustration upon discovering that the fishermen had retreated to the mountains and the bogs once a rendezvous was established.[71] Landowners also complained that they were not offered a fixed quota of men as formerly, and were unhappy with Fanshawe's assurances that a larger quota would protect the rest.

As for Guernsey, the island was positively hostile to the appearance of the press believing that it had a legal immunity to it. Sir James Saumarez had difficulty raising men there in 1793, but with the resumption of war in 1803 this resistance exploded when HMS *Hazard* fired upon a local privateer because it refused to bring to.[72] In retaliation, men in the harbour seized the press boat and carried it through the streets in triumph, threatening to burn it at the New Grounds. To show their contempt of the press gang, they attacked it with billets of wood and scraps of iron. Efforts to prosecute the ringleaders went nowhere, for the Royal Court of Guernsey sided with the town rather than the navy. Indeed, the court fined Captain Dobree for violating 'the privileges of the Island' rather than seek out his assailants. Dobree thought it 'the most Cruel Punishment they could possibly have inflicted upon me', but consoled himself 'in the rectitude of my conduct as an officer and a man of honor'.[73]

What was established in these and other confrontations was a local reservoir of popular memories on which the rhetoric of anti-impressment could grow. As the state's search for naval manpower became increasingly intense, so it touched the lives of virtually every maritime community. Through the Quota Acts of 1795, it touched many inland communities as well. Whatever their immediate context, violent protests against the press gang registered the increasing presence of the state in the everyday lives of its citizens.

4

## Spotlight on Two Ports: Bristol and Liverpool

Bristol and Liverpool were thriving ports in the eighteenth century and prime targets for the press.

Bristol began the century as the premier western port, combining long-standing links to Ireland and north-west Europe with a lucrative commerce in tobacco, sugar and rum. From 1670 to 1700 the tonnage of shipping into Bristol from the West Indies alone rose from 1900 to 5200 and continued to rise over the course of the eighteenth century, reaching over 25,000 tons by 1790. By that time 70 to 80 ships were involved in the trade, the most dynamic carried out in the port, employing about 1500 seamen. Altogether over 2838 seamen signed articles at the port in 1787, of whom 2470 gave Bristol as their place of residence.[1] This meant that about 5 per cent of Bristol's population were merchant seamen in the late 1780s; in terms of the adult male population, about 18 per cent. If one also includes the men engaged in riverside trades, shipwrights, ropemakers, bargemen and so forth, all of whom were eligible to be pressed into the navy, the proportion of impressible adult males in Bristol was likely to have been 25 per cent or more.

Liverpool's rise to commercial prominence in the eighteenth century was even more dramatic. In the early part of the century Liverpool had been a third of the size of Bristol, with a population of 7000 in 1708. The tonnage entering the Mersey was 14,600 in 1709, about two-thirds of its southerly rival. In the next 100 years Liverpool grew in leaps and bounds. From a strong base in the Irish staple trades, its merchants ventured into the Atlantic. Sugar imports increased from 760 tons in 1704 to 46,000 in 1810, tobacco from 600 tons to 8400 and cotton for the Lancashire mills from 2000 tons in 1785 to 64,000 in 1800.[2] Liverpool also became pre-eminent – notorious is the more appropriate word – for its participation in the slave trade. In 1750 Liverpool and Bristol successfully wrestled the trade away from the London-based Royal Africa Company. By 1764 Liverpool sent 74 ships to the coast of Africa to Bristol's 32. In the final 25 years of the slave trade, in fact, Liverpool towered over its rivals, being responsible for 75 per cent of the 3308 voyages from Britain to the African coast.[3] To boot, Liverpool also outpaced Bristol in the Irish, American and Caribbean trades, sending more ships to all these areas.[4] In the 1760s the number of seamen engaged in Liverpudlian commerce was certainly in excess of 3000, reaching 6000 by 1801.

At least 25 per cent of the male workforce was enlisted in the navy by the start of the French revolutionary wars; with 3000 shipwrights and associated craftsmen and haulers working the quays, the percentage of Liverpudlians who might be impressed was indubitably higher.[5]

The Admiralty was inevitably prepared to tap into this maritime expertise. In the wars of the 1740s they did so only intermittently, using naval ships that plied the coast. In 1740 Captain John Peddie dropped in on Liverpool on his way back from Whitehaven, where he discovered that Sir James Lowther and company had too many protections from the press to recover a good haul of seamen. Peddie found that without a rendezvous and a tender the number of men he could enlist in Liverpool was limited. Once the tender arrived, he and his colleagues also faced protests from the local merchants when they attempted to impress vigorously, especially with respect to a mate who was drowned attempting to escape.[6]

Further attempts to impress from the Mersey occurred a few years later. In 1744 the crew of the *Tarleton* resisted impressment at the hands of HMS *Winchelsea*, swearing 'they would fire upon the King's Boats before they would be impressed'. When Lieutenant Gideon of the *Winchelsea* barge persisted in attempting to board her, shots were exchanged and the crew ran the *Tarleton* into the dock and disappeared into the town. The following year, at the time of the Jacobite invasion of England, three vessels of war used marines to impress approximately 50 men in the harbour. The town protested vigorously, so much so that the mayor refused to sanction further raids 'for fear of being murder'd'.[7]

In Bristol impressments proved as controversial. In the spring of 1742 Lieutenant James Roots attempted to board an outward bound ship for Jamaica, the *Queen Mary*. The captain and crew refused to heave to, on the grounds that the ship was a fully licensed privateer with protections for its crew. Yet Roots, believing that the surgeon and others were attempting to escape and that their exemptions from the press were likely spurious, ordered his men to fire upon them. They dangerously wounded one seaman named Clarke in the knee and groin and badly injured some others. The Bristol magistrates committed Roots and seaman William Ferrier to Newgate for their intemperate actions. Fellow merchants declared their determination to prosecute Roots 'to the utmost'.[8] This they did at the Bristol assizes, where Justice Denison reprimanded Roots severely. 'He knew of no Authority that a man of war's crew had of firing balls upon mariners ... in order to oblige them to bring to', he declared, 'and that there was no evidence to prove the assertion.'[9] As a result the jury awarded a permanently crippled Clarke 120 guineas, and another seaman £40. The press-gang officer and ganger were also detained in gaol, perhaps on some technicality, with the result that Lieutenant Roots died there after 'a tedious and lingering illness'.

While Roots was languishing in jail, further trouble broke out in the Bristol Channel. In April 1743 nine gangers boarded the Bremen factor bound for

Lisbon off Weston Bay. The crew was compliant, save for Alexander Broadfoot who hid among the pipes of wine with a blunderbuss. When the gang discovered him, he fired at them, killing Cornelius Callahan with a shot to the forehead and wounding another in the chest. An unrepentant Broadfoot was put on trial at the summer assizes before Sergeant Foster, the City Recorder. Foster agreed with Broadfoot's counsel that the press warrant had been improperly executed, no regulating officer being present at the time of the boarding. He therefore advised the jury to find Broadfoot guilty of manslaughter rather than murder, and Broadfoot was sentenced to be burnt on the hand.[10] Although some commentators later took Foster's argument to justify resistance to illegal impressment, it really defended the legitimacy of the press while advising gangs to observe due process in its implementation.[11]

The Bristol merchants and magistrates certainly got the message. They served notice on the Admiralty that they would not tolerate arbitrary actions from the press gangs. When the regulating officer Samuel Graves presented his credentials to the Lord Mayor in February 1756, at the beginning of the next war, he was told peremptorily there would be no pressing of men with protections or men not seaworthy. This was clear advice to proceed with caution, but it was not advice that Graves particularly heeded. Graves arrived in the middle of a heated by-election and started impressing ex-seamen, or people he thought were ex-seamen, who also happened to be voters. Whether Graves was set up to do this is unclear, but his actions incurred the wrath of the Bristol Tories in particular, who thought Graves was deliberately attempting to influence the election in favour of the Whig corporation. The Tories' local caucus, the Stedfast Society, subscribed 50 guineas towards the defence of the freemen so impressed. In no time Sam Graves found himself at the centre of several vexatious lawsuits. Thomas Dennison, a local butcher, sued Graves and his gangs for 'knocking him down, striking him on the head with cutlasses and bludgeons, and ill treating his wife and servants'.[12] Although the judge did not think Graves had acted maliciously, the jury awarded Denison £200 plus costs. This allowed him to pursue the lieutenant of the gang through the courts for almost a decade.[13] Two of Graves' other officers in charge of the *Dispatch* tender were also accused of raping two girls on the Pembrokeshire coast, while one of his midshipmen, Valentine Ryan, was sued by a cooper for assaulting him and his wife. These legal suits mired Graves' reputation, and within months the Admiralty reassigned him to captaining a ship stationed at Plymouth. His continued presence in Bristol could only have compromised the attempt to establish a viable rendezvous there.

The Admiralty had no more success with subsequent officers. Captain Thomas Gordon, who arrived in Bristol in January 1759, was advised by the corporation to concentrate upon impressing men in the King's Road from the homeward-bound boats. Gordon feared that men might easily escape to the banks of the

Avon, and he probably had no wish to alienate the pilots who were responsible for ferrying craft down the narrow meandering river that was navigable for only 4–5 hours of floodtide every day. He thought he might do better in 'the Heart of the City' where many sailors resided, although he recognized 'they can easily assemble in large Bodys'.[14] And assemble they did. When Gordon's men began to beat up for volunteers on the last day of January, he reported, 'upwards of three hundred Seamen gathered in a riotous manner, almost killed a person whom they thought belonged to us, wounded the drummer & destroyed the drum'.[15] Against such a formidable quarry, a gang of twenty men had no chance, at least not without civic or military support; and so Gordon urged the Admiralty to pressure the corporation into backing press warrants and solicited the support of the army to search for seamen hiding in Somerset and Gloucestershire. Once the word got out that Gordon intended to bring in reinforcements, the seamen assembled once again, 'vowing destruction to us', reported Gordon, 'and bidding defiance to the magistrates'.[16] Gordon managed to get a few men aboard the *Caesar* tender, most of them debtors or vagrants, but he quickly met the wrath of the seamen. His gangs were assailed with 'vollies of small shot'. There was an affray in Marsh Street in which one sailor was killed and several of the gang wounded. 'As the seamen are in general well armed', he observed, 'we have been very fortunate to escape so long [with relatively few injuries] as we have had many Broyles.'[17] Eventually these broils took their toll. One of the lieutenants, Stephen Hammick, fell ill of fatigue, spitting 'a vast Quantity of Blood'. Gordon's key ganger, a prize fighter and ex-sailor named Cornelius Harris, was brutally murdered on the Ashton road by a gang of privateers while searching for seamen evading the press.[18] To further complicate matters some of his gangers fell out with the military now quartered in the city, making co-operation between the press gang and the army difficult. By June Gordon reported, 'I have not one Man in the Gangs but what is wounded or recovering of their wounds'. Unless he had reinforcements, he advised, 'the [King's] Duty cannot be carried on in this large and Populous City where we have everything to contend with'.[19]

Between riotous mobs and a tetchy mercantile elite, Gordon did not have a lot of room for manoeuvre. In late August 1759 he reported that recruitment in Bristol had come to a virtual standstill. Crimping landlords, he reported, had sent many sailors among the harvesters to await key berths on the merchant ships. And the merchants were eluding the gangs by sending their ships down the Avon with skeletal crews, filling their complements by picking up men at assigned places along the Somerset or Glamorganshire shore.[20] He could only wait, Gordon said, for the homecoming crews from the West Indies and trust that he had enough tenders and good intelligence to locate them. Attempting to impress with Bristol itself had become too tricky a business. The magistrates had dragged their feet about search warrants and sailors in hiding were desperate and well armed. In January 1760 he remarked: 'We have had three killed and upwards of Sixty wounded which obliged me to keep our men well armed or else quit the City, and as we have often been overpowered, many swords and pistols have been lost.'[21] Eventually Gordon managed to bring in 164 men for the period October 1759 to October 1760, but it was substantially less than Gravesend and Dover and no more than 40 per cent of the catch in Newcastle.[22]

Establishing a viable rendezvous in Bristol was a troubling and problematic exercise during the Seven Years' War. This was also true of Liverpool. When Captain John Fortescue arrived at the port in January 1759, he thought that the only way he could impress the 300–400 seamen milling about the town was by bringing in two men of war and using 100 men from their crews to confront them. Without this backing, he assured the Admiralty, 'we have little Hopes of Success'.[23] Fortescue also advised the Admiralty to consider winning over the publicans and crimps by offering to pay off some of the small debts of the sailors. That way he might recruit a few volunteers and perhaps gather up a press gang.

The mayor of Liverpool was not sympathetic to this strategy. He said he could offer the press gang no security on shore in the light of the port's overriding hostility to impressment. While he was prepared to top up the existing bounty to volunteers with a further two guineas from the corporation, he strongly advised Fortescue to concentrate his efforts on impressing homeward bound men on the Mersey. He had neither constables nor jails for a major press onshore, and the idea of establishing a rendezvous seemed out of the question.

It took Captain Fortescue three months to raise a gang and requisition a tender. Initially he had to send the men he enlisted to Chester Castle or Parkgate, and this meant additional expense and inconvenience, for some of the men, volunteers as well as press men, deserted. To boot it was an uphill battle. The mayor and merchants protested when Fortescue's gangs entered houses to impress seamen, an action that technically required a search warrant executed by a constable. The mayor threatened to remove the city's bounty for volunteers and to expose the gang's intrusions in the newspapers. Every seaman was 'fought hard for', remarked Fortescue in April 1759, 'there being a number of men in their Town continually armed to defend themselves against my Gangs, and to rescue what men they can from us'.[24] By the middle of May he reported he had secured 120 men, about half of whom were impressed, but between the prevarications of the merchants and the hostility of the mob it was hard going. 'The frequent applications, pictures of Distress, and Natural Dislike by the Inhabitants makes this a most Disagreeable & Difficult piece of Service to perform', he complained.[25]

A letter two and a half months later illustrated just how difficult it could be. In early August Fortescue reported that Captain Nightingale's crew on HMS *Vengeange* had impressed between 70 and 80 sailors that week, 'tho at the risque of many of our Lives, being stoned by the Mob upon us of near Three

Thousand People, and opposed by every letter of Marque [privateer] that came in'. Apparently Nightingale had been warned not to press on shore but he had persisted in doing so, even having the audacity to take up some Greenland whalers when they were at the Customs House renewing their protections. As they were taken into custody and led along the streets, one of Nightingale's party recalled:[26]

> Several hundreds of old men, women, and boys, flocked after us, well provided with stones and brickbats, and commenced a general attack; but not wishing to hurt them, we fired our pistols over their heads, in order to deter them from further outrage; but the women proved very daring, and followed us down to low water mark, being almost up to the knees in mud.

Within a week Nightingale's crew also tangled with a returning slaver-cum-privateer from Tortola, the *Ingram*. In this encounter the privateering crew imprisoned the commander so it could focus upon eluding the *Vengeance* and the press cutters in the Mersey, a course of action that so outraged Captain Fortescue that he had some of the crew whipped for their defiance.[27]

Merchants were up in arms over these activities, and complaints were made to the Admiralty about the lawlessness of the gangs. Captain Fortescue protested that the damage inflicted by the gangs was minimal. The only casualty was a woman who was accidentally shot in the thigh when Nightingale's gang had fired pistols in the air to disperse a 'Mob of women who were ready to devour us'.[28] But the wear and tear of the service was beginning to get him down. He told the Admiralty he simply could not continue impressing on shore without better help from the civil power. As it was, the threat of legal action disposed him to send his gang to Plymouth with the tender so they would not be arrested. The result was that when the Jamaica fleet returned to Merseyside a few days later, Fortescue did not have a tender or gang to impress any of the sailors.[29]

Fortescue broke up his rendezvous a few days later and for almost two years captained the *Barfleur*. He returned once more in July 1761 to try his luck at establishing a viable press-gang presence in the port. The same problems confronted him. The mayor and magistrates were reluctant to back warrants on shore, because of the hostility of the populace to impressment and the consequent threat to law and order. The mobs themselves were large, armed and militant; so intimidatory, in fact, that Fortescue could not get men to consider joining a gang for less than a guinea a day. Merchants and crimps screened the best men from the gangs in any case, sometimes through the liberal distribution of protections to so-called 'mates' and 'apprentices'. Some of the latter were as old as 26 or 27 years of age.[30] All in all it was a rum business raising recruits for the navy. 'There is not a seaport in England where a man fights so much uphill to carry on the impress service at Liverpool', Fortescue complained. 'What with shipwrights, carpenters, boatbuilders, pilots &c, 400 protections was laid before me to protect them before I could begin to press a man. Then ye merchant contrives every stratagem to prevent our taking his men, the common people the most riotous of any, under no subject of subjection to ye mayor and corporation.'[31]

Fortescue toiled on, but his efforts to establish a rendezvous in the port came to nought. In September 1761 'a riotous mob assembled with fire Arms and different sorts of weapons' and threatened to pull down the rendezvous at the Talbot Inn. The Mayor was called in and drew up a company of soldiers before reading the riot act. At first, this had no effect whatsoever, but ultimately, with entreaties from some of the merchants, the crowd backed off, threatening to return if the gang attempted to press on shore.[32] Even so, Fortescue recognized that there was little he could do unless the press gang on shore in Liverpool was increased to about 50 men. In December he reported that the 'sailors and commonalty of the town have begun to form themselves into Mobs, with Cutlasses and firearms, on my pressing a few hands, & are going up & down the Town all night, threatening to cut to pieces my Officers and People wherever they can meet them'.[33] By February 1762 the situation had reached fever pitch. On 18 February a mob of 200 rioters swore revenge for the 25 sailors who had recently been pressed in the town and attacked the Talbot Inn once again. They wounded the few soldiers of the Invalid regiment sent to protect the pub.[34] Sergeant James Tinkler lost his right eye in the affray and cracked two or three of his ribs. Andrew Dally lost the thumb of his right hand, which subsequently prevented him from following a trade. Others sustained cuts to the temple and head, bruises and stabs in the leg.[35] The house was gutted and everything destroyed. The mob then directed its fury at the lodgings of Fortescue and his lieutenant, only to be thwarted by the Mayor and more soldiers. In the aftermath of the attack, two of the rioters were arrested and sent to Lancaster gaol to be tried at the next assizes. But no legal action could offset the deterrence of the raid. 'I am afraid this Riot has Stopt us for the present from Impressing so many men from the Shore as we might have', reported Fortescue in March 1762.[36] The magistrates were once more adamant that such impressments should cease until the military presence in the port was substantially increased.

Fortescue feared that Liverpool might become a sanctuary for seamen. The picture he painted for the Admiralty was of a port under mob rule, deterring both press gangs and magistrates from doing their duty.[37] The arrival of one hundred of the Flintshire militia eased his own fears of reprisal from the mob, but the magistrates continued to prevaricate about pressing from the shore and were reluctant to provide much help. When Lieutenant Rogers ventured out in August 1762 in a town full of seamen from homeward bound voyages, 'a mob of some hundred arose with firearms & cutlasses' and fired two pistols at the officer. He only saved himself from being 'cut to pieces' by escaping over the roof of a house. Since then, Fortescue dolefully reported, 'his, mine and everybody's life is threatened'. 'This town is become so opulent in trade', the captain reflected, 'that pressing there [sic] seamen is opposed by every Individual from high and low', with the crimps doing a roaring trade for the merchantmen.[38] Even the magistrates had proved uncooperative, with the mayor threatening to send any ganger found impressing on the streets to Lancaster jail.

Fortescue did have some modest success impressing from the water, but the difficulties of so doing were formidable. The tidal fluctuations on the Mersey were great and often rapid, which meant that boats could only get into the harbour on rising tides, and with the help of pilots to navigate the shoals and sand banks.[39] This lent some predictability to the timing of impressments, but it also meant that they were potentially more confrontational. Homeward-bound ships from the Caribbean had crews of 30 to 90 seamen, many of them armed, and cannons to keep Admiralty sloops at bay. When the *Dove* tender with eighteen hands attempted to bring the *Fame* to submit to Admiralty authority, it was confronted with a merchant ship with almost three times the crew and 22 guns, including some nine pounders. As the *Fame* rounded the Rock and entered the Mersey, its crew fired on the tender and intrepidly declared 'they wou'd all die sooner than one should be taken and brandished their cutlasses at them'.[40] This became a familiar scenario: merchantmen openly defying the gangs and refusing to hand over men without a fight. In July 1759 the *Golden Lyon*, a Greenlander with a 60-strong crew, opened defied a naval man of war holding the recruiting lieutenant hostage while the ship made for the docks.[41] In September 1762 the *Christian* cutter attempted to engage two ships from Virginia whose crews had put off for the shore in open boats. But once within pistol shot, the lieutenant was wounded in the left arm by a musket shot and one of the more valuable crew members, Gabriel Devereux, received a shot through the jaw which incapacitated him for life. Fortescue thought the outright defiance of the Virginiamen tantamount to piracy, but he was exasperated by his inability to do much about it. 'I have pushed the service here farther than ... any regulating Captain ever did before me, but without their Lordships and the Laws ... support, nothing farther of any consequence can be done.'[42]

At the end of the day Fortescue did not have much of a return for his efforts. In May 1762 he calculated that of the 15 to 20,000 seamen who had poured through Liverpool during the war, 'not above one in a hundred could be secured for the service'.[43] Without a frigate, homeward-bound ships would defy the press gangs with impunity, and gales off the Irish Sea battered and even wrecked his cutters. On the quays, mobs jostled officers and shielded men from the gangs, with the magistrates little more than passive spectators. As in Bristol, the wear and tear of the service had destroyed the morale of his men. Some were unserviceable because of the wounds they had sustained. Others cracked under the pressure.

Two of Fortescue's officers could not stomach a night's duty 'without keeping (to) their room a month afterwards'; one of them, Lieutenant Skryme, seemed more or less deranged.[44] As in Bristol, the attempt to launch the impress service in Liverpool during the Seven Years' War looked a signal failure.

In the subsequent two wars, however, recruitment in these two ports stabilized. In Bristol, recruiting officers managed to establish a working relationship with the corporation and its powerful ally, the Society of Merchant Venturers. In one estimate of recruitment drawn up in April 1779, and probably for approximately a year, Bristol's press gangs, 24 officers and men, raised 664 seamen, an average of 28 men per ganger.[45] This rate of return was comparable to two other thriving ports that since the 1750s had attracted considerable Admiralty attention: Edinburgh and its port of Leith; and Newcastle and its subsidiary ports of North and South Shields down the Tyne. Both of these areas had raised over 1000 men each, but with rather larger recruiting parties. Liverpool's contribution was 735 men, but with only sixteen officers and men.[46] This was a return of 46 recruits per ganger, a figure matched only by Dublin and London among the larger ports.

Liverpool's performance was, indeed, spectacular. Whereas in the first two years of the Seven Years' War Liverpool had scarcely raised 200 men, in the comparable years of the American war it was recruiting five times that number. Part of the reason for this was economic. The escalating conflict with America, with its non-importation agreements and blockades, had disrupted Liverpool's commercial traffic in Atlantic waters and had even stalled the slave trade. Many seamen found themselves idle in port, as many as 3000 according to the *Annual Register*.[47] These were potentially good recruits for the press gang. The dire economic situation was underscored by the seaman's riot of August 1775, when seamen on a Guineaman reacted violently to the owner's offer of a 30 per cent reduction in wages by demolishing the rigging of the ship and leaving it on deck. The ringleaders were arrested and committed to prison, but two thousand tars armed with handpikes and clubs descended on the gaol and rescued them despite a reading of the riot act. In the triumphant parade that ran through the night, one terrified slave merchant fired on the crowd, believing his house was threatened. As a result, he and other Guinea merchants had their houses looted with the contents thrown on the street. 'The household furniture was very rich', one letter reported, 'with an abundance of china, and chintz bed furniture, all of which were torn to shivers, and linen, plate, &c tumbled into the street' and 'thrown about in fragments in the air'.[48] From here the sailors and their supporters moved on to the Exchange, breaking the windows and forcing out the frames. Merchants and special constables attempted to defend this symbol of commerce from the raging mob, and eventually dragoons had to be brought in from Manchester to restore order. Three people were killed and fifteen wounded in this day of destruction, while 60 people were arrested and sent to Lancaster gaol.[49]

The Liverpool merchants were clearly troubled by this explosion of violence, especially since it threatened to become a pretext for settling grudges. 'I could not help thinking we had Boston here', wrote one, 'and I fear this is only the beginning of our sorrows.'[50] More of them become disposed to helping the press, which could be usefully deployed ridding the streets of Liverpool of recalcitrant sailors. The general political disposition of the corporation helped consolidate this support. The majority of the Liverpool common council was in favour of the American war against the rebellious colonies. Its address to the crown in September 1775 talked of bringing Americans to a 'true sense of their duty' and acknowledging the sovereignty of parliament.[51] This loyalist stance inevitably disposed the corporation to supporting the war effort and accommodating the press gangs within their city. While there were dissenting voices to this policy within Liverpool – some of which coalesced around the person of Sir William Meredith, the independent member for Liverpool until 1780[52] – this opposition was unable to disrupt the activities of the press gangs in a manner comparable to London, where opposition alderman were in positions of authority.

The support that the Liverpool corporation gave to the recruiting officers manifested itself in two ways. In March 1777 the corporation offered Captain James Worth, the new regulating officer, and his second in command, Lieutenant Clarke, the freedom of the borough, possibly the first time this had been done by a municipal body in Britain.[53] Subsequently it provided the recruiters with a rent-free press room close to the quarters of the Invalids regiment. In keeping with this new spirit of accommodation, Captain Worth acceded to the request of the Liverpool Chamber of Commerce to respect the protections of seamen who kept to their own ships and did not ramble into town. He also intervened in a dispute between the master of the *Union* tender and a deputy water bailiff who had attempted to get his brother released from the press, even though the manner of the release, a writ to arrest him for a debt of £20, was likely spurious.[54] Generally speaking, Captain Worth attempted to keep the contentious issues of impressment at bay, for which he was thanked by the local inhabitants who told him 'they never were so quiet as at present'.[55]

Two matters nonetheless plagued Worth in discharging his duty. Hard winds and slow recruitment sometimes kept tenders in the Mersey for weeks on end, exasperating men who were locked down in fetid holds, especially in the summer months when typhoid fevers were likely to break out. The result was a continual trickle of desertions from the tenders, even by volunteers.[56] Sometimes these desertions collectively amounted to mutinies, with men prying open the hatches and gratings and even smuggling in saws to cut away at small beams.[57] Eight such mutinies occurred in the years 1777–80, two every year. Sometimes the numbers who escaped were high; 56 seamen escaped from the *Fisher* tender in September 1780, ten of whom were volunteers. According to the master Samuel Edwards, the recruits had been boisterous and unruly all day, and when he ordered the hatches to be nailed down and came to remonstrate with them he was surprised by 20–30 men armed with handpikes and broken staffs. Faced with this mutiny, many of the tender's crew abandoned Edwards, who was locked down in the hold himself and threatened with death if he dared shoot at the mutineers.[58] In this instance, as in others, one suspects that some of the crew members were complicit in the mutiny. The turnover in tender crews was often high, and some of the men, impressed themselves, were not inclined to linger when the going got rough, whether because of fractious recruits or noxious 'distempers'.[59]

What also troubled Worth were the activities of the privateers. Liverpudlians were passionate about privateering, and the slump in trade during the war disposed many to transfer their boats and investments to this sector. From August 1778 to April 1779, 120 privateers were fitted out in Liverpool amounting to a total tonnage of 30,878 and crewed by 8754 men.[60] Some of the privateers were as small as 45 tons, but others were substantial, often 180–400 tons and owned by substantial men. A perusal of the letters of marque for 1779 reveals that a fairly broad spectrum of trades were engaged in privateering, including a slopman, a cooper and a cabinet maker and a few who were likely too small to be included in the local trade directories. But it also reveals that many of the prominent merchants had an interest in privateering. They included members of the Backhouse and Tarleton families, men who were active in the Chamber of Commerce as well as the corporation; Henry Rawlinson, who became MP for the City in 1780; John Kennion and John Chorley, committee members of the Chamber of Commerce; William Crosbie, town bailiff in 1775 and its mayor in 1779; and William Boats, a common councilman reckoned to be 'one of the principal merchants of the town'.[61] Nineteen of the privateer owners, including all those above save conceivably Rawlinson, were slave traders who in wartime transferred some of their investments into other ventures.[62]

Captain Worth seems to have been aware that the privateering interest had supporters in the highest places in Liverpool. In July 1778 he remarked that the Leeward Islands and Jamaica fleets had arrived in port, disgorging a thousand tars onto the streets of the town. He told the Admiralty he would do his best to secure them for the navy, but he noted that they had come on shore 'in large body's armed' and that the Merchants were snapping them up for the privateers, whose crews were 40 to 60 strong.[63] Two weeks later Worth's letters revealed his frustration at not getting as many men as he had hoped. He wrote that the privateers were deliberately hiding men from the navy and began to take a hard line with the mayor, town clerk and magistrates over disputed exemptions, believing there was a 'set of traders who make use of every art they can devise to secret seafaring Men from the Public Service for their own purposes'.[64]

Worth was also aware that some privateering crews were giving his men the run around, concocting stories about the seamen they had on board 'being aware no force I had could prevail with a ship well armed and sixty men on board'.[65] Indeed, these crews were sometimes brazen enough to pull some of their own men from the rendezvous if they happened to be taken up and regulated. In late August 1778 Worth reported that 'Gangs are formed among their crew not only to invite but absolutely press men. This morning my lodgings was surrounded by a large Body who came to demand a man belonging to their party, impress'd in the course of the Night by our Gang.' Worth was intimidated into releasing the man if another could be found in his stead, which was quickly accomplished. He protested to the Admiralty that 'nothing should have obliged me to listen to any Terms from a Mob' but he feared his lodging would have been destroyed and his gang 'insulted and abused by a lawless crew that were at no loss to find hiding places'.[66]

Two months later Captain Worth suffered the humiliation of having his own rendezvous raided by the privateers. He reported that 'a large Body of Armed men' had broken open the doors of the press room and had carried off two impressed men. He complained to the mayor, who issued a notice forbidding privateering crews from assembling in such an unlawful manner, and threatened to call in the military if such behaviour persisted. Yet as Worth remarked, 'its Effect as yet amounts to a mere nothing'.[67]

Newspaper reports suggest that Worth had better luck impressing privateers in the following year. The *London Evening Post* reported that Liverpool had 'suffered much by the press' with 1300 men being taken from outward-bound ships, 'privateers as well as merchantmen'.[68] But a subsequent letter in the *Shrewsbury Chronicle* suggested that the gangs were really scraping the bottom of the barrel, even to the point of picking up shop assistants. Certainly there is continuing evidence that privateers were not about to let their more experienced crew members fall into the clutches of the press gang. In January 1780 Lieutenant Hayworth picked up fifteen seamen on their way to Liverpool from Ormskirk and had them sent to the rendezvous. But the lieutenant of the *Stag* privateer, one Spence, arrived that evening and demanded their release. This was refused, and so Spence and his comrades broke down the door with crowbars and stormed the press room, wounding two of the gang in the process. One of the men sustained cuts to the nose, shoulder and head, the latter very close to the temporal artery; the other ganger had four cuts to the head, one on his wrist and left cheek, a stab wound in the right shoulder and another in his groin near his scrotum. He was in a 'deplorable condition' remarked the surgeon, and his recovery was 'very doubtful'.[69]

Privateers were a thorn in the side of Captain Worth throughout his tenure at Liverpool. Even so, the return of seamen from that port continued to be noteworthy. In the first two years of Worth's tenure, from December 1776 to

December 1778, he brought in 1103 recruits including landsmen, of whom 781 (71 per cent) were impressed men. In the subsequent two years, Worth enlisted another 1242 men of whom 1053 (85 per cent) were impressed. In other words, the few humiliations that Worth suffered at the hands of privateers did not seriously disrupt the momentum of impressment. This is also evident from the monthly returns. During the Seven Years' War Worth's predecessor, Captain Ferguson, had often been unprepared for the homecoming fleets from the West Indies, from which the largest catch of seamen could be made. In August 1759, for example, he complained that the absence of a man of war and tender in the Liverpool Road prevented him from taking hundreds of seamen who had just arrived with the Jamaica fleet.[70] Captain Worth, by contrast, had greater success impressing these fleets. There was a noticeable surge in the number of impressed men in July–August of the years 1777–80 when the main sugar fleets arrived from the West Indies, and while Worth had initially complained of the lack of a space to take recruits from six homecoming merchant ships from Jamaica in March 1778, he soon reported that a general press on shore had picked up many of them.[71] In these endeavours he likely found the Liverpool merchants more co-operative than his successor, especially once their own privateering crews were on their voyages. Besides, the merchants' demand for convoys to protect commercial shipping always meant there were limits to how far they might obstruct the business of the Royal Navy. In the years 1779–82 this was an especially pressing problem because the Royal Navy was outnumbered by the combined fleets of France, Spain and America. In the predominantly loyalist Liverpool of the American war, a rough and ready understanding had been established between the press gang and the mercantile elite about the needs of both the navy and commercial enterprise. In the year from October 1780 to October 1781, Liverpool delivered more men to the navy than any port save London.[72]

The understanding between the impress service and the Liverpool merchants threatened to become unstuck at the beginning of the French war. The divisions in local politics about the American war were palpable enough, but those concerning the French Revolution were more acrimonious. In the months prior to the outbreak of war the Enlightenment reformer William Roscoe had successfully mobilized moderate opinion in Liverpool in favour of a loyalist address to the crown that advocated parliamentary reform. The mayor, Clayton Tarleton, brother of the war hero and local MP Colonel Banastre Tarleton, attempted to thwart this with a 'true blue' address more in line with one already passed by the Common Council, but Roscoe's motion passed by a significant majority.[73] Tarleton and his corporation allies, however, raised a loyalist mob to intimidate the moderates from signing Roscoe's address and to shred it in pieces, leaving the way clear for a set of hardline loyalist resolutions to the crown.

None of this might have mattered had not Clayton Tarleton been closely associated with the naval mobilization in Liverpool. The mayor and prominent slave trader was very eager to back press warrants long before the regulating officer was ready to receive seamen, and long before the bureaucracy for paying volunteers a municipal bounty could be put into effect.[74] However misguided, this frenetic enthusiasm, combined with a deep depression in the cotton industry and a corresponding dislocation of trade, helped the press gang raise almost 1500 men in their first six months of duty.[75] This was a spectacular haul, well in advance of any other northerly port; Greenock and Newcastle, both thriving ports, could only bring in little more than half that number.

Unfortunately for the press gang, there was a price to be paid for this success in a politically contentious climate. In mid-October, Clayton Tarleton processed the town in the customary manner with a Mr Baker, 'a very respectable merchant' whom Tarleton wanted as his mayoral successor.[76] The freemen of the city, however, including many linked to the port trades, were not disposed to take his advice. A few days earlier, a broadsheet addressed to 'Brother Seamen, Carpenters and Coopers' ironically applauded Tarleton as a 'Chip from a good stock', a 'lad that will stand all Weathers' who never allowed 'lawless Ruffians called Press-gangs to parade the Streets of Liverpool' while he was mayor.[77] It was an ominous warning of trouble.

Tarleton sought to frustrate this opposition by using the press gang to clear the streets of demonstrators. He had Captain Coffin of the *Melampus* frigate make a 'general sweep' of the town on the eve of the mayoral election. The local regulating officer, Captain Child, refused to go along with this plan and events proved this to be a very wise decision. Coffin and his crew from the frigate, along with a few extra men from the *Ann* tender, fell in with some seamen from a sloop from Newry and attempted to impress the mate. The master of the sloop, one Felix McIlroy, remonstrated with one of the midshipman about this and in the ensuing scuffle was shot dead.[78]

The coroner's jury in Liverpool brought in a verdict of wilful murder, but the mob were not prepared to wait for the legal proceedings to take their course. It swore revenge on the press gang. On 18 October, the day of the mayoral election, 400–500 seamen and carpenters descended on the rendezvous in Strand Street and New Quay and started to gut them, throwing the furniture into the street.[79] Both of the landladies of the two pubs were subjected to popular reprisals, and amid the fury of the mob Captain Child and his men steered a very wide berth. When the mob threatened the life of Captain Child, ex-mayor Tarleton attempted to mobilize the Warwickshire militia to protect him. This intervention only fuelled local grudges. The new mayor, Henry Blundell, who was an ally of the Roscoe circle, refused to call out the militia to prevent the crowd from wrecking the two rendezvous. In fact one report suggested he was a 'Spectator of the Enormities' which lasted seven hours.[80] Believing the gang had provoked the populace, Blundell subsequently refused to back the press warrants, with the result that Child's recruiting campaign ground to a halt. As he wrote to the Admiralty, 'there is every reason to apprehend that Prest Men just on board the receiving tender would be liberated and there is too much reason to suppose that an attempt to Press on shore in our present situation would occasion the Death of every officer and men'.[81]

This was exactly the sort of predicament regulating officers were advised to avoid and it boded ill for future recruitment in Liverpool. Yet despite the physical hazards of impressing in the port, Liverpool's recruitment proved to be among the most impressive of the provincial ports. The destruction of the two rendezvous only momentarily affected the momentum of the recruiting drive. In the years 1793–95, Liverpool raised 3016 men at a cost of £1-4s per man. No other northerly port delivered so many men so cheaply, not Greenock, Edinburgh and Leith, Newcastle, Hull or Yarmouth. Rear-Admiral Pringle, who collected these figures, noted that tide and wind sometimes meant unavoidable delays in the departure and passage of the tenders to Plymouth, with the result that desertions, even mutinies, remained a persistent problem. He also believed that homeward-bound vessels were often landing their crews before they rounded the Rock and entered the Mersey, a situation that might be remedied if a 'stout cutter' was stationed in the estuary.[82] These reflections were hardly news to the regulating officers of the port, all of whom had stressed the dangers of mutiny aboard tenders and the need for a stronger naval presence in the Mersey. But they did not detract from the fact that impressment in Liverpool had become something of a success story.

In Liverpool, then, we have something of a paradox. In terms of affrays and anti-impressment riots, Liverpool was one of the most violent ports of the country. During the period 1739–1805, it witnessed 66 serious acts of violence against the press-gang and its supporters, a figure that overshadowed all other provincial ports, with Newcastle and the Tyneside ports of Shields recording 40 affrays and Bristol 36. On at least three recruiting campaigns rendezvous were sacked and the press-gang officers sustained serious injuries. Moreover, it was extremely difficult to obtain any legal redress from this sort of violence. Liverpudlians refused to testify against ringleaders and local juries were reluctant to indict, even where there was hard evidence against them. The few riotous seamen that were successfully tried were brought to the assizes courts in Lancaster or even to King's Bench. There was, in fact, a substantial conspiracy of silence among the population at large about the whereabouts and activities of seamen in port. Those who disclosed information about straggling seamen to the press gang were sometimes severely punished. One woman who informed on her common-law husband and bigamist was stripped, ducked and nearly drowned by some 'riotous people'.[83] At the time of the attack upon the rendezvous in 1762, two women were even killed for being suspected as informers, a reprisal which certainly deterred others from co-operating with the press gang.[84]

And yet Liverpool was a successful recruiting centre once the Admiralty had established some sort of working arrangement with the mercantile elite and more or less accepted the fact that some privateering crews were off limits. This was again evident in the 1803–5 returns, when once again Liverpool brought in over 2000 seamen and landsmen and 421 boys more cheaply than anywhere else.[85] In order to tap the maritime manpower of this burgeoning port, of course, the Admiralty also had to form gangs that had the physical grit and mental toughness to confront a seafaring population that was endemically hostile to its presence. By 1805 the rendezvous with its large naval flag hanging from the window was an established feature of the Liverpudlian scene, and from contemporary accounts it seems that gangs often ventured into hostile territory picking up men engaged in night brawls and revels.[86] Still, it took courage to do this. We get a sense of what a hardened gang looked like from the memoir of the Irish-American John Caldwell, who in 1809 was picked up by a gang led by Irish John, an ex-United Irishman who had plea-bargained his way into the navy after his participation in the Battle of Vinegar Hill during the 1798 Irish Rebellion. Apparently John, an expert pikeman, was given the opportunity of a reprieve from execution by Sir Ralph Abercrombie if he could unhorse 'a braggadocio of a dragoon' without causing him injury, which he promptly did. According to Caldwell, Irish John led a 'motley crew of desperadoes' made up of 'blue spirits and gray, blacks, whites and mulattoes'.[87] He was in frequent scrapes, and during Caldwell's brief visit to Liverpool, Irish John was twice nearly torn to pieces by the mob and had his rendezvous gutted and the furniture burnt in the street. Caldwell may well have embellished his story a little, but one gets the impression that only tough outsiders like Irish John, skilled with the pike or shillelagh, could handle the salts who ventured to this rough and resourceful port.

But what of Bristol? How did this port fare after the initial skirmishes of the Seven Years' War when the press gangs were virtually beaten into submission and when legal judgments such as Sergeant Foster's defended impressment but insisted upon due process of law? Unlike Liverpool, where the regulating officers ultimately strove to capitalize upon the dramatic growth of the port by weathering the storm of popular opposition to impressment, Bristol's captains over time adopted a less confrontational approach. Like their Liverpudlian counterparts, Bristol's regulating officers sought to improve relations with the local magistrates whose aid was always essential if the going got rough. John Nott, who was the press-gang captain during the short Falkland Islands crisis of 1770, persuaded the mayor and council to raise the bounty for volunteers so that crimps might be better disposed to handing over their men. He also sought to secure some seamen from the jails for the service, including John Cummings who had been prosecuted for perjury in a murder case aboard a slaver in Old Calabar and was lingering in a debtors' prison because of his inability to pay court fees and charges.[88]

This policy brought in a fair crop of volunteers, both seamen and landlubbers. What it did not do was gather up unemployed seamen who had no wish to join the fleet. Nott organized a hot press in December 1770, but the return was disappointing. He only raised 25 seamen, he said, because 'all the Men here belonging to the Ships are gone into Kingswood among the Colliers, where we dare not go after them'.[89] This was troubling on two accounts. The Kingswood colliers had the reputation of being a lawless and 'ungovernable People', defiant of authority and active in previous decades in some formidable turnpike and bread riots in the Bristol area.[90] In 1759, when Captain Gordon sent some members of his press gang into the country to avoid confrontations with the military who were stationed in Bristol, the Kingswood colliers had roughed them up badly, wounding eight of them.[91] Their proximity to Bristol meant their pits were always likely to be a near-permanent sanctuary for straggling seamen who wished to evade the press gang. What also improved the seamen's chances of eluding the gangs there was the fact that some crimps were supplying the tars with provisions and arranging mercantile berths for them. Captain Nott's hope that high bounties might crack the crimping trade in Bristol had not proved very successful.

This issue continued to plague Bristol's regulating officers. There were plenty of places on the Somerset coast where sailors could disembark before reaching the estuary of the Avon. 'It has always been the practice for the homeward bound ships to land their Men to the Westward', reported Captain Hamilton in 1779. They then 'march through the country to Kingswood', he continued. The shipmasters pursued this strategy so that they could rely on much the same crew for the outward-bound voyage. In Hamilton's view, it was 'not possible for any tender lying in Kingroad to prevent it'.[92] Hamilton persuaded the Admiralty to hire two skiffs that were to be employed off Ilfracombe to reconnoitre the homecoming fleets as they came up the Bristol Channel and accompany them to the King's Road.[93] But he also recognized that these scouting vessels would need reinforcements, perhaps from a sloop of war off the isle of Lundy, if runaways from the homeward bound fleets were to be impressed. One tender at the estuary would not be satisfactory. 'Most of the ships from this port now are ships of force', the captain declared, 'and the men are resolute. It would therefore require a superior force to prevent bloodshed.'[94]

Hamilton did register some modest success in preventing the premature departure of homecoming seamen, or so he reported in May 1781.[95] But the bigger ships continued to defy his officers. In the same month he reported that the crews of three ships had fired at his skiffs and had successfully disembarked their men on the Somerset shore off Bridgwater Bay. Hamilton advised the

Admiralty to establish a gang in that vicinity to handle these seamen, but there is no evidence they did so. The result was that Bristol's regulating officers had to tolerate a continual drain of potential recruits as seamen routinely landed on the Somerset shore and tramped through the countryside to places like Kingswood or perhaps to Clutton and Radstock in the North Somerset coalfield, where they might find temporary work before landing new berths. Captain Hawker complained in 1793 that seamen were flying to Kingswood in droves, and a decade later it was thought to be the sanctuary of hundreds who all 'bid defiance to the gangs'.[96] Not that the coalfields were the only places of refuge. Hawker advised the Admiralty to send gangs to Bridgwater, or further up the Severn to Chepstow, and Newnham, on the edge of the Forest of Dean, all places where seamen lurked.[97] The latter was a resort of Severn trowmen who were threatened with impressment and it was not surprising that deep-sea sailors ventured there as well.[98]

The press gang simply had to live with the disappearance of many seamen before the homecoming fleets reached Avonmouth. What also contributed to the elusiveness of homecoming seamen was the fact that the pilots of the River Avon were increasingly venturing out beyond Flat Holm and Steep Holme to navigate the incoming fleets past Sand Point and up the western coast of the Severn, facilitating the escape of impressible seamen in the process.[99] This was troubling to the Admiralty and it probably aggravated the searches that took place at the estuary. Even so, the searches did not generate as much controversy as those earlier in the century, when press-gang members were shot and sometimes incarcerated for overly aggressive behaviour. Crews threw six-pound shots on press-gang lieutenants and even fired on boarding parties.[100] But there were few fatalities in the King's Road that generated deep controversy.

The real trouble on the Avon came from the press gang's relations with the pilots, most of whom lived at Pill, on the Somerset side of the river. They were essential to the economy of Bristol for without them no traffic could move up and down the muddy labyrinthine river to the town. This induced the pilots to think they had not only an immunity from the press but the ability to harbour seamen and facilitate their escape from the gangs.[101] Press gangs complained continually about their obstructive attitude to impressment and threatened to take them in. Usually the stand-offs between the gangs and the pilots moved to the latter's advantage, as the merchant elite quickly intervened so that Bristol commerce would continue to flow. In 1777, for example, Lieutenant Carlyton impressed several pilots whom he knew had helped straggling seamen evade the gangs, with the result that the river ground to a halt. The Merchant Venturers immediately protested, and Captain Hamilton could do little but accede to the requests for the pilots' discharge.[102]

The Pill pilots were a thorn in the side of the press gang for much of the eighteenth century. They made impressments on the river more difficult and potentially more vexing. Yet there were other reasons why the press gangs had to act cautiously in this western port. Unlike Liverpool, where the corporation was basically loyal during the American war, Bristol's elite was divided. Edmund Burke and the Rockingham Whigs encouraged the Merchant Venturers and merchants outside the elite circle to send conciliatory petitions to parliament in favour of addressing American grievances, but by the end of the year, as support for coercive measures increased, the hawks and doves were more evenly balanced.[103] This polarization continued for the rest of the war, both in the corporation and at Merchant Hall. It forced the press-gang officers to tread warily lest their indiscretions became part of the political battle about the ends and means of the war effort where there were discussions about raising a volunteer regiment and also raising the bounty on seamen to twelve guineas.[104]

The situation became especially acute in the summer of 1779, when the advent of the Dutch into the American war meant Britain now faced three European enemies as well as its former colonists. Desperate for seamen, the Admiralty issued an order to press from all protections, statutory as well as administrative, in order to re-man the fleet. In the first dramatic hot press of that summer, the Bristol gangs picked up 640 men, an intake that surpassed that of Hull but was less than Liverpool where the number of gangers was smaller.[105] This big sweep occurred at a time when the Whigs and Tories were battling for the advantage in city councils, and it inevitably proved controversial. Merchant Hall demanded the return of some pilots, and the mayor, Sir John Durbin, told Captain Hamilton to release a freeman sail maker named William Lewis for fear that his impressment would compromise the Tory motion for a loyalist address in Common Council.[106] Hamilton reluctantly complied with these requests but hard on the first press the Bristol gang seized James Caton, a prominent merchant and former skipper with American sympathies, as he was conducting business at the Exchange. Caton was probably taken up to settle some personal political score in the City, with the press gang an unwitting accomplice to this malice. But the affair certainly fuelled protests against the press gang. Caton was kept in solitary confinement and then taken to the tender in Kingroad. All requests to see him were denied. Fortunately for him, Edmund Burke and the lawyer-cum-politician John Dunning took up his case and secured his release with a habeas corpus at King's Bench.[107] Caton subsequently sued Captain Hamilton and Lieutenant Michael Lane for false arrest and imprisonment, claiming he had only served as a master of a vessel and was therefore always exempt from the press. According to the *Annual Register*, Caton asked for £5000 damages, an enormous sum even for four days' confinement and the disruption of his business and reputation.[108] At the Bristol Guildhall before Justice Nares Caton was awarded only £50, but Hamilton and his lieutenant still had to face costs of over £160.[109]

The Caton affair was but one of a series of onshore incidents in which the press gangs were entangled during the American war. In 1777 a local woollen draper raised a mob to rescue a man from the press gang, beating up the midshipman in the process. In the next two years there were several confrontations in pubs in which one of the parties was fatally wounded; in one instance, the victim was a crimp named Farrell, the landlord of the Shakespeare at the Gibb.[110] These confrontations signalled that onshore hostility to the gangs remained high, perhaps not as high as during the Seven Years' War, but certainly substantial enough to keep gangs on their guard.

During the French wars gangs faced further crowds bent on rescuing men from their clutches. The most dramatic incident occurred on 25 March 1803, when Captain William Prowse of HMS *Ceres* was ordered to help the regulating officer remove some impressed men from the guard room of the first regiment of Dragoons and put them aboard a tender bound for Plymouth. Prowse sent his lieutenant to do the job, but upon his arrival Lieutenant Norman encountered a crowd in an ugly mood, 'huzzaing and using language of the most inflammatory kind'. The previous night soldiers had lined the bridges of Bristol while a press gang scoured the streets and quays looking for possible recruits. Two hundred stragglers were reportedly taken up in this nightly raid and those considered fit for service were ready to be escorted to Rownham, where the tender awaited them. Norman did not like the look of the crowd and requested a detachment of dragoons to help him escort the men to the quayside, expecting trouble. And trouble there was. 'A Multitude of People variously armed with Bludgeons … repeatedly attempted to rescue the impressed men', Prowse informed the Home Office. Consequently Lieutenant Norman ordered the troops to fire over the heads of the people in an effort to intimidate them. This only had the opposite effect. 'The mob became outrageous and closely assaulted the party', Prowse reported, and the marines, jostled and bruised, retaliated by firing on the crowd halfway along the Hotwells Road, killing a boy and wounding several other people.[111] Norman succeeded in getting the men to the boat, but a warrant was issued for his arrest and his party. Norman was not detained very long, nor were the two privates who did the shooting. A coroner's inquest decided that the death of the lad was justifiable homicide. But the incident was a bad start to the new wave of recruiting that began as the Peace of Amiens crumbled and a resumption of the war against Napoleon loomed.

The upshot of these violent quayside confrontations was that the Bristol press gangs tended to concentrate their efforts at the estuary of the River Avon rather than in the alleys and backs of Bristol's quays. Part of the reason for this strategy was that Bristol's gangs included a number of local men who had little wish to alienate portside communities to the point where their own families were threatened. Yet it is also clear that the memory of the bloody confrontations of the 1750s were seared into the consciousness of the gangs. Subsequent affrays and rescue attempts reminded them of the eruptive power of Bristol's crowds and the difficulties of recruiting in a city where merchants were tetchy, if not politically hostile to their activities.

This meant that the navy received relatively small pickings from this western port. Although Bristol's press gangs did not have to deal with powerful privateering crews to the same degree as Liverpool, they did not get Bristol's top sailors, who were surreptitiously screened from the press by merchants and shipmasters. Press gang officers also realized very quickly that they could not easily impress the trowmen and coasters who supplied the city with vital provisions and industrial products from the West Midlands, despite belated efforts to open up this populous sector of seamen to the navy on the grounds that the Severn was 'open sea'.[112] Some headway was made on this score, but it usually evoked protests from the Merchant Venturers and mayor. It was not until 1806 that the navy was able to persuade the Association of Severn Traders to hand over one in every ten to the navy, about 60 trowmen, an offer begrudgingly accepted after the group received an unfavourable decision in the Court of Exchequer about the juridical status of the Severn.[113] As for the pilots of Pill, they remained a pretty fractious fraternity, openly defying the gangs by helping seamen evade them. Efforts to discipline the pilots with a few exemplary impressments brought the river traffic to a standstill, much to the consternation of the Merchant Venturers and the Corporation.[114] In 1803 the mob at Pill, angered by the impressments of some of their pilots, even prevented the Cork packet from sailing any further than their village, having assailed the crew with stones and boarded the vessel to bring her to.[115]

In the 75 years from the war of Jenkins' Ear to the battle of Trafalgar, Bristol contributed proportionately more volunteers, more landsmen and fewer pressed men than did comparable ports such as Liverpool and Newcastle upon Tyne. Whereas over 60 per cent of the seamen enlisted by the regulating captains of these two ports were impressed, the corresponding figure for Bristol was seldom more than a third.[116] To some extent this pattern reflected the changing priorities of the Admiralty, its disposition to tap the resources of ports in their most dramatic decades of growth. Bristol's period of growth was earlier than those of other provincial ports, ebbing in the period after 1760. Yet recruiting priorities were also shaped by the experience of the regulating officers and their ability to bring in men as cheaply and smoothly as possible. Impressment was unpopular in Bristol, and if Sergeant Foster and others said it was technically legal, many thought it palpably unjust. In those circumstances the Admiralty wanted a disagreeable service carried on with a minimum of fuss, especially when a more aggressive policy might raise the hackles of the powerfully placed Merchant Venturers and mire the officers on the ground in legal suits.

There was a price to be paid for this policy. In Bristol it appears that the more experienced seamen, particularly those who arrived with the West Indian fleets, became very adept at evading the gangs by disembarking in droves on the Somersetshire coast before they arrived at the Avon estuary. Unless the Admiralty was prepared to guard that coast with extra skiffs and cutters, regulating officers stood little chance of bringing in a rich harvest of experienced seamen. To attempt to capture the seamen from their sanctuaries – places like Kingswood, where the colliers and quarrymen had a reputation for militancy – was to invite the sort of violence that Thomas Gordon's gangs had experienced in the 1750s. No ganger or regulating captain wanted that sort of trouble. As Captain Thomas Hamilton remarked to the Admiralty in 1781, if they required him to institute a hot press, he would need the backing of the militia. Many seamen flocked to Kingswood, he noted, 'where there is no going without an armed force, & that pretty strong'.[117] The easier path was to flatter and chivvy the mercantile elite into providing the kind of financial inducements that might attract raw men in their twenties and hope that other ports, or impressments offshore, would provide a sufficient number of seasoned jack tars to man Britain's wooden walls. From the 1770s onwards this was certainly the preferred option for regulating officers in Bristol. Unlike Liverpool, where recruiting officers weathered storms of protest for a relatively rich harvest of seamen, Bristol's press gangs tended to adopt a low-key approach to impressment, fearful that mercantile interference might entangle them in legal suits and encourage crowds to defy them.

5

# Manning the Navy in the Mid-century Atlantic

On a Saturday night in October 1744, in the English harbour of Antigua, the crew of the *Mercury* were living it up. The occasion was the capture of a Dutch sloop, or at least of a sloop flying Dutch colours, that had been marauding colonial shipping and the seamen were no doubt looking forward to receiving the windfalls of the prize. Between 10 and 11 o'clock, the sentinel on duty spied a smaller craft approaching the ship. He hailed it to little avail. Amid the noise of drums, trumpet and general merry-making, the watch could not identify the approaching vessel, nor comprehend the muffled response of its seamen, some of it in French. The captain was alerted. 'Warm' with drink and armed with a pistol, he demanded that the boat bring to. The commander of the vessel, the master of a local tender, pleaded with the captain not to fire 'for there were only Negroes that were with him in the boat'.[1] Nonetheless, Captain Montagu, concerned that the intruders might be French, 'snapped his piece'. The pistol misfired, but on his second attempt Montagu shot indiscriminately into the boat, severely wounding one of the seamen in the thigh. The injured man was brought on board, but the ship's surgeon was too drunk to dress his wounds properly and so the surgeon from HMS *Lynn* was called for. By the time he arrived, the wounded man had lost a lot of blood. The second surgeon patched him up as best he could, but the man died the following morning. Crudely sutured with needle and thread, with only a small 'roller' over the dressing, he bled to death on the deck.

Captain William Montagu of the HMS *Mercury* was hardly perturbed by this incident. The dead man was not just black, he was a slave, one of the 'King's negroes' belonging to the yard at Antigua whose job it was to careen the vessels of the Royal Navy. As far as he was concerned, his action merited at best a fine and some monetary compensation to the government for the loss of one of its slaves. This was all the laws of Antigua demanded, he informed the Admiralty. He had not committed a wilful killing, 'much less was it done illegally or wantonly', he continued. It happened because of the 'wilful default of those in the Boat, in not answering when haled to'. In his opinion, the 'whole island' and other crews in the harbour 'looked on it in this light'.[2]

Montagu was astounded when Commodore Charles Knowles, the illegitimate son of the fourth earl of Banbury, sent him home to face a court martial. Knowles' decision, Montagu complained to the Admiralty, meant that he lost his share of potential prizes and his place in the officer hierarchy. Equally important, he also suffered 'greatly in his Honour and Reputation'.[3] Among other things, he had to endure the humiliation of spending seven months aboard HMS *Eltham* as a virtual prisoner of the commander, Captain Durell. The lords of the Admiralty, for their part, sympathized with Montagu's predicament, as indeed did Governor William Shirley of Massachusetts, who had talked over the matter with Captain Durell.[4] No doubt their lordships were influenced by the fact that Knowles was locked in a dispute with the crown over the distribution of two Spanish prizes and had caused them some embarrassment over a rash press in Antigua.[5] While they did not question Knowles' decision to send Montagu home, they did not initiate a court martial either. Indeed, the only court martial to eventuate from the affair concerned the surgeon of the *Mercury*, and this for professional negligence.[6] Rather, the Admiralty quickly restored Captain Montagu to the command of another vessel at the Deptford yard and had him carry volunteers and pressed men down to the Nore. Within a month or two, Montagu found himself reconnoitring off the French and Spanish coasts where he picked up a French ship bound for Bordeaux loaded with cocoa and cayenne: a catch, he informed their lordships, 'which I believe will turn out to be a very good prize'.[7]

The incident at English harbour is a tragic story of racial contempt and of the incredible insouciance of a naval officer, who by the racist standards of the day thought himself above reproach. But it is also about the predatory world of the mid-eighteenth century Caribbean, where the spoils of war were fierce and competitive. And it throws an oblique light upon the different labour regimes that made up that world and shaped the manner in which Great Power struggles could be fought in it.

More than one servile labour force faced one another at English harbour in October 1744. Apart from the poor slaves who were subjected to Captain Montagu's intemperate actions, his own ship contained seamen who had been brought to the Caribbean against their will and were consigned to serve in His Majesty's navy for the duration of the war. Precisely how many pressed men were aboard the *Mercury* in 1744 is uncertain, for the muster books provide no reliable indication of the numbers who were coerced into service rather than those who volunteered. Yet it seems likely that approximately a third of the *Mercury*'s crew were impressed men.[8] They were part of a larger resistance to naval service that at its most violent generated widespread anti-impressment riots, the most dramatic occurring at Gravesend where a 'great Mob of People' rescued pressed men from the local gaol.[9] In fact, there were at least 55 affrays against the press gangs from the inception of the war to the incident at English harbour. Despite the hoopla that surrounded the war at home and the jubilations that greeted Admiral Vernon's early victories at Porto Bello and Fort Chagre, despite hard winters and souring bread prices, the reality was that the Admiralty had to scour the jails and streets to find a sufficient quota of men. As Sir Charles Wager remarked to Vernon at the very outset of the war, 'We must do as well as we can, but we find great Difficulty in getting Seamen enough for our ships, which has been our Case in all our considerable Sea Armaments'.[10]

Serving on his Majesty's ships was a poor substitute for the high wages that a seaman might enjoy on a merchantman, or for the windfalls of war that might be won on a privateer. But the reluctance to serve in the 1740s was amplified by the fact that the main theatre of war was in the Caribbean. This torrid zone was well known to be a death-trap. The risks of war were underscored by the popular comparison between Vernon's victory at Porto Bello and the fate of Admiral Hosier's expedition some twelve years earlier, when 4000 seamen had died of yellow fever. In the 1740s the death roll never reached these alarming heights, at least for seamen, although it has been computed that at least two-thirds of the soldiers who embarked on Caribbean expeditions in the 1740s died of tropical diseases.[11] Yet in proportion to the number of seamen borne, the death rate was formidable enough. In the cramped quarters of the lower deck, an early exposure to malaria could decimate crews. Of the two squadrons stationed at Jamaica in 1741, some 2514 men, over 17 per cent of the total, were discharged dead, while another 5 per cent were off duty sick.[12] On some ships the proportion of men who went down to either scurvy or malaria topped 30 per cent. Without adequate hospitals in which to house them, the lower decks were seething cellars of disease. As the former surgeon's mate Tobias Smollett so graphically represented in *Roderick Random*, bilious fevers and inappropriate prescriptions could cut a swathe through crews and render lower decks foul and putrid.[13]

In an effort to offset the inevitable mortality of crews in Caribbean waters, the Admiralty adopted a number of strategies. Crews were supplemented with supernumeraries on setting sail from Britain, but this was only accomplished with difficulty when hostility to impressment ran high.[14] Another alternative was to impress men in the colonies, either from the colonial ports or from homeward-bound vessels. The crews of Guineamen were especially vulnerable on this score, for slavers routinely augmented their complement in anticipation of slave revolts on the middle passage. The Royal Navy customarily attempted to impress up to one in three Guineamen on their return voyage and up to one in five from other merchant ships. Sometimes there were complaints that commanders were taking more.[15] Admiral Davers, for instance, was criticized for pressing too many men from outward bound vessels in 1745, although he claimed he only did so where they were regarded as 'mutinous and dangerous fellows'.[16]

The difficulty with this policy was that the flow of men frequently ran in the opposite direction. Once hospitals were built in the major ports of the Caribbean, men of war frequently anchored to discharge their sick men; and because all ships were regularly infested with the toredo worm found in tropical waters (at least until the introduction of copper sheathing in the 1770s[17]) they frequently had to be careened in dry dock. The consequence was that naval seamen had real opportunities to desert. And desert they did. About 4 per cent of the Jamaica squadron deserted in 1741, over 6 per cent in 1747. These figures approximated those who disappeared while on general leave at home, but on some ships the proportion was in excess of 20 per cent.[18] One storeship, the *Astrea*, lost virtually its whole crew between March and December 1741. Lured by the high wages offered by merchants for homeward bound runs, or by the prospects of privateering, seamen were ready to jump ship.

Naval officers did all they could to prevent this drain of men. In April 1744, five men belonging to HMS *Plymouth* were each given three dozen lashes for desertion, a punishment that must have drenched the gratings in blood. Very occasionally a deserter was hanged from the yard arm 'to deter others' remarked Commodore Knowles in 1744, 'for no corporal Punishments have been able to do it'.[19] In the following year Admiral Davers executed two men because 'the continual Desertions from his Majesties ships & the hospital obliged me to make examples of them, as Offenders of the worst kind'.[20] Yet punishments of this magnitude could only be used sparingly, for in the end the navy wanted men not bloody backs and broken necks. Consequently the Admiralty also attempted to deter seamen from desertion by recommending that they should lose not only their wages but their prize money, the latter being regarded as a form of private property which seamen could claim through the prize courts. This prohibition was achieved by an Act of 1744.[21]

None of these actions diminished the level of desertion as long as local merchants offered high wages for the homeward-bound trade and privateers inveigled men from the service with the promise of ever larger spoils. Every commander on the Jamaica station recognized this to be the crux of the problem, yet none proved able to resolve it. Admiral Vernon attempted to bully the merchants into compliance, only to witness the desertion of more than 500 men from the hospital at Port Royal lured, so he claimed, 'through the temptation of high wages and thirty gallons of rum'.[22] When he scoured the taverns of Port Royal and cracked down on the North American traffic in his quest for men, he so alienated the Jamaica merchants that his second in command, Sir Chaloner Ogle, nearly came to blows with the governor, Edward Trelawny, over the issue. Ogle and Vernon were troubled by the complaints of Jamaican merchants, particularly from one Samuel Dicker, that the navy was interfering with the commerce in crucial supplies from North America on which the slave economy depended. Ogle thought Dicker 'a scoundrel and a rascal'; Trelawny defended him, and to the dismay of Vernon and watchful servants, Ogle began to draw his sword in what might have been a very unsavoury skirmish in the governor's residence. Vernon expeditiously intervened to prevent this happening. As Trelawny recalled, 'I put my hand to my sword with intention to draw in my defence, but Mr Vernon who was between us clapped his hand on me, which joined with the rustiness of the sword, I could not draw it'.[23] Trelawny was so outraged by this affront to his authority and hospitality that he went on to prosecute Ogle in the highest court of Jamaica.[24]

The confrontation of July 1742 revealed just how far tempers could fray over the manning problem in the Caribbean. The situation was not alleviated by the disposition of many Jamaican and American masters to go privateering, the sort of opportunistic venture that attracted disgruntled seamen, especially since an act of 1708 purportedly exempted privateers from the press.[25] In a competitive maritime market, confrontations between press gangs and privateers were predictable. In May 1743 Captain Charles Knowles was upset by the decision of merchants in the lesser Antilles to hire a privateer to accompany their ships rather than accept his naval convoy. He retaliated by impressing its crew when it returned to English Harbour in Antigua. In the confrontation that ensued each side took hostages, and the privateering interest badgered the governor to remain neutral in order to make an example of the errant captain and his commander. Consequently Knowles found himself posting a huge bail of £12,000 to keep himself out of jail and was later sued to the tune of £4000 for damages resulting from the dislocation of commerce. As he ruefully reflected, naval officers sometimes had to 'suffer in their private fortunes' to pursue the king's business. In the end only the diplomatic intervention of Sir Peter Warren kept Knowles out of hot water.[26]

This was the first of several confrontations in the lesser Antilles. In St Kitts another privateering crew mobilized the populace against a recruiting officer, this time Captain Abel Smith of HMS *Pembroke Prize*. They threatened to burn his launch if Smith did not release the press men, and complicit merchants subsequently sued him for £500 damages.[27] When France entered the war in 1744 and the scope of privateering increased, Knowles, now a commodore and the new commander in chief, strove to persuade the merchants that the privateers were seducing their crews and that it was in their mutual interest to restrain their commissions. But he failed to convince them this was so and had to tolerate the harassment of his gangs at the hands of privateers and conniving magistrates. His captains, he complained, were 'insulted by 50 Arm'd men at a time' when they came on shore looking for men, and were 'obliged to take shelter in some Friends houses'. He was bitterly critical of the magistrates who, rather than quelling the riots, 'encouraged the Privateers Men to knock the Men of Warr Dogs (as they call them) on the head'.[28]

Part of the intractability of the manning problem in the Caribbean was that the local imperatives of commerce did not easily square with the imperatives of war. Island planters and merchants wanted safe convoys for their sugar, rum and molasses, open channels of trade with the North American colonies upon whom they depended for provisions and lumber and a sufficient privateering force to ward off enemy predators and to capture enemy cargoes. In other words, they wanted the best of all worlds. They were quite willing to take naval officers to court over matters of impressment. The captain of the *Deal Castle*, for instance, found himself facing damages of £2000 for an alleged 'trespass' upon merchant property following an aggressive impressment exercise in St Kitts.[29]

If the manning problem in the Caribbean was dire, it was hardly better on the North American seaboard. Earlier in the eighteenth century, governors and naval officers had come to blows over the rights and responsibilities of impressment. In 1702 Captain Robert Jackson of HMS *Swift* had raided Boston harbour of an eighth of its seamen in an attempt to recover some ten deserters from his sloop. Harrassed by merchants, Lieutenant Governor Povey demanded that Jackson release the men he had taken. Jackson refused, but he was prevented from sailing from the harbour by cannon shots from Castle Island, one of which struck the capstan, killing one of his seamen and wounding others. An angry Jackson returned to Boston to confront Povey and other officials. Beside himself with rage, he maligned the lieutenant governor, threatened a judge with his cane, and nearly assaulted a councillor. Povey, for his part, dismissed Jackson from the *Swift* and packed him off to jail to await transportation home.[30]

Confrontations such as this, and complaints from 150 merchants that impressment was ruining British commerce, led to the passing of a statute in 1708. This made it illegal for naval officers to impress mariners serving or retained to serve on privateers or trading vessels 'in any part of America', save for naval deserters.[31] This hastily contrived act did little to resolve the problem. It did not clarify whether the impressment of *all* merchant seamen in the colonies was illegal, or indeed whether governors, as the juridical arm of the crown, could still impress in emergencies. Legal opinion in Britain thought governors retained a residual prerogative power to impress, and the solicitor general recommended that this be clarified in some further statute. But no clarification was forthcoming, and indeed well into the century governors were asked to observe 6 Anne, as the statute was called, without any additional instructions that they were empowered to impress.[32] To add to this confusion, it was not at all clear whether 6 Anne expired or not with the end of the War of Spanish Succession in 1713. The Attorney General Sir Edward Northey said it did, but down to 1723 at least naval commanders in Atlantic waters were instructed by the Admiralty to observe 6 Anne.

None of this mattered crucially in the years of peace, but the advent of war with Spain in 1739 and the subsequent scrambling for men, demanded that the legal status of impressment in colonial waters be regularized. In Britain the attorney and solicitor generals declared that 6 Anne had expired, but in the colonies there were many merchants and mariners, although not governors, who thought otherwise. This spelt trouble. At Charleston in 1740, Captain Samuel Bathurst of HMS *Tartar* was indicted for murder as a result of an impressment affray aboard the merchant vessel *Caesar*. Three years later, Captain Charles Hardy reported that 'this Spirit of Prosecuting on that Stature [6 Anne] reigns her more than ever; Insomuch that I am informed the Merchants have Entered into a Subscription to Prosecute Captain Hamur ... for every Man he Impressed'.[33] In Boston a mob armed with cutlasses, clubs and axes besieged Captain Scott in his residence when he attempted to impress with the backing of the governor. In a second press the following winter Scott managed to alienate prominent Boston merchants with his actions, with the result that both houses of the Massachusetts legislature complained to Governor Shirley about the 'intolerable Violence and Injury done to the Liberties of His Majesties Subjects of this Province, their Trade and Business'.[34] This sort of pressure placed Governor Shirley in a difficult position. He was anxious to mobilize men for an expedition to Louisbourg so he did not wish to relinquish any of his power to impress; at the same time he did not want to allow naval commanders to impede the flow of colonial and coastal commerce that was Boston's lifeline. Keeping a handle on just who could be impressed was none the less a tricky business. When two naval captains received the nod from the lieutenant governor of the province to search for deserters in 1745, there was an affray in the North End of Boston in which two merchant seamen were mortally wounded. People were incensed. One commander, Captain Forest of HMS *Wager*, fled to his quarterdeck, damning the Bostonians as 'an incensed unmerciful People governed entirely by their passions and prejudice'. 'If some Check is not put to that inveterate Humour among them', the Admiralty confided to Lord Granville, 'we fear it will get to such a Head, when they find it Attended with Immunity and Success, that it will be impossible to recruit Seamen in those parts, and consequently our Ships will become useless to His Majestys Service.'[35] As for the other officer, Captain Rouse of HMS *Shirley*, he was only saved from the mob by the intervention of the sheriff. 'He dared not set his foot on shore', he later confided to Admiral Warren, 'for fear of being prosecuted on the [6 Anne], or murthered by the mob for pressing.'

Resistance to impressment was rising in Boston. Quite apart from the obstreperous crowds, the Boston Town meeting submitted a petition to the House of Representatives in March 1746 remonstrating against illegal impressments and complaining that the issuing of press warrants by Governor and Council was a 'Breach of Magna Charta, and the Charter of this Province, and an Act of Parliament [6 Anne].'[36] The town meeting subsequently backed down from this position, but it did put pressure on the Bostonian elite to reconsider what 'advice and consent' was necessary for press warrants. Within months parliament had passed an act that echoed that of 6 Anne. It allowed the navy to impress deserters, as before, but it also permitted impressment when an invasion was imminent or when there was 'any other unforseen and emergent necessity'.[37] More importantly it also specified that impressment could only be undertaken with the assent of a governor or colonial assembly. Yet crucially, it applied only to the sugar colonies, not to those of the mainland, even though the petition from the planters and merchants 'trading to America' had put a re-enactment of 6 Anne on the political agenda.[38] In effect, parliament had heeded the powerful sugar lobby in its demand to attune impressment with the imperatives of commerce, specifically the need for critical supplies from British North America. But it did nothing for the supplier, perhaps because the Americans were suspected of trading with the French under neutral flags of truce. For the first time it became patently clear that North America was to be vulnerable to impressment in ways that their Caribbean counterparts were not.

The Bostonian response was the riot of 1747. On 16 November 1747 Commodore Knowles ordered a sweep of Boston's harbour to recover or replace the 30-odd seamen who had deserted his fleet while it anchored for repairs at Nantasket Island. As far as the commodore was concerned, he was well within his rights. Captain Blyke, who was assigned the task of picking up the men, even promised that 'he would not keep a man that belonged to the town or the Colonys; that he wanted nothing but strangers'.[39] The promise was not kept. Knowles' men not only picked up local seamen, they took some from outward- not inward-bound vessels, flouting the conventions of impressment in the process. Some accounts even suggested that they ransacked the wharves in the search for men. The result was that about 300 privateers and Guineamen reacted to this press by searching for naval officers as hostages, just as their Antiguan counterparts had done before. According to Thomas Hutchinson, they seized a lieutenant from the *Lark* who was ashore on other business. A local sheriff from Suffolk county unsuccessfully tried to free him, but eventually Hutchinson, the Speaker of the House of Representatives, managed to do so, quickly removing him to the governor's house. This brought an angry and swelling crowd to Governor Shirley's door. Shirley parleyed with the crowd, and one spokesman accused the governor of backing press warrants. Shirley denied the charge. He also thought the man 'a very impudent Rascal for his behaviour; and upon his growing still more Insolent, my son in Law, who happen'd to follow me out, struck his Hat off his Head, asking him if he knew who he was talking to'.[40] At the same time, Shirley's men seized some of the other hostages the mob had taken. These included Captain Derby of HMS *Alborough* and the purser of the *Canterbury*, Knowles' flagship. The mob, in its turn, threatened to ransack Shirley's residence if they were not returned and seized one of the deputy sheriffs, carrying him away in triumph and setting him in the local stocks.[41]

The following day the House of Representatives discussed the causes of the riot, and expressed their concern that Bostonians had been 'forcibly carried on board his Majesty's Ships of War'. While a crowd of several thousand threatened to storm the Council Chamber, Hutchinson and others pleaded with the governor to placate the mob by promising to use his powers to release the impressed Bostonians and the outward-bound seamen. Shirley agreed to parley once more with the crowd, who remanded the lieutenant in his custody and reminded him that no one had been executed for the press-gang murder of 1745, a clear indication that Bostonians were putting Knowles' actions within the broader context of arbitrary impressments. Shirley for his part promised to speak to Knowles, who refused to release any seamen until his own men were securely in his care and even threatened to bombard the town. The mob for its part kept up the pressure, manning all the wharves to ensure that none of the hostages retaken by Shirley could leave town. It also rounded up other naval seamen, taking some from the navy hospital, and held Captain Erskine of HMS *Canterbury* on his own recognizance at the house of a local militia colonel.

The stand-off continued as long as the militia declined to mobilize, many of the militiamen now being part of a mixed crowd of apprentices, blacks, seamen, and local craftsmen and householders. Eventually the General Court passed resolutions demanding the release of Captain Erskine and offering rewards for the discovery of the ringleaders of a riot that had escalated to potentially dangerous proportions. At this point the riot subsided, the militia came out, the hostages made their way back to the fleet and Commodore Knowles released most of the impressed inhabitants. Some of the ringleaders, largely mariners, were eventually tried, but only three were found guilty. By eighteenth-century standards they walked off with relatively light sentences in the light of the affront they offered to authority. All in all it seems the town, which quickly became implicated in the spontaneous actions of the privateers, wanted to make a point without aggravating the colonial authorities or reducing a legitimate set of grievances to a matter of law and order. As Shirley wrote to their lordships in London, Bostonians were aggrieved that they were excluded from the 1746 Act and to all intents and purposes believed 6 Anne was still in force.[42]

They may well have been correct. The British parliament did not repeal the 1708 statute until 1775 and various lawyers, including John Adams, were prepared to argue for its legitimacy until then.[43] In fact, knowing the disposition of the ports and the temper of the local courts, commanders often trod warily when it came to impressment in American waters. Commodore Samuel Hood told the captains of his boats blockading Masschusetts Bay in 1769 to exercise restraint and politeness in implementing a press; to ask first for volunteers, to avoid taking a master's favourite seaman and to refrain from taking those who were married.[44] Not all officers, of course, were as diplomatic as Hood would have hoped. One of his lieutenants from the frigate *Rose*, Henry Panton, threatened to impress the mate of the *Pitt Packet* if he would not summon his eligible seamen. In attempting to ferret the resisting tars from the brig's forepeak, he quite literally got it in the neck from a harpoon, dying less than an hour later. Lieutenant Frodsham of the *Winchester* cursed resisting seamen in New York as a 'parsill of Raskills'. He was quite prepared to fire across their ship's bow to intimidate the crew to bring to. Once again there were casualties, this time among the crew of the privateer *Sampson*, an incident that simply amplified the resistance to impressment in the American ports.[45]

The fact is that the Royal Navy failed to tap the thousands of seamen who sallied forth from the North American ports with the expansion of the colonial economy after 1740. In this respect the Knowles riot of 1747 proved something of a landmark. The only really successful portside raid occurred in New York in May 1757, when the combined resources of Lord Loudoun and Admiral Sir Charles Hardy, which included no less than 3000 regular troops, swept up some 800 men from the taverns and wharves for an amphibious attack upon Louisbourg.[46] This was an unprecedented press. Other in-harbour recruitments proved violent and contentious, with crews firing on the recruiting parties or mobs carrying press boats through the streets, and sometimes triumphantly burning them. With lawyers resorting increasingly to natural rights arguments to vindicate resistance to the press (a strategy that was first outlined in the aftermath of the Knowles riot by Sam Adams) and juries offering a sympathetic ear to them, naval commanders found it more efficacious to impress at sea.[47]

Popular resistance and legal proscription hampered the navy's recruiting efforts in the mid-eighteenth century Atlantic. In the North American context, naval commanders could count on only the help of the governors, for colonial assemblies became increasingly outspoken in their opposition to impressment.[48] In the Caribbean, the Act of 1744 increasingly hemmed in commanders. Captains who abrogated the Act were liable to a £50 fine for every seaman illegally impressed by the navy. In 1780 Sir Peter Parker thought his subalterns liable to hundreds of suits against them because of the litigious nature of Caribbean merchants, and protested that the navy was being destroyed by 'iniquitous Judgments obtained by means of interested Juries'. With the constant drain of men into the merchant ship or the privateer, he was reduced to recommending that the army pick up straggling soldiers and transfer them to the navy.[49] Others considered confiscating letters of marque from privateers whose masters encouraged men to desert, or closely monitoring those ships flying flags of truce that brought out a surfeit of seamen from Britain for the American or homeward bound trades. Although colonial authorities sometimes co-operated with the navy in ridding their streets and taverns of straggling seamen and vagabonds, this seems to have been a relatively rare occurrence. Admiral Rowley complained that the assistance he received from the magistrates and inhabitants of Kingston, Jamaica, was deplorably slight. He informed the Admiralty that he had increased the bounties in an attempt to reduce the appeal of the privateer, and had ventured as far afield as the Mosquito Shore in the search for men.[50]

In the circumstances, what were the options? One was clearly utilizing the rapidly increasing black labour force that drove the plantation economy. Once a treaty between the planter elite and the Jamaican maroons had been concluded and the prospect of slaves escaping to maroon enclaves minimized, this was at least a possible solution to the manning problem. To be sure, the 1739 treaty did not eliminate the prospect of slave rebellion, of which there were several minor outbreaks in the 1740s, and more with the advent of subsequent wars, when the armed presence of white soldiers and militiamen was precariously stretched. Yet the planter elite was prepared to hire out black slaves for the military expeditions of the early 1740s. Why did it not similarly commit blacks to the fleets, however temporary their service might have been?

Certainly it was not a matter of skill. Black slaves were sometimes seasoned seamen. Some were hired out by their masters to provision plantations or ships in local harbours. Slave codes attempted to regulate their movements and to ensure that they sailed with white masters or overseers; or in the case of Jamaica, with certificates of leave.[51] But maritime slavery was certainly growing, constituting perhaps 3 per cent of the total slave population in Nevis in 1765, and roughly the same proportion in Jamaica a decade later.[52] In the Carolinas, the proportion of skilled slaves who were mariners was as high as 9 per cent. Consequently the presence of black seamen could be very conspicuous in the American trade to the Caribbean, especially when white seamen boarded privateers or were troubled by the presence of the navy in southern coastal or Caribbean waters. A spot check of the vessels lying in Kingston harbour in mid-December 1743 from Boston, New York, Rhode Island and Bermuda revealed that 30 per cent of the crewmen were black, and some of these slaves rather than freemen. In the Bermuda vessels, in particular, blacks routinely outnumbered whites aboard ship, a pattern that deeply disturbed Governor Trelawny.[53]

Blacks also achieved enviable reputations as pilots in Atlantic waters, where swift currents, shifting winds and shoaled passages could be extremely dangerous to commercial traffic. In the windward passage between Jamaica and Hispaniola, for example, the currents were known to be 'very irregular' and 'seldom set in the same direction for two days altogether'. At Plumb Point off Port Royal, it was imperative to get the aid of a pilot, remarked Charles Roberts, 'so useful body of men that every encouragement ought to be given them both here and elsewhere'.[54] Not surprisingly, black pilots were often venerated for their skills and knowledge of local waters and poached by Britain's enemies. At the end of the war of Jenkins' Ear, Spanish brigantines were reported off the Mosquito coast looking for able pilots among the blacks before they set off on a raiding expedition to the Cayman Islands.[55] During the war with America, United States patriots were keen to capture or kill a black pilot named Sampson who was helping 3000 Highlanders, Hessians and New York loyalists cross the bar of the Savannah river. One exceptional pilot in the British navy, John Perkins, was even promoted to lieutenant by Sir Peter Parker in 1782. Two years later Rodney gave him an unofficial commission as commander of the *Endeavour* brig by virtue of his success in acquiring prizes of war, but he had to wait until 1797 for his status to be confirmed. He subsequently commanded two frigates on the Jamaica station and retired from the service because of ill health in 1805.[56]

Placing slaves on board men of war was not unprecedented. French ships had recruited slaves from Saint Domingue during the war of the 1690s.[57] But the planters in the British colonies were very averse to following suit. They had only agreed to the recruitment of black auxiliaries for the 1740–2 military expeditions with the utmost reluctance, as exceptional concessions to the British war effort. Indeed, the vast majority of these slaves acted in an unarmed capacity, as 'pioneers' or general drudges rather than as 'shot negroes', as they were popularly known.[58] Given the general uncertainty about internal rebellion, and the fear that some slaves would avail themselves of the wartime situation to desert their masters, it was hardly surprising that the planters were averse to volunteering their slaves as naval seamen. Like their counterparts in Virginia and the Carolinas, they thought maritime slavery would corrode bonded labour because of the mobility and worldliness it encouraged.[59] If they did agree to set their slaves afloat, it was in privateering vessels rather than men of war, and only then because of dramatic shortages of white seamen. In 1745, for example, John Curtin, a planter and owner of the privateer *Dowdall*, was forced to put fourteen of his own slaves on board his vessel because too many of his men had been impressed aboard HMS *Adventure*.[60]

Planters sometimes deplored the way in which the navy inveigled slaves aboard men of war and kept masters at bay through the 'licentious and uncontrouled Behaviour of the Seamen'.[61] Certainly there were officers who had little compunction about bringing slaves on board and paying them the same wages as ordinary seamen. During the American war, slaves were actively recruited into the navy following Lord Dunmore's declaration offering them freedom if they fought on the British side.[62] But this was an exceptional precedent dictated by the circumstances of the continental campaign. In earlier decades officers such as Commodore Douglas manned his private sloop with slaves, some of whom had been free before they were captured as prisoners of war.[63] Yet if slaves were recruited informally in the decades before the American war, it was more likely on small craft rather than frigates and men of war. When officers allowed conspicuous numbers of blacks on board, there were complaints from planters and crackdowns from commanders. In 1775 Admiral James Young ordered five of his vessels to enter no more than four slaves per vessel, and then to consign them to menial duties such as cooks.[64] The same was true of Admiral Sir George Brydges Rodney, who ordered slaves taken from St Vincent to be restored to their owners, and criticized Captain Saxton of HMS *Invincible* for taking up slaves from St Eustatius with a view eventually to selling them.[65] Judging from the muster books – admittedly an imperfect record for this sort of detective work – it would appear that officers were generally reluctant to sign on slaves without the consent of the owner.

The main reason for this restrictive policy was that naval captains upheld the proprietorial nature of slavery. But it may also have been prompted by a general reluctance to mix two servile labour regimes. Slaves were, after all, among the spoils of war. Although the mid-century wars seldom degenerated into the general manhunt that characterized the War of Spanish Succession, when enemy plantations were raided with impunity, slaves were part of the prizes captured by British men of war. In 1744, for example, Commodore Knowles' fleet captured two slave ships from the Guinea coast and Angola, the first with 400 blacks on board, the second with 650.[66] These prizes would have been worth about £30,000 and shared, albeit very unevenly, among the crews involved. Such rewards were one of the few tonics which kept seamen aboard ship in these torrid climes. Admiral Vernon believed they induced 'a good will for the Public Service'.[67] Bringing large numbers of slaves on board to serve in the navy would likely have unsettled already fractious crews and complicated relations on the lower deck. Slaves capturing slaves was, of course, one of the historical paradoxes of Caribbean warfare, but it was best left to privateers rather than the large crews of the Royal Navy to negotiate the contradictions it might have involved.[68]

This did not mean that the Royal Navy did not bring any slaves on board ship, only that it did not actively recruit them in large numbers. Although it is attractive to think of ships as 'microsystems of linguistic and political hybridity', one should not assume that they were racially very diverse. The current assumption that one quarter of the crews on British naval ships were black in the late eighteenth century is frankly fanciful.[69] It is based on an off-hand speculation by a colonial commissioner in the 1920s, and has somehow entered the historical lists as a compelling factoid for all those who wish to see the ship as the nucleus of an international, multi-ethnic Atlantic.[70] Yet while merchant ships were sometimes racially diverse, this was not so apparent in the British navy. On the Leeward Islands station, the proportion of blacks in the Royal Navy was probably no more than 4 per cent; and that is assuming that all born in the empire, the USA and South America were seamen of colour, which is very unlikely. Other muster books reveal that seamen from North America and the Caribbean rarely constituted more than 5 per cent of a ship's crew in the Napoleonic era and significantly less 50 years before that.[71] On HMS *Implacable* in 1808, the seamen from the Americas, the Caribbean and India did not exceed 8 per cent of the total crew; on Nelson's

*Victory* no more than 6 per cent.[72] So, even allowing for a reasonable proportion of racially mixed crews from London and Liverpool, the magic figure of 25 per cent simply cannot be reached. Instructively, the percentage of black seamen among American prisoners of war in the war of 1812 was only 9 per cent.[73]

Seamen of colour were conspicuous enough to attract the eye of a Rowlandson. They added to the exoticism of the senior service. Naval officers were sometimes accompanied by black servants whom they had purchased, as was Olaudah Equiano by Captain Pascal during the Seven Years' War.[74] So, too, was the odd ship's carpenter. In the muster book of HMS *Plymouth*, for example, James Caesar, a carpenter's servant, was entered on 25 July 1745 along with his master, who collected his wages until his discharge two years later.[75] Quite possibly a few runaways were recruited at Caribbean ports, especially when desertion rates ran high and complements were perilously low. On HMS *Lenox*, for example, which lost nearly a third of its crew through death or desertion on the Jamaica station, we find that William Quasshy was entered as an able seaman at Port Royal, and John Quamino as a boatswain's servant six months later. On HMS *Canterbury*, where the ship's complement was down by 25 per cent, we discover entries at Barbados for Hilkia Moor and Black Emmanuel.[76] Whether these men were runaways or free blacks it is impossible to say. Free blacks certainly found their way onto men of war, either as impressed men or as volunteers who feared re-enslavement on the islands if they were without work.[77] It was not without its risks, for capture by the enemy could lead to re-enslavement. Admiral Frankland disliked using the 'woolly race' in vessels of war and when he came across a French privateer filled with black mariners, he had no compunction about selling them. He was quite prepared to defy the courts and ignore certificates of freedom to do so. Commodore Douglas followed his example, telling the governor of Martinique he should do the same.[78] Even so, some free men of colour took their chances, for the prospect of re-enslavement on land was not exactly slim. Among those aboard HMS *Litchfield* until his desertion in 1740 was John Henzer. He was described as having 'a swarthy mulatto complexion and black lank hair, aged about 28 years', 5 ft 7 in high with 'a large scar on the inside of his shoulder'.[79] Yet men like Henzer were not as visible in the Royal Navy as they would be later in the century, when the free black population in the British colonies was considerably larger.

Slaves and ex-slaves, then, did find their way on board British men-of-war, but not in numbers that would have made them a conspicuous minority. The only exception to the rule were the Jamaican maroons who volunteered for HMS *Princess Louisa*,[80] and after the 1739 treaty they were clearly a special case. By and large the British navy followed the army strategy of using slaves as auxiliaries. Thus the captain of the *Deal Castle* reported in early 1744 that he sent his carpenter, a gang of men and '8 Negroes ashore to Cutt Timber'. Later a further '6 Negroes' were brought in from Spanish Town to assist in the work.[81]

In Jamaica and Antigua, the British government even purchased its own slaves to careen, caulk and repair the ships. With their own women and children they formed small companies, 30 or so in size, known as 'His Majesty's Negroes'. From time to time the British navy hired other slaves to supplement this small but skilled workforce. In Antigua, Governor Matthew arranged for 100 blacks to help the navy rebuild its wharf and careen its ships. In Jamaica in 1748, Commodore Knowles asked Governor Trelawny for 250 blacks to assist 'in heaving the ships' in order to careen them.[82] He was reluctant to commit his own seamen, he said, because too many of them had been enticed away by the high wages offered by merchants for the 'run home'. Besides, he added, echoing the prejudices of his day, blacks were acclimatized to heavy labour in the sun in a way that most of his seamen were not. As one contemporary writer asserted, 'Drudgery in the Sun cannot be borne by the *Europeans*'.[83]

In segregating its servile workforce by race, the British navy inevitably found itself continually short of men on board ship. Ostensibly the colonial authorities co-operated with the navy in its search for deserters. Laws were passed imposing heavy fines on anyone who harboured them.[84] Yet frequently they were honoured in the breach. Too many colonial officials had links to merchants and privateers to take the regulations seriously, and when navy press gangs scoured ports to track down deserters, they were sometimes opposed by colonial forces. In 1746 the search party of the *Falmouth* was arrested by the militia in Spanish Town on the grounds that its unruly behaviour threatened the town on what was a 'negro holiday'. When the Admiral Davers complained to Governor Trelawny, he retorted that the actions of the militia officer were 'prudent'.[85] Davers thought otherwise. It was indicative, he informed the Admiralty, of the way in which the service was being compromised by officials whose first allegiance was to the merchant and planter elite.[86]

The tug of war over manning the navy inevitably led commanders to adopt other expedients. Prisoners of war were sometimes given the option of serving in His Majesty's Fleet rather than languishing in close quarters. Some accepted, for the muster books of the 1740s are littered with Spanish names in particular. Indeed, free black or mulatto seamen from Spanish vessels had a special inducement to enlist, for there was a very real prospect that they might be enslaved if they reached British ports, especially if they could be construed as part of British prizes.[87] Together with the pressing that took place offshore from privateers or from merchant ships on the homeward run, even from vessels flying flags of truce,[88] the navy strove hard to hold on to a minimal complement of men. In 1744 Commodore Knowles complained that he could only man his squadron in the Leeward Islands by exchanging prisoners with the French, a frustrating experience because island governors deemed such exchanges to be within their jurisdiction and frequently turned them over to privateers.[89]

In these circumstances, the strain upon crews was severe. It was registered by squabbles over prizes and near-mutinies when commanders lost sight of valuable spoils, or were thought to be dealing with local merchants over contraband goods that would otherwise have been condemned as prizes and redistributed to the crew.[90] One seaman, who had been pressed into service 32 months previously and had little respite from the service beyond a brief sick leave in Gibraltar, was sentenced to 36 lashes of the cat for describing HMS *Eltham* as a 'prison', despite the fact he had worked his way up to being a quartermaster.[91] In the following month, on another man of war that had done long service in the Leeward Islands, two men were hanged from the yardarm for deserting their ship and for drowning the midshipman as they escaped. The bosun's mate who had abetted their escape was sentenced to 300 lashes of the cat o' nine tails, one that if rigorously executed would surely have killed him.[92]

Deserting a ship was an easier matter in America than it was in the Caribbean. It was easier to blend in with the local population, and the range of seafaring opportunities was arguably higher. Deserting in the Caribbean was a riskier business. It was especially risky in the hurricane season between July and mid-October when merchant shipping was virtually at a standstill, leaving seamen little choice but to linger in port. Without contacts, seamen could easily fall into the hands of local crimps who would consign them to the highest bidder. A deserter's chances of getting home were best when the large merchant convoys were about to sail in the spring and early summer, although the chances of detection on the voyage were high. The other alternatives were finding some space for survival on the Caribbean frontier or joining a privateer, of which there were over 400 in Caribbean waters in the peak years of 1745–47, not to mention those rigged out by the Spanish and French.

Historians have sometimes suggested that the profits of privateering were little better than the prize money that a seaman might obtain aboard a man of war. Yet in the Caribbean at least, the prospects were better because the distribution of prizes was more equitably distributed among the crew, with only a third of the share going to the owner rather than the half that prevailed in European waters.[93] Much, of course, depended upon chance, upon the capture of a lucrative prize; for privateering crews were not always paid any wages. But the rewards that accrued from captured cargoes of sugar, molasses, tobacco, coffee and indigo were often more than double the average wage paid to merchant seamen and six times the Royal Navy's monthly wage.[94] Besides, there were opportunities for running contraband trade to enemy islands, and even trafficking in slaves. The Bahamian privateers, in particular, seem to have been notorious on this score. They routinely captured slaves from open boats and canoes off the coast of Hispaniola as well as supplying that island with much needed provisions.[95]

Naval officers sometimes expressed disbelief that seamen with two or three years' back pay would desert for a privateer, but the lure of spoils was great. In any case, the discipline aboard a privateer was not as harsh as on a man of war, where naval officers had armed marines to back up their decisions. The promise of shorter cruises, usually seven months in all, was also attractive. Among other things, it gave British seamen the opportunity of getting back to British North America and from thence home, for the principal ports from which privateers hailed were New York, Newport, Boston and Philadelphia.[96]

As a last resort, a seaman might seek a haven to hide in for the duration of the war. In the early eighteenth century Curaçao was a favoured resort; over a thousand were said to be there before the passing of 6 Anne.[97] But when Knowles ventured there in 1743 in search of men he could only find Dutch mulattoes to fill his complement. In the Caribbean of the 1740s, the number of places where one might eke out such an existence was more limited. Most islands and isthmuses were rapidly becoming part of the plantation zone, one in which there was a significant growth of large estates at the expense of poor white settlers. The one obvious frontier for British colonists in the mid-eighteenth century was in Central America, among the logwood settlements of the Bay of Honduras or further south on the Mosquito coast, where handfuls of white settlers lived alongside the Mosquito Indians and mustees descended from coastal Indians and shipwrecked black slaves. The Mosquito Shore was of little economic importance. Its main significance was strategic, for the British had cultivated good relations with the Mosquito Indians, and indeed paid for their goodwill, as a counterpoint to Spanish ambitions in the area and as a reserve force for putting down slave rebellions in Jamaica. The logwood enterprises, on the other hand, were important to the British woollen industry for their valuable dyes. They were largely seasonal settlements, run with slave labour, despite the fiction of patriotic discourse in Britain which portrayed them as industrious territories of free-born Englishmen vulnerable to the lawless depredations of the Spanish. In fact the Baymen were quite prepared to engage in illicit trading with the Spanish who claimed the territory, and also with the Dutch and northern colonists who received the lion's share of the lumber. There was no semblance of government to talk of. 'The modern settlers, as well as their predecessors', remarked Edward Long two decades later, 'have lived hitherto in a kind of republican state, having no governor appointed over them.'[98] Governor Trelawny of Jamaica thought the whole coastline 'a retreat for Pyrates and disorderly people averse to all Government' and had been so for 40 years.[99] Captain Nathaniel Uring, who had spent some time among the logwood cutters earlier in the century, was of the same opinion. He thought them a 'rude drunken crew', a motley group of ex-pirates and seamen whose 'chief delight' was 'drinking'.[100]

Naval deserters certainly ventured to the area during wartime. When the Jamaican government decided to build a port and garrison on the island of

Roatan as a centre of operations against the Spanish, some of the seamen jumped ship.[101] A few may even have joined the various expeditions against the Spaniards that the adventurer Ralph Hodgson organized on behalf of the government, expeditions that were compromised by the Mosquito preference for marauding and enslaving local Indians. Others may have joined the privateers who cruised the coast, or the raids on Spanish settlements in Truxillo and Omoa in the aftermath of the war.[102] Some of them would have been confronted by their own kind; for in the retaliations of the Spanish along the Mosquito coast by two brigantines, half of the crews were said to be English or Scottish. 'A little hanging for these renegadoes, if they can be catched', remarked Hodgson, 'would be extremely wholesome.'[103]

The continuation of hostilities up and down the Mosquito coast in the early 1750s points to the difficulties that many seamen had in coming to terms with the armistice of the great powers. Seamen who became habituated to privateering, or to trafficking in contraband goods under flags of truce, sometimes found it difficult to return to normal commerce once war was terminated. Captain Henry Osborn remarked on the shift from privateering to piracy at Montserrat, and recalled an attempt to do this off Barbados aboard the *Chesterfield* privateer.[104] The same happened at New York. When several French prizes were not condemned before the declaration of peace, a number of crews mutinied, became 'very arrogant & desperate', remarked Governor Clinton, '& threaten publicly that they will cut out some Vessels, and hoist the Black flag'.[105] Among those who did so was Owen Lloyd, a seaman who persuaded the masters of two Rhode Island sloops to steal the cargo of a Spanish galleon moored in Ocracoke inlet in Pamlico Sound and venture south to Caribbean waters. One of the sloops ran aground, but peg-legged Lloyd successfully charted the other to Spanish Town, Jamaica, and then onwards to the Virgin Islands, where he reached his own treasure island, one called Norman's, south of Tortola. There, on an uninhabited island that was a regular rendezvous for privateers with contraband goods, he unloaded 50 chests of Spanish dollars and church plate, 120 bales of cochineal and 70 bags of indigo and tobacco.[106] It was a spectacular heist, worth perhaps £100,000. Lloyd's own share of the catch appears to have been a tenth, about £10,000, a princely sum for a seaman and one that likely set him up for life.

If he managed to get away with it. Owen Lloyd's haul not only paled in comparison with the windfalls of war that accrued to admirals, several of whom received £100,000 or more in prizes, but the risks were incomparably greater. The golden age of piracy was over. Under the vigilance of the Royal Navy, the pirate community had been broken in the 1720s, dwindling in numbers to little more than 200 men. The great powers of Europe were not about to tolerate its revival 30 years later, once the war had been concluded. Although some captains feared that wartime privateering would 'breed up a Nursery of Pyrates',[107] policing operations and trials were the order of the day; aided and abetted by the privateering owners themselves, who in the last year of war transferred their investments to less predatory activities.

British seamen of the 1740s were more likely to go 'upon the account' on Hounslow Heath than they were on the not-so-Spanish Main. As one English commentator remarked, the end of the war in 1748 would 'loose upon the Nation Twenty Thousand *Sixpence-a-Day Heroes*, with perhaps a Crown in their Pockets, and very little Inclination to starve for want of recruiting out of other People's Property'.[108] In this struggle for survival there were few cross-cultural alliances that extended beyond the lower deck. Indeed, the camaraderie that seamen fostered during the war tended to be concrete and specific to their own crews. According to John Brown, a vicar from the thriving port of Newcastle upon Tyne, it was this sort of comradeship that made the British navy such a formidable fighting force.[109]

Although there have been recent attempts to situate Atlantic mariners at the centre of a rebellious, multi-ethnic proletariat in the eighteenth century,[110] there is actually little evidence that seafaring solidarities extended to other subaltern groups in the Caribbean, or indeed in North America. In the incident at the English harbour of Antigua with which I began this chapter, there is fleeting evidence that some of the crew disapproved of Captain Montagu's intemperate actions. Several had refused to fire into the long boat and the mate had attempted to intervene before Montagu fired his second shot.[111] There were also a few occasions when blacks alerted white seamen to the threat of impressment, joining them (among many others, propertied and un-propertied) in their protests during the Boston riot of 1747.[112] But such support was fleeting and fragmentary. There is no evidence that seamen sympathized with slave revolts in the Caribbean during this period; sailors helped repress the Tacky rebellion of 1760 in Jamaica, and were called in again during the 1776 Hanover revolt.[113] And while there was some collusion between Irish soldiers garrisoned at Fort George and the slaves who worked along the New York waterfront in the conspiracy of 1741, the New York seamen were conspicuous by their absence. The only seamen clearly implicated in the plot to burn the houses of the royal governor and well-heeled citizens were Spanish speaking, free men of colour who had been sold into slavery when their sloop, *La Soledad*, had been condemned as a prize of war. These men had a particular grievance against Captain John Lush, the man who had differentiated them from their whiter-skinned crew members and had sold them in New York. They protested that 'if the captain would not send them to their own country, they would ruin all the city'. Amid threats of burning the town, 'killing all the people' and bragging that they could kill twenty times as many people as an equivalent group of 'York negroes', they looked forward to the possibility of the French or Spanish invading New York and facilitating their emancipation.[114]

These were hardly sentiments that were revolutionary or conducive to forging more permanent solidarities among the diverse subalterns of the Atlantic world. Rather, they were very much part of the particular conjuncture of eighteenth-century war, its adventure capitalism and racial inequities. Nor did the other known sailor who was involved in the conspiracy show much solidarity with the New York waterfront. He was Christopher Wilson, an eighteen-year-old from a hospital ship, the *Flamborough*. He had been part of the fencing network at Hughson's tavern where the conspiracy was hatched, but when it came to the crunch he turned in one of the chief conspirators, a slave called Caesar who was owned by a New York baker.[115]

What is particularly damaging to the notion of a multi-ethnic Atlantic 'working class' that features sailors and slaves prominently amongst its 'motley crew' is that sailors were deeply implicated in the institution of slavery: both as pirates and privateers. Despite the existence of pirate 'commonwealths' and more egalitarian relations aboard ship, pirates were not ideologically opposed to slavery. On the contrary, pirates in Madagascar and Sierra Leone owned and traded slaves. Similarly, seamen crewing for privateers had little compunction about selling slave cargoes in time of war.[116] This was also an era when maroons tracked down runaways, and when Mosquito Indians in the service of the British enslaved their rivals and sold them to logwood cutters on the Bay of Honduras, or to Dutch and Jamaican planters. Briton Hammon, one of the few blacks to have left a record of his sea adventures during the 1740s, recalled being captured on the Florida coast by a band of Indians who 'beat me most terribly with a cutlass'. They taunted me in 'broken English', he remembered, that 'they intended to roast me alive'.[117] Later they sold him to the governor of Havana.

This is not a picture that evokes interracial harmony or some international fraternity of the dispossessed.[118] It is a violent world of marchlands, to use Bernard Bailyn's phrase, in which relatively little space opened up for amicable relations between people of different cultures, let alone the cultivation of wider solidarities.[119] As Philip Morgan has argued, seafaring may have 'blurred the binary terms in which British peoples generally encountered indigenous peoples on land' where scalping and ritual sacrifice accentuated cultural difference, but it never 'overcame the fissures of race'.[120] In fact the Atlantic world of the mid-eighteenth century threatened to degenerate into a dog-eat-dog society whose predatory actions flowed from the predatory nature of war, the state conflicts that licensed that predation within very specific international divisions of labour, and the sheer struggle for survival among the marginal and exploited.

It is a picture, however, that should be contrasted with the prevailing discourse in mid-eighteenth century Britain, which saw the 1740 struggle with Spain and subsequently France as a pre-eminently patriotic venture, a veritable derring-do. The fervour that greeted Admiral Vernon's victory at Porto Bello expressed a libertarian, bellicose mercantilism in which trade and the accumulation of wealth were revered as the highest national and individual good, a felicitous welding of national and imperial interest, of participatory politics and Protestant destiny. Within this context the Caribbean became the site of freedom of trade, freedom from Catholic absolutist rule and, through the growing popularity of sugar and tobacco, of consumer desire. Slavery was deeply implicated with production and colonial grandeur within this discourse but all too frequently in an elliptical way. The slave was periodically recognized as the raw but necessary muscle of the sugar economy, surfacing abruptly at the Stono rebellion of South Carolina in 1739 as a simpleton seduced by Catholicism and hopes of freedom at the hands of the perfidious Spanish.[121] The seaman, by contrast, was foregrounded as the victimized tar of the Spanish *guardacosta*, or as the sturdy arm of a masculine nationalism. In the same issue of the *London Daily Post* as the Stono rebellion, there was an account of Vernon's assault upon Fort Chagre, the headquarters of the *guardacostas*, in which seamen stormed the fort and struck the colours. Such valorous tales were commemorated later in the year with a print representing Jack Tar as the British Hercules; the stuff of imagined communities but not of the experience of the lower decks in the Atlantic, least of all in the tropical zone.

Chelsea pensioners reading the Waterloo dispatch

# 6

## The Navy and the Nation 1793–1820

In 1822 David Wilkie exhibited his painting of the Chelsea pensioners reading the gazette of the Battle of Waterloo. By all accounts, it was enormously popular, at least for those who had the time and the money to visit the Royal Academy, where it was cordoned off by special barriers so that it would be protected from the crowd. The painting depicts an aged pensioner, a veteran of the battle of Quebec by which Britain secured Canada from the French, reading the news of Wellington's victory against Napoleon to a captive and enthralled audience. Clustered around him are a variety of soldiers from different regiments in the British Isles – Welsh, Scottish, Irish – some of whom did service in the far-off posts of the empire. Across the table is a young black military bandsman who leans forward eagerly to learn of the event. And further afield, under the windows of the Duke of York, are the wives and sweethearts of other soldiers, rapturously attentive to the disclosure of a most signal victory.

The painting self-evidently attempts to capture an upsurge of patriotism in the summer of 1815 that transcends race, class, gender and even age. In the estimation of Linda Colley, it is 'one man's very perceptive interpretation of both the variety and roots of Britishness'.[1] Indeed, it is the opening image of her concluding chapter of *Britons*, a synecdoche of the military experiences that she believes shaped British identity in the long eighteenth century.

In fact, Wilkie's painting is more than paean to Britishness. Commissioned by the Duke of Wellington in 1816, it went through a variety of revisions in the next five years. Initially, the Iron Duke said he simply wanted 'a parcel of old soldiers talking over their stories'. Then in 1819 Wellington decided he wanted younger soldiers in the painting, not simply Chelsea pensioners. David Wilkie, flattered that the Duke had personally approached him in the first place, was more than willing to oblige, and by the spring of 1820 he had begun to line in the perspective. At this point in its production, the painting remained apolitical, with no hint of Wellington or Waterloo – and it lacked the central focus of the gazette. But some time in early October 1820 David Wilkie deliberately made Waterloo and its victor the resonating theme of his work.

It is unlikely that Wilkie simply did this for the money, even though the fee he requested, 1200 guineas, was a little pricey. It is more likely that Wilkie was troubled by the flagging fortunes of his patron. Wellington was the hero of the

Peninsula War and then of Waterloo, the decisive battle of the campaign against Napoleon.[2] In the 1820s he was still able to draw considerable cachet from his status as Britain's pre-eminent general. At the parade of his regiment on the anniversary of the battle in June 1820, Mrs Arbuthnot reported 'the mob was collected in immense numbers & received the Duke with most tumultuous applause'.[3] At the same time, the Duke's stature had been tarnished by his endorsement of the government's repressive policies towards the post-war radical movement and its strategy of mass petitioning. Wellington had applauded Sidmouth's defence of the yeomanry cavalry at St Peter's Fields, Manchester, when they stomped and sabred members of the crowd whom they believed to be illegally assembled. He supported the Six Acts. Ultra-radicals despised him. One of them, James Ings, a bankrupt butcher from Portsmouth, attempted to kill him when he was walking from the Ordnance Office in London.

This adventure could be written off as the reaction of a lunatic fringe, at least by people like Wilkie. But Wellington's close association with the new king, George IV, in his efforts to ban his estranged wife from regal status, was more troubling. In the prints of the day Wellington was associated with the contemptible Milan Commission. This was the inquiry which sought to find incriminating evidence of adultery on the part of Caroline of Brunswick when she was gadding about the continent while her husband was cavorting with a variety of mistresses at home. It was a classic case of the double standard, and it placed Wellington solidly within the aristocratic cohort of libertine Old Corruption as well as part of a reactionary, anti-democratic, government. On the first appearance of the Queen in London in 1820, when crowds demanded lights and championed her name, Wellington had to prevent Lord Sidmouth from being dragged from his coach. By the opening of Queen Caroline's 'trial', Wellington himself was the object of scorn. He was hissed by the crowd, much to the amazement of the *Morning Post*, who asked 'Will England credit it? Will the world believe it?'[4] A few weeks later a mob attempted to unhorse the Duke as he was riding from the Lords and crowds upbraided him with the words 'No hero! We want no hero!'[5]

All this must have been troubling to David Wilkie, who tried to stay out of the polarizing politics of the times.[6] From his studio in Phillimore Place, he must have been uncomfortably aware of the chanting crowds and hoopla that greeted the Queen's supporters as they paraded along Kensington High Street to Brandenburg House, Hammersmith, to pay their respects to Queen Caroline. Represented among those supporters were a wide range of people, middle and working class, including petitioners from the ports of Tyne and Wear and London, the latter in the shape of the British seamen of Middlesex. Ten thousand seamen were said to sign petitions in favour of the Queen.[7] These were men with wartime experience, proud of their country and their contribution to Britain's wooden walls, flying flags that represented men of war and Hearts of Oak, but also ones that demanded 'Freedom and Justice'.[8]

At the peak of the Queenite agitation, Wilkie changed his painting to re-appropriate patriotism for the Duke. The signifiers in the painting are very explicit about this. Waterloo is cast as the culmination of a struggle against the French dating back to the Seven Years' War. The painting invokes memories of battles on three continents, including Wellington's own victories at the Battle of Assaye in India and Vittoria during the Peninsular War. Wilkie's friend Walter Scott, the novelist and royal choreographer, approved of its sentiments; so too, of course, did Wellington. When it was finally exhibited at the Royal Academy in April 1822, it was placed with Jackson's portrait of the Duke of York on one side and Lawrence's portrait of Wellington on the other. Wilkie thought it 'one of the happiest arrangements I ever saw'.[9]

The 'Chelsea Pensioners', then, is not an innocent representation of Britishness, nor is it one that could stake a strong claim to be a synecdoche. It is a deliberate intervention by Wilkie to resuscitate his patron's fortunes at a time when people were beginning to debate what the war effort had been all about. Leigh Hunt understood this when he mischievously observed: 'We are right glad to see at least one good result from the dearly-bought victory at Waterloo.'[10] What Hunt's remark gestures towards, and what Colley's interpretation glosses, is the contested terrain of patriotism that emerged so strikingly at the end of the war when de-mobbed soldiers and sailors faced hardship, repression and nothing in the way of citizenship for their efforts. Perhaps the kind of patriotism they strove for and dreamed about was rather different than its establishment variety? Perhaps the making of Britishness was a more tortured and ambiguous narrative than Colley portrayed? I propose to test this out by looking at those jack tars who rallied to the Queen and whose commitment to king and country was hardly straightforward.

Naval historians tend to think of the British seaman as an essentially apolitical being, tetchy about his privileges and perquisites, but loyal to good officers and compulsively patriotic. Peter Kemp writes: 'In general he appears as a rather simple sort of fellow, ready to follow to the death when led by officers his trusted.'[11] In many representations, certainly, this is how he appeared. Prints revealed popular admirals sharing a jar with the hardy tar. Pub songs celebrated his infectious optimism and courage in the face of the enemy. In *A Garland of New Songs* (a collection of songs from Newcastle), John Bull is told that 'Your sailors are true stuff,/Just point at what you want, John,/To them – that's quite enough'.[12] Such intrepid service sometimes came at a price, but even in George Cruickshank's subtly ironic *Sailor's Progress*, the disabled sailor is still raising his jar to king and country, jocose to the end.

Successive mobilizations had taught the Admiralty to be rather more wary of the patriotism of the British tar, and the French wars of the late eighteenth century were no exception. At a time when John Reeves and his associates were ringing the tocsin of popular loyalism in an effort to mobilize the country against Revolutionary France and isolate republican sympathizers, the Admiralty was facing its greatest challenge. Recruitment campaigns faltered in the face of massive resistance. In the first year of the war the press gangs confronted angry mobs on at least 27 occasions. Although the number of anti-impressment affrays had been higher at the onset of the Seven Years' War, the scale and intensity of resistance was more formidable in 1793. At Liverpool large mobs of seamen and carpenters pulled down the two central rendezvous. At Whitby there were similar threats to sack the press gang's headquarters, forcing Captain John Shortland to beat a quick retreat. In Cork there was a mutiny aboard the tender, while in Greenock a crowd of seamen and sympathizers attempted to burn the open boat of the tender in the public square. As the regulating officer there reported: 'The lower class of People of Greenock became very riotous and proceeded to burn everything that came in their way, and about 12 o'clock they hauled one of the boats belonging to the Rendezvous on the Square and put her into the fire, but by the timely assistance of the Officers and Gangs supported by the Magistrates & a party of Fencibles, the Boat was removed tho' much damaged.'[13]

The scale and variety of resistance was most impressive on the banks of the Tyne and Wear, where crowds of seamen and inhabitants rescued men from the tenders and besieged the press gang in its rendezvous in Sunderland. At South Shields, one magistrate reported, hundreds of rioters carrying a banner 'Liberty for Ever' drove the Press Gang through the streets in ritualistic humiliation, with their jackets turned inside out.[14] According to the *Newcastle Courant*, 'a numerous mob' took the gangers to Chirton bar and told them that if they ever returned they would be torn limb from limb.[15]

The protests that ranged up and down the Tyne were diverse. Running people out of town with their jackets inside out was a conventional form of hazing. In the early months of 1793 it was used by striking joiners to bring some of their workmen into line. At the same time, striking keelmen forced one of their uncooperative brethren to ride the stang.[16] Yet seamen did not only employ the familiar forms of folk justice in their opposition to the press gang. They held meetings, talked of their entitlements, demanded higher pay and better provision for their dependents.[17] Angry that the normal statutory protections offered colliers did not seem to be recognized, seamen struck the sails of coal ships and deliberately disrupted the trade. Commenting on the striking seamen – who were also bargaining for better wages in return for carrying coal to London – one JP observed that they had shown 'a degree of system & order unknown in former riots, so much so, as to make the Part the Magistrates had to act, embarrassing and difficult'.[18]

This was not all. Under the guidance of a Magna Carta club, seamen voiced their concerns about the unconstitutionality of impressment and circulated their grievances to other ports.[19] As I suggested earlier, these forms of association betokened more sophisticated modes of resistance; they went beyond the usual repertoire of evasion and direct violent confrontation with the gangs. They were accompanied by whiffs of support for Tom Paine despite the efforts of loyalists to rally anti-Painite forces in Shields, Sunderland and at several industrial villages near the Crowley works at Swalwell and Winlaton.[20] Magistrate Joseph Bulwer, not one to exaggerate the scale of protest in the Newcastle area, reported that crowds on Tyneside frequently shouted 'No King, Tom Paine for ever'.[21] Bulwer had earlier informed the government that there was nothing political in the seamen's grievances; they were 'heartily attached to the Government of the Country'.[22] Now he was presumably having second thoughts. Sailors were very much part of the waterfront protests, and were aware of the radical rhetoric of the day. Sixpenny editions of Paine were in circulation on Tyneside and at South Shields, a liberty pole was erected in the marketplace, a Francophile gesture that must have shocked local property owners.[23] As at other ports such as Plymouth and Greenock, radical ideas circulated among seamen in what was an expanding but imponderable frontier of political literacy.[24]

The actions of the seamen in the winter of 1792–3 bore some relation to what happened four years later at Spithead and the Nore. Conventionally the 1797 mutinies have been interpreted as pragmatic protests against poor working conditions to which political motives were added by outsiders, whether radical artisans recruited under the Quota Acts of 1795 or the United Irishmen. While the social and political heterogeneity of the crews doubtless had an impact on the way in which the mutinies unfolded, one does not have to adopt such a bipolar perspective to explain their course. Demands for an increase in wages in the Royal Navy were voiced on Tyneside in the winter of 1792–3 and circulated to other ports.[25] Soaring prices and bad harvests gave them added urgency in the middle years of the decade; consequently petitions for an increase of wages were sent to the Admiralty in 1796. Early the following year, the Channel fleet sent more petitions to their former commander-in-chief, the popular Lord Howe, who was at Bath nursing his gout. Howe chose to ignore them, sensing that they were written by some radical agitator intent upon whipping up discontent in the fleet.[26] He sent them on to the Admiralty who decided to pre-empt any protest by having Admiral Bridport order the fleet set sail.

This strategy backfired. The sailors of the Channel fleet refused to weigh anchor until their demands were addressed. The main ones included better pay, which had not been increased for over 140 years; wholesome provisions including fresh supplies of vegetables; more liberal shore leave; full wages for men when wounded (over 800 seamen had been wounded in their fleet in the first notable victory of the war); and better pensions and care for the sick. The seamen also demanded some modification of the articles of war and a full pardon for existing deserters. The negotiation of these terms was left to a committee of delegates, two from each ship, who symbolically appropriated the space of the officer class by meeting in the cabin of Lord Howe's former flagship HMS *Charlotte*.

The Admiralty was keen to negotiate, but the officers assigned the task sometimes had trouble dealing with men whom they were accustomed to order about. At the first meeting Sir Alan Gardner lost his temper, assaulted one delegate and threatened to hang one in five in the fleet.[27] The delegates, for their part, were suspicious of the officers and sensibly wanted any deal confirmed by parliament and the king, backed by a general pardon. They refused to be bamboozled into quick agreements and resented the arrogance of the admirals in thinking they would quickly fall in line once their main grievances were settled. After a second failure to weigh anchor, tempers flared. Vice-Admiral Colpoys refused to allow delegates to convene on his flagship, the *London*; he ordered the marines to fire on the mutineers, several of whom were killed. The seamen nearly hanged Colpoys and one of his officers in retaliation, but eventually ordered Gardner, Colpoys and over 100 malevolent officers ashore. Although Bridport remained the nominal commander, the mutineers raised the red flag and took effective command of the fleet. Ultimately it took all of Howe's diplomatic skill and cachet with the lower deck to reach some amicable agreement.[28]

The mutiny at Spithead was contentious enough; the one at the Nore proved more so. The Nore was an anchorage off Sheerness dockyard, at the junction of the Thames and the Medway. It was a clearing house for new recruits and a focal point for ships coming to and from Chatham. Unlike Spithead, it had no real fleet, and certainly no *esprit de corps* equivalent to the Channel fleet at Spithead, which had seen action in the Atlantic. Only the defection of ships from the North Sea fleet provided the Nore mutineers with some experienced crews. Over a third of all the seamen at the Nore were made up of Quota men, which is an indication of the transient and heterogeneous nature of its complement.[29]

The course of the Nore mutiny was therefore more volatile and arguably more political. The demands of the mutineers were certainly more expansive, for they included a more equal distribution of prize money, pay advances for pressed men, court martial by jury and a veto on all returning officers. The last two demands, in particular, struck at the heart of the navy's hierarchy of command, and the Admiralty was not disposed to negotiate any further on the seamen's grievances beyond offering a general pardon. Richard Parker, the elected President of the Nore, refused this offer and the conflict escalated. Once the government cut off supplies, the mutineers cordoned off the Thames, removed provisions and water from passing merchant ships and attempted to put pressure on London. Parliament responded with two acts banning communications with the mutineers and punishing those who encouraged mutiny. The government then went on the offensive, and, with no navigation buoys to guide them away from the Nore, the mutiny collapsed as ship after ship defected.

The mutineers emphasized their service to their country in both the American and French wars in advancing their demands. The tars talked of themselves as 'British seamen' and even at the Nore, in the final phases of the mutiny, celebrated the king's birthday. Some of this was clearly strategic and rhetorical, although there was a populist edge to some of the sentiments voiced during the mutinies that was critical of the Pitt ministry and of the naval and social hierarchy. Much of this was couched in democratic rhetoric, and provides clear evidence that radical ideas had penetrated the navy. Tom Paine's *The Rights of Man* was found on board the *Espion*.[30] Mutineers in 1797 declared that they 'did not want to be treated like the dregs of London streets, nor the Footballs, Shuttlecocks, and Merry Andrews of a set of Tyrants who claim from us ... their Honours, Titles and Fortunes'.[31] They demanded their 'Liberty, their Invaluable Priviledge, more particularly inherit [inherent] to an Englishman – the Pride and Boast of Brittains – the Natural Rights of all'.[32] Richard Forester of the HMS *Monarch* at Spithead thought himself 'a Briton'; 'He had spirit', he said, 'and he had read Magna Carta and the History of England ... he was as good Flesh and Blood as They [the officers] were.'[33] Sentiments such as this led to demands that courts martial should be handled by juries of seamen, not boards of officers. They signalled that the rough-and-ready naval paternalism of the past was over.

Some seamen wanted to use the mutiny as a strike for peace. Thomas Ashley, a seamen on the *Pompee* at Spithead and a committed democrat who confessed he 'could not discover any Good Quality belonging to George III', was one such advocate.[34] He told his shipmates that he had received communications from London that disclosed that the mass petition for peace had failed. The sailors were now the last resort of the friends of peace. He wanted the crew to reopen negotiations with the government to force Pitt from power and tried to get supporters to swear an oath 'to ever stand true till death in promoting the cause of freedom with equity'.[35] Although seamen at Spithead were aware of soaring prices and shortages in Britain through contact with their families, they were not about to renege on the limited concessions the government had offered. The result was that the plot to retake the *Pompee* collapsed and the ringleaders were confined by the crew. Even so, the political dissatisfaction readily apparent among some members of the crews at Spithead revealed a real sympathy for the move for peace among radical and Whig circles.

More serious were the signs of disaffection at the Nore, where the aspirations of the United Irishmen made themselves felt. These radicals likely enlisted early on in the war, when there was a big push to increase recruitment from Ireland. Among the 9 per cent of Irish seamen at the Nore, it is very likely that some were in contact with radical cells in Dublin, especially on ships such as the *Pylades*, the *Repulse* and the *Inflexible*, where a disproportionate number of Irish were tried for mutiny.[36] Some of them were defiantly dismissive of monarchies. Thomas Jephson, court martialled for refusing to play 'God Save the King' when Admiral Buckner boarded the *Sandwich*, exclaimed, 'By Jasus, it is an old stale tune and I care nothing for Kings and Queens. Bad Luck to the whole of them'.[37] Irishmen like Jephson were among those who wanted to defect to the French. This possibility had actually been mooted before the mutiny began and became more vocal once the committee of delegates at the Nore rejected the settlement that had been offered to them. It drew some fierce dissent from those who cherished the seamen's traditional role as Britain's wooden walls. One sailor on the *Neptune* declared that 'English sailors were once the ornaments of their Country but he was afraid they were about to do something that would clap an eternal stamp upon their character'.[38] Defecting to France was a minority view, closely associated with the radical Irish, but it did add to the kaleidoscope of opinions about the war within the fleet in which consensus proved impossible. Far from proving a melting pot, the navy represented the varied positions of the public at large as it struggled with the war against France amid spiralling inflation and the government's crackdown on sedition and radical dissent.

The mutinies of 1797 were the closest the British seamen came to being classified as not simply disloyal but treasonable. The lack of deference shown many officers, and the sheer organizational sophistication of the mutinies in which officers were ditched and delegates communicated with each ship, terrified members of the ruling class. One writer thought the mutiny 'more ... dangerous in its tendency than any thing of the kind that ever occurred in this, or perhaps any other country'.[39] The pro-peace, liberal *Morning Chronicle* put it more irreverently: '*Representative Government* actually established on board the British fleet, and a Commissioner of Admiralty gone to treat with a *Convention of Delegates* is an aera in the annals of our Navy which no man who madly gave his suffrage for the present War of Disorganization ever expected to see. Good God, what a spectacle for England!'[40]

Consequently, after the hanging of the leading mutineers at the Nore and the studied gestures of mercy, real efforts were made symbolically to accommodate the British tar seamen within the panoply of king and country. The opportunity came with the naval victories that marked the end of 1797 and continued with Nelson's spectacular assault on the French fleet at Aboukir Bay the following year. Amid sheep roasts and generous libations of beer, bumpers were raised not only to the victorious admirals but to the plucky tars of Old England.[41] One poem described them as 'valiant tars who fight for Freedom and the Throne'. After Admiral Duncan's victory at Camperdown, the London Common Council described the seamen as the 'guardians of the realm', while a song written to the familiar tune of 'Hearts of Oak' portrayed them as 'undaunted and steady', the worthy defenders of Albion.[42] As far as the *Oracle* was concerned, the formerly mutinous seamen of the North Sea fleet had atoned for their crimes. Commanders and men had agreeably contributed to 'our Internal Tranquillity'.[43]

After Camperdown, the press could once more expatiate on the seamen's bravery. 'The coarse pleasantry of our sailors is proverbial', remarked the *Worcester Herald*. 'Jack will have his joke though Death stands staring him in the face.'[44] Loyal, hearty, intrepid, the British tar was seen as reverting to form, putting behind him the deviations of a Spithead spring and an insurgent Nore. At the thanksgiving of December 1797, 200 seamen and 50 marines paraded behind the colours captured from Britain's foes in its memorable naval battles. They were received, reported the *True Briton*, 'with the loudest acclamations that perhaps were ever uttered'. Such plaudits transcended contemporary politics and the continuing efficacy of the war. 'However much we may deplore the calamity, or condemn the impolicy of the war itself', declared the *Morning Chronicle*, 'it is with pride and pleasure that we witness the exploits of our defenders on our natural element, and that we see our Country saved against the incapacity of Government by the courage of our Tars'.[45] Such was the solidity of the seamen in the public sphere of celebratory exultation that the *Gentleman's Magazine* could remark: 'The anchor of Great Britain is the constitutional courage of her seamen.'[46]

Yet the berth of the good ship Britannia was not so stable, despite the significant shifts in public opinion at the turn of the century. The 1790s had been a dramatic decade when loyalists were pitted against Francophile radicals and anti-war liberals and when the necessity of domestic repression was hotly debated. With the advent of Napoleon, more people became reconciled to the need for a defensive war against an aggressive imperial France. This was especially so during the invasion panics of 1803–5, when voices from many quarters impressed upon British people the duties of resisting a likely invasion and the benefits of British rule. Historians such as Linda Colley have seen the resumption of the war in 1803 as a transformative moment in the history of British nationalism, a moment when ordinary British people pledged their allegiance to king and country by their willingness to take up arms against Napoleon. What light do the activities of British seamen throw on this phenomenon?

In the first place it is clear that the anticipated invasions did not reduce the resistance of seafarers to the prospect of rejoining the navy after the Peace of Amiens in 1801. The abolition of impressment had not been part of the mutineers' official demands; in the context of the war it was not really a negotiable proposition, as Conrad Gill noted many years ago.[47] But impressment was a smouldering grievance that was constantly discussed by the mutineers. For one thing it was linked in seamen's minds with the issue of shore leave. It surfaced in some of the songs that were delivered to Admiral Keith on HMS *Repulse*; and its abolition was prophesied by one mutineer when he visited a pub in Leman Street, London. Furthermore, impressment was addressed in a petition.[48] 'As for English Tars to be the Legitimate Sons of Liberty it is an Old Cry which we have Experienced and Knows it to be False. God knows, the Constitution is admirable well Callculated for the Safety and Happiness of His Majesty's Subjects ... on Shore; but alas we are not considered as Subjects of the same Sovereign, unless it be to Drag us by Force from our Families to Fight the Battles of the Country which Refuses us Protection.'

It also formed part of the address of the Nore mutineers to their brethren on shore. 'Liberty', article 2 ran, 'this Invaluable priviledge, more particularly inherit to an Englishman – the Pride and Boast of Brittains & the Natural Rights of all – has always been denied to us who they allow to be the bulwark and glory of Britain & whose services have render'd this Kingdom at once the Envy the Admiration and the Immitation of all Europe.'[49]

Opposition to impressment returned with a vengeance in 1803 with as many as 88 riots and affrays occurring between March and December 1803. Unlike the protests which greeted the French revolutionary wars, which centred conspicuously on the north and south east, the resistance of 1803–5 was more evenly distributed across the country. Every major port in the country was affected. The most dramatic protests occurred in the south west, especially in 1803. In Bristol, where the Admiralty instituted a hot press to pick up some 200 stragglers for the navy, a mob of men, women and children attempted to block the Hotwells Road when a company of marines escorted the impressed men to Rownham Ferry. Shots were fired and one boy was killed in the melee, although the coroner judged the matter justifiable homicide. Further south, at Portland Bill, stonemasons joined straggling seamen in confronting a press gang that had come to enlist them. Three men were killed in a showdown at Easton, two quarrymen and a blacksmith, and the local coroner's jury was so incensed by the intrusive activities of the gang that it brought in a verdict of wilful murder against the regulating officers. It did not stick. At the Dorsetshire assizes the press officers were acquitted because it was felt that the mob had aggressively opposed a legitimate press, and that marines had been obliged to fire to save their officers' lives. But the passions raised by the episode revealed that even the southerly coasts were not always prepared to support the military emergency if it meant the loss of incomes and manpower.

More promising were the projects set afoot to create companies of sea fencibles to guard the coast. As a naval volunteer force, sea fencibles had first appeared in 1798, but in 1803 a concerted attempt was made to create 30 districts around the coast, with a predictable concentration on the south coast closest to the continent. With three captains per district, the Admiralty's intention was to mobilize all seafaring men who were not eligible for the navy into the fencibles, a force that was to be protected from the press gangs. This was intended to include local fishermen, those who worked in the coastal trades around Britain, pilots and ferrymen in the main estuaries, and perhaps the odd sailor who was really too old or invalid for active service at sea. A letter to the lords lieutenant of the counties talked of enrolling seafaring men 'not applicable to the service of the navy'.[50] The Admiralty presumed that most of these men would be settled members of their communities, married, perhaps owning part of their boats or some other small property. Many of these seafaring trades had previously received formal or informal exemptions from the press, and it was predicted that the captains would have no difficulty sorting out those who would be eligible for the fencibles from those who were fit for the Royal Navy.

In practice this proved more difficult than anticipated. The Admiralty's own capacious definition of who was eligible for impressment did not help, for many fishermen were technically eligible for the press. Nor did the disposition of some fencible captains to enrol anyone who wanted to join, on the grounds that any enlistment was a contribution to the war effort. Sir Ralph Milbanke, the commander of the fencibles in the Whitby district, fell out with the local recruiting officer over this matter, believing that first priority of the government should be 'the most perfect unanimity between all Corps acting for the defence of the King and Country'.[51] Whether seamen enrolled in the fencibles or the navy was secondary. The same was true of Captain Jonathan Clements, the fencible commander at Leith. He enrolled 200 journeymen shipwrights, ropemakers and sailmakers into the corps, although he did not think they all fitted the bill. Many were single rather than family men and had been to sea rather than simply working on rivers. But 'they are a fine body of men', he remarked to the Admiralty, 'and in order to prevent any check being thrown at present upon the loyal spirit of the people, I have given them a favourable reception.'[52]

Their lordships at the Admiralty were not amused. They ordered Clement to stick to his instructions. As the Navy braced itself for another confrontation with the French, tracking down every eligible seafarer became an urgent priority, especially as it became increasingly clear that the country was experiencing a serious shortfall in its naval recruitment. The result was that in December 1803, Vice-Admiral Hugh Phillip was sent on an extensive tour of the districts to discover how successfully the fencible captains had recruited the right people and how many seamen might be recovered for the navy.

The result was something of a comic disaster. Fencibles sometimes refused to muster, especially in areas where hostility to impressment was rife. Those that did, like the mackerel fishermen of Pevensey and Eastbourne, proved to be really eligible for the navy. In this district Phillip estimated that near two-thirds of the recruits were really navy material, although he despaired of catching many of them, especially the so-called pilots of Hastings who he thought were actually operating smuggling cutters out of the port. 'Unless some precaution is used' with these rough characters, he concluded, 'they cannot be easily impressed.'[53]

All that Phillip's inquiry seemed to do was to illustrate how many men were eluding the navy. This included not only those enrolled as fencibles but also those like the herring fishermen of Yarmouth and the whalers of the North Yorkshire coast who simply moved inland at the first sign of the gangs.[54] Visibly alarmed, the Admiralty sent in another vice-admiral to re-investigate, but he came back with essentially the same story. The seamen were using the fencible system to evade the press, especially in Cornwall, where the rates of evasion were sometimes 66 per cent or more. 'A very considerable portion of the finest Seafaring Men have sheltered themselves under the protection of the Sea Fencible System', Berkeley observed, 'and have by this means evaded all the services to which every other class of men in the country are subject.' In fact it angered Berkeley to see that 'exemption from the Impress & Ballot is now claimed as a sort of Right by these men, established by custom & rivetted by the Sea Fencible System'. On 'many parts of the coast', he noted, 'every sort of service has been absolutely refused which could in the least interfere with their private occupations'.[55]

Berkeley hoped to enrol the fishermen of the south west in the navy, many of whom were struggling to make ends meet with a wartime slump in the pilchard and mackerel industry.[56] Yet he found many fishing towns and villages hard to penetrate. In towns like Fowey, the press gangs were reduced to picking up stragglers from the shore because they lacked the necessary military reinforcements to sweep the pubs and quays.[57] In other places local magistrates were reluctant to back press warrants without military support. When the navy tried to press from the sea, they found that the fishermen took refuge in the small coves off the Cornish coast that were inaccessible to frigates and revenue cutters. The fishermen, moreover, managed to survive on the odd catch and the time-honoured custom of smuggling goods to the continent. Berkeley was outraged to find the south-west coast littered with smugglers, with many innkeepers and farmers having a stake in the clandestine trade. The government offered an amnesty to smugglers in an attempt to strengthen the security of their ports, for smugglers were potential informers for the enemy. But active smuggling gangs continued to be found in Bridport, Lyme Regis and Seaton, and in Polperro, Fowey and Portscatho in Cornwall, as well as at Ilfracombe and Porlock on the North Devonshire and Somerset coasts.[58]

Berkeley eventually decided that the only way to align the sea fencibles with the overall imperatives of naval defence was to ballot them like the militia, subject them to martial law, and provide the officers with the financial incentives to turn errant or phoney fencibles over to the navy.[59] In some instances he recommended consolidating the fencible command with the impress service, because some fencibles were actively screening seamen from the press. In Bristol, for example, many fencibles were recruited from the pilots of the River Avon, men who often abetted the escape of seamen aboard homeward-bound vessels before they encountered the press tenders in the King's Road.[60] On the Isle of Purbeck, the fencibles hid seamen from the Newfoundland trade who had been dropped off at Chapman's Pool or Lulworth Cove before their ships entered Poole. Drawn principally from the local quarrymen, they occasionally armed themselves and 'turn'd out' against the press gangs that sought straggling seamen among the clay pits.[61]

As a defence strategy, the sea-fencible scheme was never put to the test; as a mobilizing strategy, it was a failure, at least from the government's point of view. Although the Admiralty hoped to use the regular coastal trade as a form of naval defence without impinging upon the drive for seamen, it proved unable to accomplish its goal. Seafaring men used the new service as a means of evading the press, at least for as long as they were able to get away with it. It was a classic example of how fishermen and coastal seamen might occasionally work the system in their favour.

But what implications does this wholesale evasion of full naval duty have for our understanding of popular attitudes towards war, towards the French, towards defending one's country in 1803? These are trickier issues, dependent upon fragmentary evidence and a thin skein of inference. Yet it is important to hazard some speculations.

Enlisting in the sea fencibles to evade the press was not necessarily an anti-war protest. Although demands for peace had informed the naval mutinies of 1797, the period 1803–5 was one in which the country as a whole was fixated on the very real possibility of a French invasion and the genuine dangers of an occupying army that could make life very uncomfortable for the civilian population. Cobbett noted that in their invasions of other countries the French had not observed 'the maxim of war to the palaces, peace to the cottages', an observation that struck a chord as news of the French army's ill treatment of the Hanoverian population filtered across the Channel. 'To spread nakedness and hunger, to introduce misery and disease among all ranks, seems to have been their uniform desire', he thundered, but the 'lower orders of the people' were 'the object of their direct malignity'.[62] This message was transmitted more crudely in broadsides and ballads, all of which emphasized the threat to hearth, home, family and liberty from marauding foreign soldiers. One such ballad, sung to 'Hearts of Oak', urged Britons to defend their shores from Bonaparte and his army for 'our Wives, Children, Freedom'.[63] So, too, did the broadside entitled 'The Sailor to his Messmates', while another addressed to the 'Navy of Britain' declared that a 'war of plunder and massacre' was about to be waged 'against our Fields, our Homes, our Parents, Wives and Children'. As the 'peculiar objects' of Napoleon's 'rancour' British seamen were especially vulnerable, the author reminded his audience, for 'Every Tar has his Sweetheart on shore, and even she is held out to the Republican slaves as a lure to the venture'.[64] Whereas the loyalism of the 1790s played upon the contrast between English liberty and French anarchy, between plenty and scarcity, the rhetoric of the post-Amiens years stressed consular tyranny and the ravaging of the civilian population. It was a more inclusive, populist pitch that avoided the patronizing tone of early loyalist appeals to the plebeian classes. At the same time it foreclosed a sustained discussion of the merits of monarchy and constitution amid frothy eulogies to king and country and commonplace appeals to Britain's libertarian past. It was a bottom-line message that in the conjuncture of 1803–5 invited and drew a rough consensus, however reluctant or begrudging.

To be sure, there were disaffected cells in the country, most of them connected in some way with the United Irishmen or affiliated groups. Yet after the arrest and execution of Colonel Despard, loyalism in its most capacious idiom was undoubtedly the public language of the day, not least among the sea fencibles. When Horatio Nelson ordered the sea fencibles to man their vessels in 1801, few actually responded. He was informed they would only muster if they were given genuine assurances that they could 'return to their homes when the danger of Invasion is passed'.[65] Yet two years later they seemed more enthusiastic. As Captain Phillip Beaver observed of the Malden sea fencibles: 'So far as I am able to judge from the short time I have been here, there seems to be an honest & true English zeal, and patriotic feeling in the whole body of Seafaring persons employed in the fishing and Coasting Trade of this District, and a very general willingness to come forward and enrol themselves.'[66] Beaver may have misconstrued just how disinterested the Malden men were in taking on this assignment, but like the Margate fencibles whom Nelson encountered earlier they would probably have manned the guns and taken sail once the enemy had embarked on an invasion. General Sir John Moore certainly thought so. Writing from Dungeness, where rumours of invasion were rife, he reported that the sea fencibles had turned out and were 'very cheerful – not at all dismayed at the prospect of meeting the French'.[67]

Defending one's country as a last resort was one thing; doing one's 'loyal' duty in the navy was another. Pondering the possibilities of creating a naval reserve in the summer of 1803, General John Maitland believed the seafarers had 'every degree of attachment to their country, & to the cause in which we are engaged'. Yet they had a deep aversion to enlisting in the navy and would 'abscond and submit to every distress rather than put themselves in the way of being pressed'.[68] Maitland attributed the unpopularity of the Royal Navy to the harsh discipline on board ship, a grievance that had been voiced more aggressively in the 1790s when crews complained that their 'usage was more like Turks than of British seamen'.[69] But discipline in the navy was not relaxed after the mutinies, despite efforts by the Admiralty to regulate it. Some officers, troubled by the lack of deference that seamen showed them during the crisis, probably concluded that indiscipline was the source of the problem. In any case, the difficulties of dealing with more heterogeneous and unskilled crews seem to have prompted more punishment. Floggings on first-rate men of war continued with persistent regularity. Nelson's flagship the *Victory* witnessed a tougher regimen of floggings than Admiral Rodney's flagship in the 1780s, when Rodney was pursuing de Guichen and pushing his men to the limit.[70] Moreover, the incidence of summary floggings, not to mention the practice of 'starting' and running the gauntlet, likely increased. They certainly proved difficult to regulate, despite efforts by the Admiralty to do so in the last decade of the Napoleonic wars.[71] In the short term, the arbitrary punishments that were at the root of the mutineers' grievances in 1797 showed little sign of abating.

The hard discipline and humiliations of serving on the lower deck were not the only grievances keeping men out of the navy. Although the mutineers of 1797 had managed to raise seamen's pay, it still lagged woefully behind commercial rates, and, despite further increases in 1806, never reached the 40 shillings per month demanded by the Tyneside seamen at the beginning of the war.[72] Although some pay was technically paid in advance under the 1758 Act, often to help out families, seamen seldom received a good recompense for their labour until they were actually discharged. Then there were delays because the Pay Office had to calculate what each man was owed as he was turned over from ship to ship. When it did materialize, pay came in the form of tickets that could only be redeemed at the Navy Office, a predicament that tempted the reckless seamen to discount it at 5–6 per cent to innkeepers and brokers. So not a lot was gained from the pay increases of 1797 in the larger scheme of things, and on other matters, relatively little. Restrictions on shore leave were not relaxed until 1809 when 48 hours' leave was given to those crews whose ships were paid off. Prize money, often reckoned one of the great incentives of joining the navy, was tardily paid and not always very accessible for seaman who were turned over to different ships.[73] Even with changes in the pay scale in 1808 – which was largely to the benefit of petty and warrant officers at the expense of the captain and commander-in-chief – it remained grossly weighted in favour of the officers despite popular demands for a better redistribution to the lower deck. Often prize money brought little for the common seamen relative to the risks involved. At Trafalgar, where cannons blasted one another at perilously short distances and wrought a death toll of 449 British seamen with an additional 1214 wounded, the common seamen received under £10.[74] Finally, impressment continued to be a central recourse of the navy once the pool of initial volunteers was exhausted. Pressed men were treated as criminals, locked up in foetid holds in the tenders until they were crawling with vermin and virtually suffocating.[75] Moreover, families whose men were impressed had no advances or bounties to rely on and were therefore more likely to find themselves applying for poor relief. On Tyneside poor relief tripled in the early 1790s to accommodate the families of seamen or keelmen taken up by the press.[76]

In these circumstances, loyalty to family and plebeian self-respect, especially if it was coloured by new notions of citizenship propagated in radical circles, militated against enrolling in the navy. If one's patriotic duty could be fulfilled in some other manner, so be it, especially when it allowed for some semblance of normalcy and security. Joining the sea fencibles, then, was not a high form of patriotic endeavour. *Pace* Linda Colley, it was not a crucial catalyst of national identity.[77] For a significant number of seafarers it was a perfect scam. But in an age when exemptions to military service could be bought for those who could afford it, it was an acceptable dodge among those who bridled at the fact that the burdens of war fell heaviest upon the poor and unconnected.

There remains, of course, the issue of whether the seamen were captivated by the increasingly theatrical choreography of war that was characteristic of this era. I have thus far suggested that while there were clear efforts to incorporate seamen into the national festivals of war, the actual draw of those festivals might have been brief and superficial. Certainly the continuing and aggressive hostility to impressment after the Treaty of Amiens suggests that seamen did not identify with 'king and country' in quite the way festive patrons and their publicizers hoped they would.

The tangled skein of commitment to 'king and country' can best be investigated through the figure and feats of Horatio Nelson. At first sight his spectacular victories against the French appeared to consolidate the loyalty that prevailed as Napoleon's territorial ambitions became clear. Toasts to Nelson were breathlessly paired with attacks upon French republicanism, Gallic vice and sometimes even linked to that 'English boy, Billy Pitt'.[78] Even reformers struggled to combine the celebrations of his victory at the Nile with the demand for peace with an essentially liberty-loving France. Those that did not celebrate Nelson's signal victory against the French were likely to be taunted with cries of 'Nelson and Victory'.[79] As the *Sussex Weekly Advertiser* reported after the Battle of the Nile, 'there has scarcely anything been heard but the ethos of loyalty from one end of the country to the other; the most obscure village even participates in the general joy manifested on this glorious occasion'.[80]

Yet Nelson was not a straightforward signifier of loyalism. His popularity did not rest simply upon his capacity to serve as a symbol of national deliverance from the foreign foe. Among sailors he had the reputation of a fair-minded paternalist. Although he was unsparing with the lash if he felt it was required, he recognized that sailors should get better food and healthcare than they did.

During his two years in the West Indies and the Mediterranean he was especially attentive to the victualling and purveyance of his ships and encouraged the use of stoves and ventilators below decks in an attempt to improve the health of his crews.[81] Furthermore, he also strove to ensure that his seamen received their due recompense in prize money. 'An admiral may be amply rewarded by his feelings and the approbation of his superiors', he wrote to Earl Spencer in 1798, 'but what reward have the inferior Officer and men but the value of the prize.'[82]

Nelson's paternalism was reinforced by his generosity and deep loyalty to men under his command. Unlike St Vincent, whose imperious bearing and irascibility distanced him from his inferiors, Nelson was no stickler for rank. His easy manner won him many admirers, as did his personal solicitations on behalf of officers and seamen. During his visit to Salisbury in 1800, he singled out sailors with whom he had fought to recall past exploits and to offer them presents.[83] Nelson's strong sense of camaraderie and devotion to service was such that he was quite prepared to commend controversial figures, regardless of whether their politics and aspirations matched his own. He gave evidence on behalf of Colonel Despard at the revolutionary's trial, commending his role as the engineer on the Nicaragua expedition of 1780. He even attempted to secure a pension from the government for Despard's widow.[84]

Nelson's liaison with Lady Emma Hamilton no doubt endeared him to sailors whose sexual gallivanting was notorious. No one was surprised that admirals had mistresses, but few flaunted them so publicly as Nelson, bringing his lady and her husband, Sir William, to live with him at Merton Place. The first whiff of scandal reached England as the infamous ménage à trois travelled openly across Europe in 1800, sometimes to the frosty reception of northern courts. By the time the threesome reached London in November the secret was out. Admiral Lord St Vincent believed Nelson's relationship with Emma would 'reflect eternal disgrace upon [his] character, which will be stripped of everything but animal courage.'[85] Predictably, Nelson's standing at the evangelical Court of St James waned dramatically and he was soon ostracized by much of high society. Yet he retained his cachet with the crowd. Festooned with medals, with the sultan's *chelenck* in his tricorne and Emma by his side, the one-armed Nelson was instantly recognizable. 'Lord Nelson cannot appear in the streets without immediately collecting a retinue', one American visitor remarked, 'and when he enters a shop the door is thronged till he comes out, when the air rings with huzzas and the dark cloud of the populace moves on and hangs upon his skirts. He is a great favourite with all descriptions of people.'[86] Nelson's love of the limelight, his love of decoration, his flouting of polite convention, all helped to puff his popularity. The son of a Norfolk parson who reputedly 'went into the world without fortune',[87] he was the gallant little admiral, the people's conquering hero.

Above all, Nelson's appeal was augmented by the sheer intrepidity of his actions. At Cape St Vincent, Nelson intercepted the escaping Spaniards on his own initiative; at Copenhagen, he ignored Sir Hyde Parker's orders to disengage the Danish fleet, purportedly putting the telescope to his blind eye. These were technically acts of insubordination, but they earned Nelson an enviable reputation for swift, audacious action. As the *Leeds Mercury* was later to remark, with Nelson 'courage was not a passion, but a principle, he could make even an excess virtuous and graceful, and exalt rashness into fortitude'.[88] At Aboukir Bay, Nelson totally surprised the French by attacking on both the landward and seaward sides, calculating that the draught of his ships near the shore could manage this two-sided assault. Sir John Jervis marvelled at this 'almost incredible and stupendous victory'. The *Annual Register* thought it 'the most signal that graced the British Navy since the days of the Spanish Armada'.[89]

Nelson's intrepid leadership and willingness to take risks beyond the call of rank and duty quickly entered naval folklore. One Tyneside newspaper calculated that the wound he received at Aboukir Bay was the 42nd of his career.[90] In a war that was increasingly seen in sacrificial terms, and in which perhaps one in five plebeian families was directly involved, Nelson was the embodiment of sacrifice, putting his own personal safety and heath at the service of the nation, just as thousands of seamen had done in turn.[91] With one arm and a gammy eye, he was the epitome of the gallant warrior, a vision that Thomas Rowlandson captured in his portrait of the admiral 'recreating with his brave tars' after the Battle of the Nile. Certainly the paintings of him, whether boarding the San Josef at Cape St Vincent, lying wounded in a boat at Tenerife in July 1797, or collapsing on the deck of the *Victory* at Trafalgar, evoked his outstanding courage and service to his country. Such bravery was recognized in a less decorous but heartfelt fashion by his fellow tars. As one seaman wrote from the Victory, 'All the men in our Ship who have seen him are such soft toads they have done nothing but blast their eyes and cry ever since he was killed; chaps that fought like the devil sit down and cry like a wench'.[92]

Trafalgar struck a chord with sailors quite distant from the conflict. Even John Nichol, a long-serving seaman who was constantly evading the press gang, was touched by the victory. Working as a quarryman, he recorded a 'feeling of triumph' on hearing how the British seamen defeated a combined Franco-Spanish fleet of superior numbers. 'Every now and then I felt the greatest desire to hurra aloud', he recalled, 'and many a hurra my heart gave that my mouth uttered not.'[93]

It was sentiments such as these that the organizers of Nelson's state funeral hoped to mobilize. This event was designed to represent a nation in grief, to commemorate the bravery of a fallen admiral and parenthetically his men in what was the most significant naval victory of the war. Actual sailors from the

*Victory* were incorporated into this drama. At Greenwich hospital, where Nelson's body lay in state, a representative group of seamen was greeted by the lieutenant governor, Lord Hood, and paraded before the public as 'true bred cub[s] of the British lion' who 'bore the honourable scars they received on that day'.[94] In a procession carefully calibrated by rank and hierarchy, much speculation centred on the seamen's proximity to Nelson's body. 'No sight could be more gratifying to a British Public, or more worthy of a British Hero's funeral honours', opined the *Star*, 'than to see those gallant men, the crew of the *Victory*, accompany their beloved Commander to the grave.'[95] In the event the funeral car was attended by 19 admirals, imparting to the procession a decidedly professional stamp. The seamen were placed behind the Greenwich pensioners, themselves living embodiments of sacrifice in war, with a smaller group closing the procession with the colours of the *Victory*. Even so, the evidence suggests that they stole the show. What particularly struck spectators was the perforated, bloodstained colours that the sailors bore, reminding them of the bloody honours of war. Those colours were scheduled for the crypt at St Paul's, but the seamen tore off scraps of the ensign as souvenirs. In the contest for public recognition, they arguably had the last word.[96]

The state funeral of 1806 was a national tribute to bravery and courage in battle, to sacrifice in war. But it was not without its ironies. In his own lifetime Nelson was treated a little shabbily by the British establishment. He was never much of a politician. In 1784 he did seek a seat in parliament, but within a month he told his brother that he had 'done with politics: let who get in, I shall be left out'.[97] His words were prophetic. Nelson was always a bit of a political outsider. Although he respected Pitt, he could never be counted among his supporters. He was not cut out to be a levee hunter or a parliamentary placeman, and after the battle of the Nile at least, his actions never carried the hint of political opportunism. As Cobbett remarked, Nelson's character was not deformed by party principles but informed by 'pure un-sterling loyalty'.[98]

However admirable a stance, Nelson's political marginality did not give him much leverage in the corridors of power. Nelson was reasonably content with the knighthood and the £1000 pension he received for his services at Cape St Vincent, but he was less than gratified by the honours he received after the Battle of the Nile.[99] Admirals Jervis and Duncan had been awarded greater pensions for lesser victories; they received an earldom and viscountcy respectively, whereas Nelson received a barony, the lowest order of the nobility. To a man who prided himself on his Egyptian expedition, this was a bitter disappointment, aggravated by the fact that the king of Naples had conferred on him the dukedom of Bronte with property worth £3000 a year. It led him to affect his foreign honours in a flamboyant way; he signed off as 'Nelson and Bronte', not as 'Baron Nelson of Burnhamthorpe'. In public he wore the magnificent aigrette he was given by the sultan of Turkey. Gillray's mischievous portrait of the admiral burdened with medals and plumes not only hinted at Nelson's vanity, it underscored his sense of the state's ingratitude for his services.

Such ingratitude linked Nelson to his tars. Once the war was over, the state more or less abandoned the seamen to market forces. In 1813 there were over 130,000 seamen in the navy. At the peace in 1814 about 50,000 men were paid off almost immediately and in 1816 a further 60,000 were discharged. In other words, about 85 per cent of the navy was laid off in less than two years and left to clamour for jobs in the merchant marine.

The demand for jobs began soon after the celebrations of Waterloo had died down. In July 1815 seamen boarded some of the ships in the London docks and demanded that the masters remove foreigners from British merchant ships, partly on the grounds that they were suspected of accepting a reduction in wages that the employers were now offering in a buyer's market. One man was arrested in the course of these heated discussions and the rest dispersed. But seamen kept up the pressure by parading through the streets of Shadwell with cockades, flags and music, and by sending deputations to both the Admiralty and the Lord Mayor. The Mayor protested he could do nothing to alleviate their plight; the Admiralty did nothing except allocate a few jobs on the peace establishment and counsel patience, noting that the return of peace would automatically reduce the proportion of foreign seamen in any crew on a British vessel.[100]

During the summer of 1815 strikes broke out in several ports including Hull, Yarmouth and the Tyne and Wear, spreading later to Leith, Aberdeen and Clydeside. Seamen were angry about the dramatic reductions of wages coincident with the peace and with the paucity of jobs. Unlike London, where the docks were heavily policed, provincial seamen were able to prevent ships from sailing, removing crews and striking the sails in order to advance their claims. The authorities were alert to the random disorder these confrontations might produce, but they were more troubled by the organization and collective strength of the sailors. Seamen had 'established Rules and have a kind of subordination amongst themselves',[101] Lord Sidmouth was informed. In several ports committees had been created to co-ordinate the protests. They disciplined errant sailors and regulated the passage of boats from the harbour, allowing some to sail if they would contribute to a sailor's relief fund. Sidmouth was alert to the possibility that these organizations might be a criminal conspiracy under the terms of the Combination Acts and wanted clear evidence of oath-taking.[102] Some commentators thought the organizational regularity of the sailors evoked the discipline of the 1797 mutineers; it was even rumoured that the secretary of the late Richard Parker was 'president' of the men in North Shields. Other sources, including *The Times*, thought the combinations were inspired by the writings of Tom Paine and republicanism.[103]

The most protracted conflicts occurred in the north-eastern ports of the Tyne and Wear: they caught the public eye and necessitated the vigilance of the authorities. The disputes here were only partly about wages. In wartime the owners of the colliers had been offering as much as £8, even £9 a voyage to London, but with the coming of the peace they wanted dramatically to reduce these rates. The sailors on the Tyne struck for £5 a voyage in winter and £4-10s in summer; those on the Wear settled for slightly less. These demands were negotiable, at least for a short-term contract, for while the strike threatened to drag on for a month or more, the ship-owners and coal-owners calculated that they could afford such rates as the price of coal soared. The real sticking points were the other issues.[104] In wartime the ship-owners had continually resorted to 'apprentices' to man their colliers, partly because they were cheaper than skilled seamen and partly because they were exempt from the press. What constituted an apprentice, and how many should be allowed on a collier's crew, now became a contentious issue. Seamen feared a dilution of labour at precisely the time that jobs were at a premium. This situation was aggravated by the fact that the ship-owners had skimped on maritime labour during the war; they had quite cynically undermanned their boats and increased their insurance premiums in case their colliers were shipwrecked in the North Sea gales. Seamen now pushed for a reasonable but secure living. They proposed a scale that calibrated the size of the crew to the size of the cargo, an average of six men and one apprentice for every 100 tons, to be regulated by some form of public inspection. Wartime ratios on the Tyne had been only three men per 100 tons, but the seamen saw this as both dangerous and unacceptable, and certainly out of line with those adopted by the government's transport services during the war in which some of them had worked.

The ship-owners baulked at this proposal, even when the ratio was reduced to five men per 100 tons. They calculated that the new manning requirements would reduce the number of annual voyages by about 25 per cent, and they deeply resented the notion that the seamen should have a 'controlling power over their property'. It would impair their ability to manage their assets, 'a principle subversive of the General Law of Property' and possessed of dangerous ramifications to other trades.[105] Eventually the ship-owners of the Wear came to some accommodation with the sailors over the manning rates, largely through the mediation of a local magistrate, the Reverend William Nesfield. But the Tyneside owners refused magisterial invention and calculated that the organizational solidity of the seamen would sooner or later force the government to take military action.

In this they proved correct. Sidmouth and his own Home Office informants had no particular liking for the owners, who were considered both devious and avaricious. But they became increasingly alarmed by the actions of the seamen who were highly organized and were winning considerable local support. Discipline among the seamen was harsh. Delinquents were tarred and feathered or ritually humiliated by being stripped naked and forced to ride the stang, a pole that was carried on men's shoulders.[106] Three thousand battle worn seamen turned out on a regular basis with their colours flying, and easily intimidated the local militias or the few soldiers in the area. One informant remarked that 'old sailors who have seen death in all its terrors' despised the yeoman cavalry.[107] Magistrates proved unable to prevent seamen from stopping ships and striking sails, and even from creating a barrier of boats across the estuary of the Tyne at Shields. In effect the seamen ran the Tyne for the duration of the strike, with committees determining local strategies, organizing relief funds and applications and hiring lawyers to negotiate with the ship-owners. To a man like Sidmouth, who believed in hierarchy and property, this was deeply disturbing, a world turned upside-down. As his informant John Cartwright reported, Sidmouth would be less alarmed by the violence of the dispute than by 'the shocking enormity of such a body of men thus overbearing the law and negotiating with (not to say commanding) their employers'.[108] Once it became clear to Sidmouth that the magistrates could neither arbitrate the strike nor maintain appropriate order, the troops were called in and a naval gunboat entered the Tyne.

*The Times* attributed the strike to troublemakers, not to the plucky tars of the war. It talked of six weeks of misrule at the hands of 'surreptitious turbulent characters' from the Nore mutiny.[109] This was nonsense. The irony was that the seamen staked a claim for a fair deal on their contribution to the war effort. In answer to the charge that Nelson would have disapproved of their actions, the seamen of Sunderland reminded their detractors that 'many of us have fought under his victorious banners, and have experienced his friendship to a British sailor ... we may say without flattery to ourselves that we have been and will continue to be the support and bulwark of England'. They went on to remind their opponents that 'if a shipowner's property has been preserved during the time we have been fighting for our King and Country, a British sailor cannot but expect to be employed on his return home as a reward for his services'.[110] This argument never received a fair press; it was buried amidst accusations that the striking seamen aspired to be the new 'naval lords', at once 'refractory' and 'misguided'.[111] Yet the wartime contribution of the seamen was tacitly recognized by the Home Secretary, Lord Sidmouth. He understood that demobilization was at the root of the problem on the Tyne and Wear, and in the round-up of ringleaders he counselled leniency. In a letter to Lord Northumberland in late October 1815, he urged that no prosecutions commence save against the most prominent offenders, 'as the Law is no longer violated'. He hoped in the aftermath of the strike that 'consideration and liberality may be manifested by the shipowners which is due to British seamen'.[112]

If the seamen were to get anything, it would come only from their employers. The government did nothing to help beyond offering a few of them a place in the peace establishment, which stood at only 28,000 in 1826. A bill to reward seamen for long service was abandoned. Pleas to retain a reasonable naval establishment in case of future wars, or to create some sort of register, were ignored.[113] And a petition from British seamen to the Lord Regent to recognize their wartime contribution fell on deaf ears, which may well explain why so many rallied to his estranged wife in 1820.[114] Market forces were to determine what recompense sailors might receive, not government largesse. In London there were reports of hundreds of seamen 'almost in a state of nudity', homeless among the brick kilns.[115] On the Tyne, where commerce did not really pick up until the 1830s, market forces meant a lost generation of workers in the coal trade, although some seamen likely emigrated to the USA, an event that deeply disturbed some nationalists.[116] The situation was worst for the keelmen, for the employment of steam tugs and the increasing use of coal spouts to deliver the coal into the holds of waiting colliers threatened their livelihood. Two strikes in 1819 and 1822 failed to win them any concessions on technological issues and resulted in redundancies for those who worked the Tyne 'below bridge'.[117]

Unemployment thus greeted many returning seamen on the Tyne; beggary confronted those who were wounded. Of the seadogs of Camperdown, the Nile and Trafalgar, Thomas Haswell later recalled: 'Scores were to be found on the quays, the wharves, the landing places and lower streets of old Shields, in every state of picturesque dismemberment – one arm, one leg, one arm and one leg ... grimly suggestive of the peculiar horror of 'tween deck fighting.' They were 'hardy, patient long-suffering fellows, whose bronzed faces spoke in every line of hardship and privation'. He found them 'cheery and good-naturedly responsive when addressed, but mostly reflective, taciturn and observant'.[118]

The sight of these men must have recalled the terms on which the seamen had staked their claim for recognition in 1815 and beyond. That centred on their wartime contribution as Britain's defenders, a line of argument that the British elite had frequently applauded during the war amid refrains of 'Britons Strike Home' and 'Hearts of Oak', but was now quite happy to ignore. Sailors had played the patriotic card but it was more than an 'invaluable' resource, to use Linda Colley's adjective.[119] It was a profoundly alienating experience which only confirmed their status as petty subjects of the realm. Sailors wanted a just recompense for their labour, their sacrifice and the hardships that their families had experienced in their absence, usually shoddily handled through the poor laws. At the very least they wanted to be recognized as free-born Englishmen, or free-born Britons, as the inheritors and beneficiaries of the rights than purportedly differentiated Britons from other nations, rights that they were exhorted to defend at sea. This was a conservative statement of the seamen's case, but it could easily be amplified into a demand for greater political inclusion as the loyalist rhetoric for king and country gave way to a policy of ignoring wartime contributions and frustrating any advance of political citizenship. Some of these sentiments were voiced at Spa Fields in London in late 1816. Others surfaced around the time of Peterloo. As one radical reminded his audience at a reform meeting at Rochdale in July 1819, they had been called 'British Heroes – Brave Lads – and the finest Fellows in the World' during the war. But, he asked, 'What do they call you now? Scum, Rabble, &c A set of People who have no Rights. Is not every Man equal? He ought to be … We are all made of the same materials … we are all equal in the sight of God – have all an equal Right & Privilege – Ponder well on these things when you go Home tonight.'[120]

# *Epilogue*

Whitby was among the North-eastern ports that aggressively opposed the press gangs in the 1790s and beyond. A town of some 13,000 inhabitants at the beginning of the French wars, it had first distinguished itself in the seventeenth century as a centre for the production and export of alum, whose rock was plentiful in the region. By the 1760s its commerce had dramatically diversified. Whitby boats now ventured to Europe, to the Mediterranean and North America, to Greenland and the White Sea. The port was intimately involved in the coastal trades of the east coast, with close links to Newcastle and Sunderland as well as southward to London. 250 ships belonged to Whitby in 1790, with a total capacity approaching 50,000 tons.[1] In fact, the port had established itself as an important ship-building and sail-making centre to which North Sea owners flocked with enthusiasm. 'The genius of the inhabitants of Whitby has a most surprising turn for the sea,' wrote Lionel Charlton in 1779. 'Very few boys will go apprentices to any other business; and if they do, they generally at the expiration of that term convert their thoughts to sea, where they see many of their associates in a fair way of making their fortunes.'[2] There were roughly 4000 seamen from Whitby during the American war, some of whom were prime targets for the press gangs. When war was declared in 1793 it was predictable that the press gangs would return for a new harvest of men.

The reception they received was rough. Whitby seamen, especially the whalers, had a reputation for roughness. 'The most resolute seamen of the North Country' was how one press-gang officer described them, men who would not hesitate to use their flensing knives to keep the gangs at bay.[3] At the beginning of the Seven Years' War they had beaten up the regulating officer and sent him packing. During the Falkland Islands crisis of 1770 the inhabitants of Whitby had helped 70 seamen escape from the *Active* tender.[4] In 1793 the town decided it did not want the press gangs at all. As soon as press warrants came down, the rendezvous was attacked by a mob of one thousand men and women. The gang held out until the evening, when the doors were broken down and the gang run out of town. As Captain Shortland was leaving Whitby in a chaise with the gang's belongings, he was told by 'a party of Seamen that stood in the street' that if he returned with his men 'I and they must not expect to live'.[5] The Inniskilling dragoons were brought in to bring the situation under control. Local worthies attempted to temper the confrontation, or perhaps exculpate themselves, by offering extra bounties to volunteers. But many were intimidated from joining up. In fact, Whitby quickly became a sanctuary for seamen on the run. 'Seamen, seeing the impossibility of pressing at Whitby,' remarked Vice-admiral Pringle, 'go to it over land from other ports, where they continue till their vessels are again ready for sea.'[6]

The government could not let this predicament stand. It launched lawsuits against three rioters involved in the attack on the rendezvous. At the Yorkshire assizes, the judge, fearful that the town's defiance would expose it to 'sedition and insurrection', found two guilty under the Riot Act. One, Hannah Hobson, had her sentence respited; the other, William Atkinson, was hanged.[7] This example simply fuelled Whitby's opposition to the press, for the costs of recruiting increased dramatically as seamen evaded the gangs. In just over two years, Whitby brought in 112 men of whom only twelve were impressed, and at an exorbitant cost of £19 per person.[8] This was eight times the cost of raising men on Tyneside, and fifteen times the cost on the Mersey.

So judicial terror did not deter Whitby. Defiance remained the order of the day. With the resumption of war in 1803, there were further protests against the gangs. In May the town confronted the crew of the *Eagle* cutter which had arrived to impress seamen, killing two of the crew. The following month, Thomasine Witham led an attack upon the new regulating officer in the streets of Whitby, assailing him with curses and stones. In July, some Davis Straits whalers rescued men from the press boat, egged on by spectators on both sides of the river. The whalers were prosecuted at the North Riding Quarter Sessions, and, acknowledging their crime, were sent into the navy as 'volunteers'.[9] What happened to Ms Witham, a local spinster, is unknown.

Gestures of mercy did not resolve the manning problem in Whitby any more than the gallows. We learn this from the next captain who was sent on this difficult assignment. Captain Richard Poulden told the Admiralty he was obstructed everywhere. The only JP in the area, a Mr Morson, was a 75-year-old former ship-builder; he was little better than an 'old woman' Poulden lamented, 'and of course particularly interested in *not* forwarding the King's Service'.[10] The same was true of the local Customs officer, who winked at the comings and goings of the seamen. 'He never furnished me with an information of a single seaman', Poulden complained, 'or even the haunts of them, altho' frequently urged to do so. He is refractory, wanting energy, in short has every negative character a man can have.'[11] As for the seamen, they lived in a 'lawless state', and eluded Poulden at every turn. Between Hull and Whitby it was estimated that there were a thousand sailors hiding in the hills. Indeed, Poulden despaired of recruiting from land; he could not find anyone willing to set up a rendezvous. In his opinion the best way to recruit men in this seaman-rich port was to station a revenue cutter in the bay and impress from incoming vessels.[12] This is what happened. The Admiralty abandoned the rendezvous at Whitby and shipped recruits to Hull. Between 1803 and 1805 it only raised 73 men and one boy, but at half the cost of the previous recruiting drive.[13]

The Whitby story is a good example of the limits of the state, for the government and its allies were flexing every ideological and administrative muscle in their efforts to mobilize the population against the French. It is indicative of what might happen where the Admiralty lacked the co-operation of the civil authorities, and where that authority was fragile to begin with. It underscores one of the themes of this book, the strength and vitality of popular opposition to the press gang, encompassing seafaring communities, and not simply seamen. But the Whitby story is also interesting for the way in which it was fictionalized and committed to memory in the Victorian era. It tells us something of how the press gangs entered literary folklore in an age not of war, but of Pax Britannica.

In the autumn of 1859 Mrs Elizabeth Gaskell and her two daughters, Meta and Julia, visited Whitby. The visit was intended as a break from Manchester for the purposes of Julia's health, but Mrs Gaskell quickly became wrapped up with the folk memory of the town and the 1793 riot upon the rendezvous, for which William Atkinson was hanged. Gaskell researched the incident, looked at contemporary comments about the press gang in publications like the *Annual Register*, and consulted people like Thomas Perronet Thompson, a radical reformer who hailed from Hull and had briefly been a midshipman before transferring to the army. Thompson was a vocal opponent of impressment as well as the slave trade. He once wrote a devastating review of a Blimp-like speech in parliament advocating its importance to national defence, unmasking its social contempt for ordinary seamen.[14]

The result was *Sylvia's Lovers*, Gaskell's fifth novel, and today one of her least known. The story takes place in Monkshaven, a fictional Whitby, at the beginning of the French wars when the press gang's presence is once more felt. The central plot involves Sylvia Robson, a capricious, lively, free-spirited women, the daughter of an ex-seaman turned small farmer and smuggler, who had had his own run-ins with the press gang during the American war and the scars to show for it.[15] Sylvia is courted by two suitors. The first is the dashing Charley Kincaid, a specksioneer, the leader of the harpooners on a whaling ship, responsible for organizing the flensing of the whale and the boiling of its blubber into oil. Sylvia learns of his womanizing, but is taken by his verve and courage in confronting the press gang and protecting the trade of the town. The other is her shop-keeping cousin, Philip Hepburn, a more prudential, staid character, preoccupied with business but desperately devoted to Sylvia. Kincaid asks for Sylvia's hand, and he is accepted by Daniel, Sylvia's father, with whom he shares many seafaring stories and values. He pledges his troth to Sylvia, but the next day, on his way to Shields, he is taken upon by the press gang with Hepburn as a witness. Hepburn knows the impressment is illegal, for by statute, harpooners were protected from the press. But he barely remonstrates about it to the gang who silence him by threatening to take him captive as well. Nor does he convey Kincaid's message to Sylvia that he will be back to reclaim her as his wife. Instead, Hepburn says nothing and conspires in the rumour that Kincaid had been drowned. Once a second tragedy befalls Sylvia, the execution of her father for a riot on the 'randyvowse' [rendezvous], Sylvia resigns herself to a marriage with Philip, although she questions him about a new rumour that Kincaid was not drowned but impressed. Philip remains silent, and lives a second lie; his deceptions predictably damn his relationship with Sylvia upon the reappearance of Kincaid. Sylvia rejects both of them and seeks solace in her daughter, but ultimately she does forgive Philip on his deathbed, then a broken, disfigured soldier. She does not live long and her daughter eventually emigrates to America.

Throughout this tragic tale, the interventions of the press gang are critical. Unlike some eighteenth-century novels, where the press gang intrudes briefly as part of a series of picaresque adventures, the operations of the gang are intimately interwoven into the plot of *Sylvia's Lovers*. Like Mary Wollstonecraft's *Maria*, we get a better sense of the domestic tragedies that were incurred by impressment, particularly the loss of income and loved ones. We also get a hint of how impressment dislocated trades and of debates within communities about its legality. In *Sylvia's Lovers* Philip Hepburn is its advocate. Impressment is the law, he insists. Echoing Charles Butler, he believes sailors, like militiamen, should contribute to the war effort in person if they really cannot pay in taxes.[16] But Daniel Robson is not persuaded by abstract arguments to 'nation'; like many sailors, he is troubled by the tangible loss of wages and earning power that impressment inflicts upon families. He hates its domestic deprivations. 'It's not fair play to cotch up men as has no call for fightin' at another man's biddin',' he declares, 'though they've no objection to fight a bit on their own account, and who are just landed, all keen after bread i'stead o' biscuit, and flesh meat i'stead o'junk, and beds i'stead o'hammocks. I make naught o't'sentimental side, for I were niver gi'en up to such carnal-mindedness and poesies. It's noane fair to cotch 'em up and put 'em in a stifling hole, all lined with metal for fear they should whittle their way out, and send 'em off to sea for years an' years to come.'[17] He believes, presumably as a small freeholder, that his local patron and MP should articulate his grievances in parliament.

What is particularly impressive about *Sylvia's Lovers* is the way in which the issue of violence radiates throughout the novel: both as the lawless violence of the gangs and as the retaliatory violence of communities. As Terry Eagleton notes, the latter is made more compelling and intense because 'violence is part of the fabric of ordinary life, based as it is on a rhythm of tense hopes for the absent whalers, fierce excitement at their exploits, and anguish for the men lost'.[18] In this respect, the theme of social conflict is handled more systematically, and less melodramatically, than in the better-known *Mary Barton*, where class conflict is sublimated into personal revenge.

Yet a case could be made that the violence of the anti-impressment riots in the novel is improbably gendered. In the protests against the press gangs, the men are always at the centre of the action; the women are part of the wailing crowd, cursing the press gang and inciting men to act. In the opening impressment of four whalers from the *Resolution*, we learn of 'women crying aloud, throwing up their arms in imprecation, showering down abuse as hearty and rapid as if they had been a Greek chorus'. In the attack upon the rendezvous, a woman 'with wild gestures and shrill voice' pushes 'her way through the crowd … imploring immediate action … adjuring those around her to smite and spare not those who had carried off her "man"'.[19] Yet the historical record suggests that women played more prominent roles than this, assailing press officers with stones, collecting missiles for the men, remonstrating with officers that they 'would have them [their husbands] or lose their lives'.[20] Perhaps Gaskell's strong sense of domestic propriety shaped her perceptions of how women responded to impressments within their communities.

One thing is certain: Mrs Gaskell saw *Sylvia's Lovers* as an historical novel. The social relations she charted, and the place of impressment within them, belonged to a bygone age. This is clear from the way in which Monkshaven is conceptualized. For all the hints of elegant buildings and commercial growth, Monkshaven remains a remote rural seascape with even intimations of its 'organic unity'.[21] Although Kincaird is impressed on an intended journey to Shields, there is little sense of how Monkshaven [or Whitby] is part of a larger commercial world, or part of a collective movement of the North-East against impressment. Placing Monkshaven in an almost pre-industrial context fitted Mrs Gaskell's evolutionary view of social development. There is a sense in which she sees this whaling port 'red in tooth and claw', both lawless and uncivilized; although it has been suggested that she remained sceptical of what progress might imply, in that there well may be an implicit comparison between the civil disturbances of Monkshaven and the more technological brutalities of the American civil war.[22]

Still, within fifty years of the end of the Napoleonic wars, impressment is cast as a thing of the past. 'Now all this tyranny (for I can use no other word)', remarks Gaskell, 'is marvelous to us; we cannot imagine how it is that a nation submitted to it for so long, even under any warlike enthusiasm, any panic of invasion, any amount of loyal subservience to the governing powers.'[23] Reviewers were of the same opinion. To the *Observer*, *Sylvia's Lovers* seemed like a 'tale of a foreign place'; the atrocities of the gangs were history. 'Fortunately', the author opined, 'we have so far improved since those days that we can read of such doings now as if they applied to Mexico or Tahiti.' Similarly, the writer in the *Saturday Review* talked of the press gang as an 'obsolete institution' and felt 'an irrepressible satisfaction, when thinking of present foreign grievances and oppressions, that such a system should have so completely passed away as to make its former existence almost incredible to this generation'.[24]

Was impressment obsolete? Politicians in power tried to avoid the question. Technically speaking, the crown's right to impress seamen remained on the books. It was a prerogative power that was never repealed. As long as Britain lacked a viable alternative, as long as it lacked the means to mobilize quickly, governments were reluctant to abandon impressment as a last resort. Ministers were quite candid about this in parliament and the principle of impressment was even discreetly enshrined in statutory form in 1835 and again 1853 by allowing the Admiralty the residual right to 'detain' seamen in a real emergency.[25] This came, however, with the rider that impressment would be reluctantly and moderately applied if it was used at all. In introducing his enlistment bill of 1835, Sir James Graham took this line. His bill asked for the compulsory service of all seamen for five years, in effect a time-limited form of impressment, to take effect once the opportunity to volunteer had been exhausted. Not everyone thought this was a departure from impressment, as Graham suggested, especially when the powers of the Admiralty to impress were retained as a back-up solution to manning the navy in wartime, but even some opponents of impressment saw this legislation as a start.[26]

Everyone was aware that the aftermath of the long war against the French was a golden opportunity to address the issue of naval recruitment. Successive governments were aware of this, and acutely conscious of the rising opposition to the old system. Motions, overt and covert, to abolish impressment were fended off in the Commons, sometimes by very small majorities, and the condemnation of the system was winning ground. To the old libertarian arguments, which still found favour with radicals like Julian Harney,[27] were added those of political economy. Thomas Hodgkin and J.R. McCulloch both saw impressment interfering with the laws of supply and demand, forcing mercantile wages to artificially high levels.[28] In an age of the imperialism of free trade, when British shipping was such a valuable resource, this was a powerful argument. It was accompanied by one that addressed the need for government economy, a truism among post-war politicians terrified with spiralling debt, and among radicals anxious about 'Old Corruption'. Hodgkin detailed how wasteful impressment was, especially when one took into account the tenders required to transport the press men and the marines required to guard them. In his estimation it cost over half a million a year,[29] a grossly inflated calculation, but one that could strike a chord with those obsessed with profligate government expenditures.

Alongside these arguments were ones that sought to touch a humanitarian nerve, tales of family deprivation and poverty, of brutal punishments and confinements in the navy. Ballads and melodramatic novellas blazoned these narratives. In an era of sentimentality, impressment invited a healthy quotient of intolerability and pamphlets gave it an extra twist by comparing it to the iniquities of African slavery. In the immediate aftermath of the war, but a decade from the abolition of the slave trade, some of these arguments had a nationalist and racist twist. Thomas Urquhart wanted to argue that British seamen were worse off than African slaves, whipped harder and more frequently, and, because of the deep-rooted traditions of British liberty, more culturally deprived because more aware of the constraints on their freedom.[30] He wanted British seamen to get their proper place in the politics of recognition, and berated abolitionists for ignoring these plucky patriots at their back door. With emancipation, however, the equivalent plight of the British tar became more compelling; it lost its racist edge. How, in an age of reform, when the wartime contribution of British seamen was still very much in popular memory, could impressment be justified? How could it be tolerated when slaves in British colonies had been given their freedom?

Like Urquhart, government politicians knew that the problem of impressment could only be resolved in the short term by some blending of the two sea services, the royal and the mercantile. This inevitably involved more than a freer mobility between the two sectors; it meant making the Royal Navy more attractive, and that in turn meant an overhaul of its terms of service, involving pay, pensions and other benefits, leave and discipline. Sir James Graham's 1735 act came up short in this respect. Based on the older registry system, which had been contemplated, tried, disbanded and debated in the first wars of the long eighteenth century, it presumed that a limited service of five years would induce men to volunteer, without really addressing the larger issues of pay, pensions and benefits. Its successor, continuous service for ten years, proved better in this respect. It increased pay, paid it between commissions, and offered pensions after 25 years' service. It did little to address the issue of discipline, the Achilles heel of the so-called reformed navy. Flogging was only suspended in the navy in 1881; it was not abolished as in the army, and the birching of boy seamen did not cease until 1906.[31] Yet the 1853 act cannily exploited the demographic explosion of the first half of the nineteenth century by recognizing that training youngsters was the real key to creating a standing navy that would sustain Britain's world pre-eminence at sea. Educational reforms helped, for the 1870 act provided opportunities for sweeping up street urchins and placing them on naval training ships. Not that coercion was necessarily needed, for as Thomas Hodgkin astutely realized, a life at sea could be viewed as 'spirit-stirring, and not dull and deadening, like throwing a shuttle or twisting a cotton thread'.[32]

The press also played its part in creating a new image for the navy, indeed for the armed forces generally, as the British empire expanded and its commitments increased. The blue-jacket, the product of the 1853 reforms, became a beloved figure and certainly enhanced the attractiveness of the service. Once the differentials between royal and mercantile pay narrowed, a permanent Royal Naval force became a real possibility. The core group of blue-jackets was backed up by a Royal Naval Reserve of volunteering merchant seamen, and in 1900 with a Royal Fleet Reserve of ex-royal seamen. This mixed force proved insufficient for the assignments of the First World War – conscripts had to be introduced – but impressment never became an issue in the run-up to the National Service Bill of 1916.[33] In the end, conscription superseded impressment even if it did not legally abolish it.

There was covert impressment during the Victorian era. East India Company seamen were periodically requisitioned for the navy, and during the Crimean War, when the navy was really stretched for men because of the mobilization of the Russian fleet in the Baltic, a 'recruiting centre' was set up at Tower Hill that looked ominously like the old rendezvous.[34] But no government had to invoke its powers of impressment in a dramatic way during the Pax Britannica. Indeed, the long peace of the nineteenth century and favourable demographic circumstances allowed the navy time to find a permanent alternative to an institution that had lost credibility among both seamen and the propertied classes. Mrs Gaskell was wrong when she assumed that impressment was long over at the time she wrote *Sylvia's Lovers*. Its necessity was vigorously debated throughout the first half of the century, and as a prerogative power, it was always in the shadows of the debates over naval reform.

Yet the question Mrs Gaskell and others posed about why impressment survived the long eighteenth century needs to be addressed. It was not as if people did not know about its oppressions; it was not as if some of the alternatives, such as a registry of seamen, or naval militia, had not been debated; and it was well known that impressment violated cherished ideas of British freedom. So why was it tolerated for so long?

One answer is timing. A voluntary register of seamen, with bounties, prizes and very modest sick benefits, had been tried during the wars of 1690–1713, but it failed to meet its desired quota of 30,000 reservists. Its inability to deliver a sufficient number of seamen was underscored by the continual resort to impressment when the fleets were desperately short of men.[35] The scheme was abandoned in 1710, and although various other schemes for a volunteer reserve were mooted during the century, they were rejected either because of their authoritarian implications or because legislators remained riveted to a stereotypical image of a reckless tar who would buck bureaucratic procedures. In any case, most of these proposals were hatched in the heat of war, or in brief intervals between wars, and there was really little time for legislative and administrative inquiry into their efficacy. The traditions of naval service also militated against dramatic changes in recruiting practice. Many officers came from seafaring families as their fathers and grandfathers before them. They constituted nearly half (48.2 per cent) of the officers at the end of the eighteenth century, and if uncles were included in this familial cohort the percentage would be considerably higher.[36] If we add the 15 per cent who hailed from army backgrounds, then it is not implausible that upwards of two-thirds of the naval officers were really part of a self-recruiting military elite. As a group their disposition was to work the system not to contemplate new departures; and given the large discretionary powers they exercised, at least before 1811 when the Admiralty attempted to monitor habits of command, it is hardly surprising that ministers shied away from novelty.

Another reason why impressment was tolerated was that it suited the priorities of the state and commerce in the eighteenth century. Just as impressment periodically demonstrated the limits of the state, so it reflected the close alliance between the state and merchant capital on which Britain's commercial expansion was built after 1650. After the Civil War experience there was a fear of overbearing government in Britain, and for all the centralizing tendencies of the military-fiscal state, the country was run from the localities as much as from Westminster or Whitehall. Premier ministers recognized that the interests of trade, land and crown were interdependent; few adopted a haughty attitude about *raison d'état*. As the Earl of Holdernesse remarked in 1757:[37]

> we must be merchants while we are soldiers: that our trade depends upon a proper exertion of our maritime strength: that trade, and maritime force, depend upon each other: and that the riches, which are the true resources of this Country, depend chiefly upon its commerce.

Impressment fitted this frame of mind, and the skein of patronage through which the social relations of the propertied were mediated in the eighteenth century. The powers of the crown were sufficient to coerce maritime interests into providing seamen for the country in an emergency. Embargoes could immobilize merchant commerce; a hot press could sweep the decks and quays; and on one occasion, in 1779, the government even ignored the statutory exemptions to impressment, apologizing to parliament afterwards.[38] Yet generally speaking, ministers tried to be attentive to the needs of commerce, recognizing that the merchant marine was the nursery of the navy, and that the manning problem was in the last analysis a local one, and made more efficacious through the co-operation of the local magistracy and mercantile groups. Through the distribution of protections in particular, merchants powerfully placed in local government could barter with the Admiralty about reconciling the needs of the state with those of commerce. Certainly impressment could be inconvenient, vexatious, and by no means inexpensive, for the fees for Admiralty protections alone were estimated at

£24,000 a year during the American war.[39] Merchants and port employers could be downright obstructive when impressment seriously impaired their economic interests, although threats to remove guardships and convoys often brought them to their senses. But these difficulties were the price to be paid for a state whose capacity to wage war had brought long-term wealth and prosperity to the mercantile classes. More bureaucratic systems of recruitment would have given merchants and manufacturers less bargaining power.

From the point of view of the propertied classes, impressment could also reinforce the fabric of authority and labour discipline. It could be used to clear the streets of undesirables and putative criminals; even vocal opponents of impressment were sometimes happy to exploit the system in this way.[40] Maritime employers also used impressment to wean the troublesome from their force, and on occasion to break strikes. In 1776, for example, a London gang was encouraged to raid a group of striking journeymen sawyers and haul them away to the tenders.[41] Shipowners were sometimes happy to rid themselves of runaway apprentices through the auspices of the press gang. Through the distribution of protections they were able to reward the loyal and reprimand the recalcitrant. Because employers were such important intermediaries in cases of contested impressments, moreover, they were able to use their power to exact deference and respect from the vulnerable. This was potentially true of all employers, for there were cases where tramping artisans or travelling apprentices were taken up by the authorities on the grounds that they were not gainfully employed, and it frequently required the personal intervention of their masters, or a character reference, to have them released.[42]

During the Seven Years' War, Lady Huntington was asked to secure the release of several Methodists who had been impressed at Hastings at the request of a local Anglican clergymen. Similarly, Lord Townshend, the leading patron of Yarmouth, was approached to secure the release of a ship's carpenter who was 'sickly & has a Wife & 4 or 5 Children in poor State' and to obtain protections for several local coopers.[43] Impressment, in other words, operated like other aspects of the law in the eighteenth century; it reinforced the fabric of patron–client relations. For these reasons, it was the preferred option of many employers and patrons to the problem of manning the fleet.

To seamen, of course, and to the labourers and craftsmen who worked the rivers, impressment was the most striking example of the intrusive and discriminatory policies of the wartime state whose imperatives so shaped their lives. When the Anglo-American seaman Jacob Nagle returned from Madras in 1795 as part of the East India company fleet, his ship the *Rose* was searched off the coast of Ireland, off the Isle of Wight, and a third time off the Downs.[44] Nagle and 26 other tars managed to elude all three of these press-gang searches, but they were so appalled by the inexperience of the ticket-men who had been put board to bring the ship up the Thames that they disguised themselves as soldiers and risked exposure by hoisting up the topsails and 'sailing trim'. At Long Reach the captain informed them that two men of war lay ahead, and so the men jumped ship, but not before they each took a brace of pistols and a cutlass to defend themselves from any press gangs. They were soon joined by ten Greenlandmen armed with harpoons, and had a pilot guide them through the back roads to London. They met fourteen light horsemen on the way, none of whom chose to confront them directly, especially when the whalers whirled 'there harpoons over there heads, shining like silver'.[45] At Poplar, however, where four press gangs were in waiting, more flamboyant measures were called for. Nagle and his fellow tars hired two coaches, stationed the intrepid whalers on the top, and raced to East India House to collect their wages, firing shots out of the carriage windows to ward off potential pursuers.

Once in the city, Nagle negotiated with an acquaintance to secure him a protection, and for a while managed to trick the gangs into believing he belonged to the *Gorgon*, then lying at Woolwich. Unfortunately he encountered Edward Tyrrell, the actual captain of the ship, while he was in the city on business. Tyrrell took a shine to Nagle, otherwise his fate might have been far less attractive. He offered him the opportunity to sign up as a volunteer for the *Gorgon*, with £35 bounty money, or face impressment on a three-decker at the Nore. In the circumstances it was an easy choice to make; Tyrrell even sweetened the choice by offering him a ticket of leave to say goodbye to his newly wed wife. Nagle didn't venture to desert; he had already tried that once when his cover was blown. He told the purser that he knew 'death would be my portion if caught again'.[46]

Nagle used disguise, guile and bravado to evade the clutches of the press gang. A less experienced Samuel Bamford had only pluck and luck to rely on. After a youthful adventure at sea aboard a collier from Shields, Bamford decided to jump ship for his native Lancashire, having seen enough of a sailor's life, he recalled, to banish the romantic notions 'with which the popular songs of the day had invested it'.[47] Tramping from London to Manchester in wartime, however, was a very risky business, and Bamford was lucky to get away with it. Outside St Albans he was recognized as a seamen and tipped off about a party of marines that were impressing men in the town. He managed to elude them by hiding in a wagon full of soldiers and their families, but at Bedford he found himself vulnerable to the press once more, 'the people almost lifting their eyes in wonder at seeing a tall, gaunt, weather-browned sailor traversing that perilous ground'.[48] This time he was stopped by a party of marines, yet Bamford did not panic, and the corporal who viewed his protection was fortunately too illiterate to recognize its invalidity. He sent him on his way, much to the surprise of some farmer spectators, who told him he was the first to escape the clutches of the recruiting party in a long time. Bamford encountered another marine in Northampton, a garrison town, but his luck held and he was not stopped. Thereafter he stuck to the back roads, although dire poverty and the need to sell some of his clothes for food forced him to linger in Leicester. It was only through the kindness of strangers, and their understanding of his predicament, that he managed to get home without falling into the hands of the navy.

The narratives of Nagle and Bamford underscore the intrusive nature of the state for the wartime sailor; they also say something about public sympathy for their predicament. Ordinary people knew that impressment was unfair and unjust even if judges pronounced it legal; that it fell hardest on the poorest members of countless coastal communities, who were forced to serve the state in ways that the propertied classes were not. As this book has attempted to show, they tried hard to do something about it, from helping stragglers elude the press to harassing gangs and collectively impairing their progress. The stories of those struggles resonated in the ballads and historical romances of the nineteenth century, although as melodrama they tended to overplay the vulnerability of the seafarer confronted with press-gang villainy. In actual fact Jack Tar and his supporters battled the gangs on many fronts, and sometimes got away with it. As David Hume perceptively remarked, impressment was a 'continued violence permitted in the crown amidst the greatest jealousy and watchfulness of the people'. The consequence was that 'Liberty, in the country of the highest liberty, is left entirely to its own defence, without any countenance or protection' and 'great violence and disorder are committed with impunity; while the one party pleads obedience to the supreme magistrate, the other the sanction of fundamental laws'.[49]

# Notes

## Chapter 1: Introduction

1. Horace Bleackley, *Life of John Wilkes* (London, 1917), p. 268.
2. Old Bailey Proceedings, 11 September 1771, OldBaileyonline, trial of Mary Jones (t17710911-32); *Cobbett's Parliamentary History*, 19 (1777), 237–8, *Newcastle Chronicle*, 3 June 1797.
3. OldBaileyonline, trial of Mary Jones (t17710911-32); *Middlesex Journal*, 8–10, 15–17 October 1771, *General Evening Post*, 12–14 September 1771, *Gentleman's Magazine*, 40 (1771), 471.
4. *Middlesex Journal*, 19–21 September 1771. See also *Public Advertiser*, 17 October 1771.
5. *Cobbett's Parliamentary History*, 19 (1777), 238.
6. *Newcastle Chronicle*, 3 June 1797.
7. Westminster Public Library, Parish examinations, St Martin-in-the-Fields, F 5063/377–8.
8. F 5065/133–4.
9. *British Parliamentary Papers*, 3 (1814–15), 238. See also Sir Frederick Eden, *The State of the Poor* (3 vols; London, 1797), vol. 2, pp. 167, 563; vol. 3, p. 837.
10. The National Archives (hereafter TNA), Adm 1/3286 (22 April 1797); *The Times*, 18 April 1797.
11. See OED and the commentary in Daniel James Ennis, *Enter the Press-Gang* (London, 2002), pp. 27–8.
12. *Cobbett's Parliamentary History*, 20 (1779), 978.
13. Under 8 Geo III c.7 section 70. In the 1750s acts were passed which allowed the army forcibly to impress recruits. See Stephen Conway, *War, State and Society in Mid-Eighteenth Century Britain and Ireland* (Oxford, 2006).
14. N.A.M. Rodger, *The Wooden World* (London, 1986), appendix III.
15. John D. Byrn Jr, *Crime and Punishment in the British Navy: Discipline on the Leeward Islands Station, 1784–1812* (Aldershot, 1989), p. 76n.
16. Michael Lewis, *A Social History of the Navy 1793–1815* (London, 1960), p. 139; Daniel Baugh, *British Naval Administration in the Age of Walpole* (Princeton, 1965), p. 163; N.A.M. Rodger, 'Devon Men and the Navy 1689–1815', in Michael Duffy et al. (eds), *A New Maritime History of Devon*, 2 vols (London, 1992) vol. 1, p. 213.
17. Rodger, *Wooden World*, pp. 145, 153.
18. TNA, Adm 1/581/86–9; Adm 1/1498 (John Bover), 15 May 1778; Adm 1/2672 (James Worth) 11 December 1778; Adm 1/1447 (James Alms) 1 October 1780. William L.

Clements Library, Ann Arbor, Michigan, Shelburne Papers, 139 no. 61. See also Roland G. Usher, 'Royal Navy Impressment during the American Revolution', *Mississippi Valley Historical Review*, 37 (1950), 673–88.
19 J.S. Bromley, 'Away from Impressment: The Idea of a Royal Naval Reserve, 1696–1854', in A.C. Duke and C.A. Tamse (eds), *Britain and the Netherlands, vol. 6 War and Society* (The Hague, 1977), pp. 168–88.
20 The most recent and complete figures are in N.A.M. Rodger, *The Command of the Ocean: A Naval History of Britain 1649–1815* (London, 2004), appendix VI.
21 See David J. Starkey, 'War and the Market for Seafarers in Britain', in Lewis R. Fischer and Helge W. Nordvik (eds), *Shipping and Trade 1750–1950: Essays in International Maritime Economic History* (Pontefract, 1990), p. 29.
22 Ibid., 29, 33. Naval net pay was 22s 6d per month down to 1797, while merchant pay was between 24 and 30 shillings in peacetime rising to 55s in 1745 and 70s per month in the next two wars.
23 For the increases in the fleet, see Rodger, *Command of the Ocean*, Appendix III, which shows that ships of the first three rates doubled in the years 1696–1778, and doubled again to 1804.
24 Baugh, *British Naval Administration*, p. 159.
25 William L. Clements Library, Shelburne papers, 139, nos. 62, 64. The figures given here are 28 per cent for 1759–60 and 23 per cent for 1780–81.
26 William L. Clements Library, Shelburne papers, 139, no. 61.
27 For figures on landsmen, see TNA Adm 1/1447 (James Alms) 1 October 1780; Adm 1/581.86–89.
28 Stephen F. Gradish, *The Manning of the British Navy during the Seven Years' War* (London, 1980), pp. 57–9, William L, Clements Library, Shelburne papers, 139, no. 62.
29 Greenland harpooners and foreigners were exempt under 1 Anne c. 16 and 13 Geo. II, c. 28. Sea apprentices under 18 years of age were exempt under 2 & 3 Anne, c. 6 and those who voluntarily bound themselves were not to be impressed in their first three years of service. The colliers were allowed one able seaman for every 100 tons, to a maximum of three men per crew. The Thames watermen had to provide 200 men when required. See Christopher Lloyd, *The British Seaman 1200–1860: A Social Survey* (London, 1968), pp. 146–7
30 See 13 Geo. II, c. 3, 17, 29.
31 TNA, Adm 7/370/ 176, 190, 197, 204; Rodger, *Wooden World*, 178.
32 See, for example, Ralph Davis, *The Rise of the English Shipping Industry* (Newton Abbot, 1972), p. 321 where Davis says impressment was 'almost entirely confined to seamen and shipyard workers'.
33 The age qualification of 18–55 years was introduced in 1740 under 13 Geo. II, c. 17. For earlier impressment, see G.V. Scammell, 'The Sinews of War: Manning and Provisioning English Fighting Ships c. 1550–1650', *Mariner's Mirror*, 73 (1987), pp. 357–9.
34 TNA, Adm 1/1784 (John Fergusson) 19 July 1756; Adm 1/1611 (James Cunninghame) March 1778.
35 *Sussex Weekly Advertiser*, 26 November 1776.
36 TNA, Adm 1/1611/159–62 (James Cunninghame); Adm 1/3681/241; Adm 1/1497 (John Bover) 21 January 1771, 21 February 1778; 1/2220 (Napier) 28 January 1780.

37  TNA, Adm 1/1498 (John Bover) 16 March 1778.
38  TNA, Adm 1/579 (Jonathan Macbride) 28 February 1795.
39  William Lovett, *Life and Struggles of William Lovett*, intro. R.H. Tawney (London, 1967), pp, 1–3.
40  Westminster Public Library, St Clement Danes, parish examinations, 1778–1779, B 1184/215 and B 1185/28. For the lighterman, see St Martin-in-the-Fields, parish examinations, F 5063/377–8. For weavers and shoemakers who spent a youthful jaunt at sea and were considered prime candidates for the press gang in Edinburgh, see TNA, Adm 1/1724 (John Fergusson) 19 July 1756.
41  Old Bailey Online, October 1746, trial of Battholomew Quickly (t17461015–9); September 1757, trial of John Flat (t17570914–24).
42  Old Bailey Online, December 1747, trial of Richard Hinton (t17471209–46). See also April 1747, trial of Thomas Powers (t17470429–14); October 1787, trial of William Sorrell (t17871024–51).
43  Guildhall Library, London, Ms. 100, the diary of Marshe Dickenson, 4 November 1757.
44  For witnesses assuming a ruckus on the street involving the press gang, see Old Bailey Online, December 1776, trial of Abraham Handrequas (t17761204–18).
45  Rodger, *Wooden World*, p. 172. Westminster Public Library, parish examinations, St Martin's, F 5063/377–8, 5064/141 and St Clement Danes, 1770, B 1176/101 & 105, 1777, B 1183/73.
46  Under 2 & 3 Anne c. 6, c. 16. For earlier impressments, see A.L. Beir, *Masterless Men* (London, 1985), pp. 161–2. See also Nicholas Rogers, 'Vagrancy, Impressment and the Regulation of Labour in Eighteenth-Century Britain', in Paul E. Lovejoy and Nicholas Rogers (eds), *Unfree Labour in the Development of the Atlantic World* (London, 1994), pp. 102–13.
47  Philonauta, *The Sailor's Happiness* (London, 1751), pp. 19–20; *Gentleman's Magazine*, 32 (1762), 53.
48  *Public Advertiser*, 6 January 1787; see also Nicholas Rogers, 'Liberty Road: Opposition to Impressment in Britain during the American War of Indpendence', in Colin Howell and Richad J. Twomey (eds), *Jack Tar in History: Essays in the History of Maritime Life and Labour* (Fredericton, New Brunswick, 1991), pp. 74–5.
49  Rodger, *Command of the Ocean*, p. 397.
50  TNA, Adm 1/581/86–9.
51  See Peter King, 'War as a Judicial Resource: Press Gangs and Prosecution Rates, 1740–1840', in Norma Landau (ed.), *Law, Crime and English Society 1660–1830* (Cambridge, 2002), pp. 97–116; Douglas Hay, 'War, Dearth and Theft in the Eighteenth Century: The Record of the English Courts', *Past and Present* 95 (May, 1982), pp. 117–60.
52  *The Times*, 2 October 1787; TNA, Adm 1/2260 (Edward Wheeler), 18 March 1755.
53  TNA, Adm 1/1912 H 298; Adm 1/3684, 10 August 1795; Adm 1/3685, 6 October 1796.
54  Gloucestershire Record Office, Granville Sharp Papers, D 3549 Box 3824, 13/3/36. The case was printed in the *Morning Chronicle or London Advertiser*, 6 March 1778.
55  These conclusions are based on a survey of twenty muster books in the period 1777–1797. Because of the haphazard entry of the ages of pressed men, these figures are only suggestive.
56  Charles Butler, *An Essay on the Legality of Impressing Seamen* (London, 1777), pp. 53–4.

57  See Ennis, *Enter the Press-Gang*, ch. 5.
58  G.L. Newnham-Collingwood, *A Selection from the Public and Private Correspondence of Vice-Admiral Lord Collingwood* (London, 1829), p. 96, cited by Tony Barrow, *Trafalgar Geordies and North Country Seamen of Nelson's Navy 1793–1815* (Sunderland, 2005), p. 40.
59  John Nicol, *The Life and Adventures of John Nicol, Mariner*, ed. Tim Flannery (New York, 1997), pp. 183–9.
60  James Oglethorpe, *The Sailors Advocate* (London, 1728), p. 11.
61  William Robinson, *Jack Nastyface: Memoirs of a Seaman* (1836; repr. London, 1973), pp. 25–8.
62  Rodger, *Wooden World*, pp. 164–82, quote p. 182.
63  Ibid., appendix IV.
64  Ibid., p. 182.
65  TNA, Adm 1/1502/306–8.
66  TNA, Adm 1/3690, 5, 19 April 1804; Adm 1/581/270–71.
67  TNA, Adm 1/581/271.
68  Peter Linebaugh and Marcus Rediker, *The Many-Headed Hydra: Sailors, Slaves, Commoners, and the Hidden History of the Revolutionary Atlantic* (Boston, 2000).
69  Linda Colley, *Britons: Forging the Nation 1707–1837* (New Haven and London, 1992).

*Chapter 2: Impressment and the Law*

1  For the depositions on this case, and the Admiralty Solicitor's report, see TNA, Adm 1/3675/343–75.
2  Gradish, *The Manning of the British Navy* ch. 3; Rodger, *Wooden World*, ch. 5. Rodger notes the litigious circumstances in which impressment was sometimes carried out (pp. 169–70) but, like Gradish, his treatment of the law regarding impressment is very summary.
3  Lloyd, *British Seaman*, p. 151.
4  Christopher Hill, *Liberty Against the Law* (London, 1996), pp. 166, 168.
5  Oglethorpe, *Sailor's Advocate*, p. 10.
6  Oglethorpe, *The Sailor's Advocate*, pp. 4–5, and [Lieut. John Mackenzie], *Considerations on the Impress Service* (London, 1786), cited by J.S. Bromley (ed.), *The Manning of the Royal Navy* (Navy Records Society 119; London, 1976), pp. 130, 139. Magna Carta was also cited by John Wilkes in a debate in the Court of Alderman on impressment, October 1770. See *Middlesex Journal*, 13–16 October 1770. For the original Latin version of the clause, see William Stubbs, *Select Charters* (Oxford, 1880), p. 300. For a translation, see *English Historical Documents III, 1189–1327* (London, 1975), p. 320. The brackets reveal there was room for interpretation, on account of the fact that 'liber homo' could mean free man or the more juridical freeman, and that 'vel' could mean either 'or' or 'and'.
7  See the arguments of Granville Sharp and James Oglethorpe, outlined in John A. Woods, 'The City of London and Impressment, 1776–1777', *Proceedings of the Leeds Philosophical and Literary Society*, 7 (1956–59), 122–25.
8  TNA, Adm 1/1783 (Fergusson) 3 February 1756. For an earlier statement that impressment was contrary to the Bill of Rights as well as Magna Carta, see *Mist's Weekly Journal*, 18 May 1728.

9   13 George II, c. 18.
10  This argument can be found in the *Sailor's Advocate*, p. 3; it also crops up in the petitions from the Fleet during the naval mutiny of 1797. See TNA, Adm 1/5125, cited in J.R. Hutchinson, *The Press Gang Afloat and Ashore* (London, 1913), p. 17.
11  *General Evening Post*, 15–18 May 1790.
12  Christopher Lloyd, *Nation and the Navy* (London, 1954), pp. 131–2. See also *Newcastle Courant*, 31 July 1790, where it is suggested that seamen should organize petitions against impressment in much the same way as abolitionists were organizing them against the slave trade.
13  *English Chronicle and Universal Evening Post*, 22–24 July 1790.
14  *Cobbett's Parliamentary History*, 7 (1739–41), 428–9.
15  *Rex v Broadfoot*, 2 Salk. 31, *English Reports* 168, 78. See also TNA, Adm 1/3675/236–40. Broadfoot was found guilty of manslaughter but not murder and burnt in the hand.
16  Newcastle seamen in 1793 emphasized that impressment, while 'countenanced by Precedent and supposed to have been a Part of the common Law', had 'never been sanctioned by the authority of Parliament'. *Newcastle Chronicle*, 2 February 1793. This was contested in the *Newcastle Courant*, 2 February 1793, 'Judge Forster' being cited as the ultimate authority.
17  4 Anne, c. 19; 4 & 5; Anne c. 6. These 1705 and 1706 acts for the 'speedier manning' of the fleet were clearly intended to be supplementary to the routine acts of impressing. Or so Foster argued. *English Reports*, 168, pp. 87–8.
18  Ibid., 84.
19  *Rex v. Tubbs*, Foster 155, *English Reports*, 168, pp. 1215–20.
20  On these cases, see John Sainsbury, *Disaffected Patriots: London Supporters of Revolutionary America, 1769–1782* (Kingston and Montreal, 1987), pp. 134–9; John Woods, 'City of London and Impressment', pp. 114–21.
21  TNA, Adm 7/299, no. 64.
22  And were to be so again. See 18 Geo. III, c. 53, and 19 Geo. III, c. 10, an abstract of which can be found in the *Annual Register*, 22 (1779), 254.
23  *Annual Register*, 13 (1770), 232; also printed in *Middlesex Journal*, 22–24 November 1770; *Felix Farley's Bristol Journal*, 1 December 1770.
24  *Sussex Weekly Advertiser*, 2 June 1777.
25  *English Reports*, 98, p. 1218; 168, p. 79.
26  On this episode, see Simon Schama, *Patriots and Liberators: Revolution in the Netherlands, 1780–1813* (London, 1977), pp. 121–9.
27  *Newcastle Chronicle*, 24 November 1792. For complaints about the 'supposed necessity' of impressment, see the speech of the Duke of Richmond in the Lords, 11 February 1771, cited in *Berrow's Worcester Journal*, 21 February 1771. For newspaper comment, see the *Whisperer*, 36, 20 October 1770, 124; *Felix Farley's Bristol Journal*, 8 December 1770, 15 May 1790; *London Evening Post*, 12–14 November 1776.
28  Gloucestershire R.O., Granville Sharp Papers, D 3549 Box 3824, 13/3/36–37.
29  *Whitehall Evening Post*, 9–11 October 1787.
30  TNA, Adm 7/298, no. 99.
31  See *Rex v Broadfoot*, *English Reports*, 168, pp. 77–8.

32  Adm 1/3678/98–9. In 1787, press warrants executed in Edinburgh and Leith were said to have been 'irregular' because they were not endorsed by the magistrates. *Ipswich Journal*, 6 October 1787.
33  TNA, Adm. 1/1486 (Baird) 1 & 4 Mar. 1755, Adm 1/3677/32.
34  TNA, Adm 1/2009 (Charles Knowler) 18 March 1756.
35  *Annual Register*, 13 (1770), 232.
36  See 'Constitutional Queries' in the *London Evening Post*, 27–29 November 1770. Later in the century, a serjeant-at-law said that press warrants, 'however … tollerated from necessity' were 'always obnoxious, as being derogatory to the liberty of the Subject and repugnant to the principles of a free Government'. TNA, Adm 1/2309 (Hyde Parker) 2 September 1791, enclosure from Thomas Anthony Minchin, dated 31 August 1791. For aldermen discharging impressed men during the Falkland Islands crisis, see *Middlesex Journal*, 30 October–1 November, 1–3 November 1770.
37  *Middlesex Journal*, 19–21, 29–31 January 1771. Faced with magisterial hostility, the Admiralty sought to ensure that its gangs were properly mustered and regulated and insisted that lieutenants accompany them. One lieutenant was dismissed from the service on account of his absence. See Ruddock F. Mackay (ed.), *The Hawke Papers: A Selection 1743–1771* (Navy Records Society 129, Aldershot, 1990), docs. 470, 473–4.
38  *General Evening Post*, 23–25 January 1777. See also Sainsbury, *Reluctant Patriots*, pp. 134–8; Woods, 'City of London and Impressment', pp. 116–17.
39  *General Evening Post*, 16–18 January 1777.
40  TNA, Adm. 7/304, no. 406.
41  TNA, Adm 1/3680/238, Admiralty Solicitor Sedden to Lords of the Admiralty, 24 July 1777, reporting on a case involving a charge of common assault against one of the press captains at Portsmouth.
42  Neither Foster nor any other judge actually said this, but this was how the legal judgments were frequently represented in the newspapers.
43  TNA, Adm 1/3680/345–7.
44  *Ipswich Journal*, 6 October 1787.
45  On lawless gangs, see *London Evening Post*, 13–15 May 1755; *MR*, 57, December 1777, 491; *Hawke Papers*, docs. 470, 473; on phoney gangs, see *London Evening Post*, 17–19 July 1739, *Middlesex Journal*, 4–6 October 1770; *Newcastle Journal*, 24 November–1 December 1770; *Whitehall Evening Post*, 11–13 October 1787.
46  *English Chronicle*, 24–26 August 1790.
47  TNA, Adm 1/3675/45–6, 88–90.
48  TNA, Adm 1/1903 (Hamilton) 17 August 1777.
49  TNA, Adm 1/3680/244, 303.
50  TNA, Adm 1/2141 M42.
51  TNA, Adm. 1/3677/ 40, 135. See also, Adm 1/3689, 23 September, 10 October 1803, the case of John Barbary, a publican of Flushing, Cornwall.
52  TNA, Adm 1/1446 (Alms), 24 July 1779.
53  Rodger, *Wooden World*, p. 166; cf Gradish, *Manning*, p. 56. On the predominately genteel or professional background of the naval officer, see Michael A. Lewis, *The Navy in Transition 1814–1864: A Social Survey* (London, 1965), p. 22.

54  TNA, Adm 1/3676/129–30.
55  TNA, Adm 1/3678/256–7.
56  TNA, Adm 1/3675/35; Adm 1/3680/390–5.
57  *Johnson's British Gazette*, 17 April 1803.
58  TNA, Adm 1/3675/191–6, 11 March 1743.
59  TNA, Adm 7/301, no. 251.
60  TNA, Adm 1/3683, 13 July 1795; Adm 1/3684, 17 August 1796.
61  TNA, Adm 1/3681/194, 200. This case concerned John Brassett, a publican in St Katherine's, London, who sued a lieutenant and midshipman for false arrest. The officers searched his pub for men but did not break down any of the doors that were shut. Brassett assaulted the lieutenant and verbally abused him, for which, as a former seaman, he was impressed. The Admiralty Solicitor, said Brassett, had been on shore too many years for this action to stick. In view of the circumstances, however, he recommended that the Admiralty pay Brassett's costs and damages of £146-17-8d and also Lieutenant Wilkinson's costs of £5-11-3d.
62  *Middlesex Journal*, 1–3 November 1770.
63  Captains sometimes requested such action to punish their assailants, fearing they would not get their just deserts before sympathetic juries. See TNA, Adm 1/3683, 13 September 1790.
64  TNA, Adm 1/3678/244–7.
65  See the case reported in TNA, Adm 7/300 no. 194.
66  The corporation of Poole was outraged when the Admiralty pulled this stunt in a case involving the death of a fisherman who had resisted impressment in Poole harbour. It tried unsuccessfully to have the two lieutenants and the midshipman of the gang tried again at the Dorchester Assizes. See TNA, Adm 1/3683, 28 February, 7 March, 15, 28 July 1795; 1/3684, 15 March 1786.
67  *Gentleman's Magazine*, 49 (1779), pp. 323, 50 (1780), pp. 72–4; TNA, Adm 1/3680/317–22.
68  TNA, Adm 1/3677/188–94, 1/3681/270.
69  TNA, Adm 1/3676/129–30. He asked for £500 in damages and received £300.
70  TNA, Adm 7/300 no. 207.
71  TNA, Adm 1/3283, 7 January 1795.
72  On seamen's wages, see Jonathan Press, *The Merchant Seamen of Bristol 1747–1789* (Historical Association; Bristol, 1976), pp. 6–8; Ralph Davis, *English Shipping Industry*, pp. 136–40.
73  Gradish, *Manning*, pp. 66–7.
74  Daniel A. Baugh (ed.), *Naval Administration 1715–1750* (Navy Records Society 120; London, 1977), p. 112.
75  TNA, Adm 1/1486 (Baird), 12 April 1755; Adm 1/4446 (Alms) 2 September 1776.
76  TNA, Adm 1/2672 (Worth), 15 April 1777.
77  TNA, Adm 1/2141 M26.
78  2 & 3 Anne, c. 16; 13 George II, c. 17. For a summary of statutory protections see Rodger, *Wooden World*, p. 177.
79  TNA, Adm 1/1503 (Bover), 20 January 1782.
80  TNA, Adm 1/1486 (Baird) 26 April 1755, 6 May 1755.

81  Under 4 Anne, c. 19 section 17. The exemption for apprentices of less than three years' standing was in 2 & 3 Anne, c. 6, section 17. For legal opinion about these statutes, see TNA, Adm 7/299 no. 165.
82  TNA, Adm 1/2220 (Napier) 22 February 1777.
83  TNA, Adm 1/3684, 20 June 1795.
84  TNA, Adm 1/3884, 13 July 1795.
85  31 George II, c. 10, section 27. The people of the Channel Islands believed that the £20 or over qualification did not apply to them – that, in effect, they were exempted from the statute. See TNA, Adm 1/3681/54.
86  TNA, Adm 1/3680/408, 420.
87  TNA, Adm 1/1498 (Bover) 22 March 1778.
88  TNA, Adm 1/2220 (Napier) 22 April 1777; for Dover, see Adm 1/3681/82.
89  TNA, Adm 1/1835 (Gordon) 23 July 1760; Adm 7/299, no. 145. A crimp was an agent who entrapped men for the armed service; often a landlord who used his credit to ensnare men into the army or navy.
90  TNA, Adm 1/3680/256; Adm 1/2220 (Napier) memorial to Napier, 20 June 1777.
91  TNA, Adm 7/299, no. 165.
92  In 1713 and 1749, for example, under 12 Anne, c. 13, sec. 1, and 22 Geo II, c. 44.
93  TNA, Adm 7/300 no. 183. The opinion of F.C. Cust in 1779.
94  TNA, Adm1/1783 (Fergusson) 19 July 1756.
95  Regulating officers were also officious about statutory protections. For example, Greenlandmen (whale fishermen) could work as colliers (sailing coal ships) in the off-season, but they could be impressed if they were found doing other types of work. See TNA, Adm 1/714, Temple West, 16 February 1755; Adm 2/522/56 27 February 1758, cited by Gradish, *Manning*, p. 68n.
96  In the 1790s, for example, the Admiralty reviewed the exemptions granted mates and apprentices in the coal trade. See TNA, Adm 7/302 no. 283 and Adm 7/304 no. 399.
97  TNA, Adm 1/3684, 15 January 1796.
98  The relevant act was 35 Geo. III, c. 34. For legal advice about the discharge of 'vagrants' for criminal but not civil cases, see TNA, Adm 1/3684, 30 March 1796.
99  On this incident, see Nicholas Rogers, 'Liberty Road', pp. 72–4.
100  For a case of a naval captain threatening to throw a writ of habeas corpus and its bearer into the sea, see TNA, Adm 1/3684, 11 November 1796. For other captains refusing writs, see Adm 1/3680/138 & 139.
101  Baugh, *British Naval Administration*, p. 203; for other examples, see William L. Clements Lib., Townshend papers 297/3/2, 21, 23, and Peter Marshall, *Bristol and the American War of Independence* (History Association: Bristol, 1977), pp. 15–17.
102  See TNA, Adm 1/3681/27–8, 64; Adm 1/3684, 11 November 1796; Douglas Hay, 'Prosecution and Power: Malicious Prosecution in the English Courts, 1750–1850', in Douglas Hay and Francis Snyder (eds), *Policing and Prosecution in Britain 1750–1850* (Oxford, 1989), pp. 365–6; Ian R. Christie, 'Great Yarmouth and the Yorkshire Reform Movement 1782–1784', in *Myth and Reality in Late-Eighteenth-Century Politics* (London, 1970), pp. 284n., 294; James E. Bradley, *Religion, Revolution and English Radicalism* (Cambridge, 1990), pp. 239–40, 404, 411.
103  TNA, Adm 7/300, no. 207.

## Chapter 3: Resisting the Press Gang: Trends, Patterns, Dynamics

1. Emmanuel Le Roy Ladurie, *The Territory of the Historian* (Brighton, 1979), p. 6; François Furet, 'Quantitative History', in Felix Glbert and Stephen R. Graubard (eds), *Historical Studies Today* (New York, 1972), p. 54.
2. E.P. Thompson, *The Poverty of Theory and Other Essays* (London, 1978), p. 220.
3. Charles Tilly, *Popular Contention in Great Britain 1758–1834* (Cambridge, 1995), p. 65.
4. Rodger, *Wooden World*, pp. 174–5.
5. Christopher Hill, *Liberty Against the Law* (London, 1996), ch. 13; Peter Linebaugh, *The London Hanged* (London, 1991), p. 67; Marcus Rediker, *Between the Devil and the Deep Blue Sea* (Cambridge, 1987), pp. 27, 59, 101, 251–2, 258.
6. Cf. Tilly, *Popular Contention, passim*, who is eager to assume newspapers can be worked into workable historical series, without considering the mediating forces at work in the social production of news.
7. TNA, Adm 1/1482 (Barnsley) 25 March 1746, also cited in Hutchinson, *Press Gang*, pp. 215–16; *London Evening Post*, 7–10 March 1741.
8. TNA, Adm 7/303, no. 381.
9. TNA, Adm 1/1529 B 620; Hutchinson, *Press Gang*, pp. 209–10.
10. TNA, Adm 1/2284 (Thos. Philpot) 14 February 1740; *Ipswich Journal*, 19 September 1741; *London Evening Post*, 4–6 June 1745; *Middlesex Journal*, 10–12 January 1771; Adm 1/1611 (James Cunninghame) f. 159; Adm 1/1611/159.
11. TNA, Adm 1/1439 (Allen) 13 March 1742.
12. *Read's Weekly Journal*, 1 May 1756; *London Evening Post*, 4–6 March 1755; Woods, 'City of London', p. 112; *Northampton Mercury*, 11 November 1776; *The Times*, 23 August 1790; *Public Advertiser*, 6 July 1779; *Bath Journal*, 19 July 1779; *Morning Chronicle*, 14 April, 11 May 1803.
13. TNA, Adm 1/2260 (Edwd Wheeler) 7 Mar 1755.
14. TNA, Adm 1/3095 (George Roach) 25 June 1803.
15. *The Times*, 22 Oct 1803; *Bristol Gazette*, 31 March 1803; *Reading Mercury*, 4 April 1803; TNA, Adm 1/2602, Sandford Tatham to Nepean, 17 November 1803; Adm 1/2141 M37, M42; Adm 1/1490 (Brown)12 May 1759.
16. TNA, Adm 1/1490 (Brown) 12 May 1759, cited in Hutchinson, *Press Gang*, pp. 272–3.
17. *Sussex Weekly Advertiser*, 4 April 1803.
18. TNA, Adm 1/2141 M42; Adm 1/3689, 10 October 1803.
19. *Ipswich Journal*, 5 January 1771; *Newcastle Journal*, 5–12 January 1771; *Berrow's Worcester Journal*, 3 January 1771.
20. TNA, Adm 1/1609 (James Chads) 3 November 1770.
21. C. R. Dobson, *Masters and Journeymen* (London, 1980), pp. 24–5.
22. Calculated from Andrew Charlesworth (ed.), *An Atlas of Rural Protest in Britain 1548–1900* (London and Canberra, 1983), ch. 3, and Roger Wells, *Wretched Faces: Famine in Wartime England 1763–1803* (Gloucester, 1988), tables 1–13.
23. TNA, Adm 1/1618 (Smith Child), 27 October, 16 November, 1793; Adm 1/579 (Pringle) February 1795; Adm 1/1502 (Bennett), 12, 16 April 1782, cited in Hutchinson, *Press Gang*, p. 164.

24 These calculations are based on the number of men who were borne in each war, subtracting the highest number from the peace establishment prior to war. The figures are to be found in Rodger, *Command of the Ocean*, appendix VI. I have worked with Rodger's 'Borne (2)' list.
25 I have located 80 affrays for the period 1739–1748, and 76 for the period 1793–1801.
26 TNA, Adm 1/3095 (Roach) 25 June 1803; Adm 1/2602 (Tatham) 17 November 1803; Adm 1/2141 (Mitchell) M42.
27 *Ipswich Journal*, 22 May 1790.
28 Wells, *Wretched Faces*, p. 94.
29 Ibid., pp. 100, 176, where Wells talks of an unpopular miller in Kingsteignton taking a severe beating and a farmer from Kingston being 'suspended' by his feet.
30 TNA, T 1/316, cited by Cal Winslow, 'Sussex Smugglers', in Douglas Hay et al. (eds), *Albion's Fatal Tree: Crime and Society in Eighteenth-century England* (London, 1975), p. 133.
31 TNA, Adm 1/2602, Sandford Tatham to Nepean, 17 November 1803.
32 TNA, Adm 1/3677/26–7, 18 March 1755.
33 TNA, Adm 1/3285, 16 December 1796.
34 *Middlesex Journal*, 27–29 December 1770; *Stamford Mercury*, 4 June 1790; *London Evening Post*, 17–20 October 1741; TNA, Adm 1/3674/350–2.
35 TNA, Adm 1/1835 (Gordon) 23 July 1760; *Bristol Gazette*, 31 March 1803; *Bonner and Middleton's Bristol Journal*, 2 April 1803.
36 *London Chronicle*, 26–29 March 1791; *Reading Mercury*, 16 May 1803.
37 *General Evening Post*, 31 July–3 August, 3–5 August 1790; *London Chronicle*, 3 August 1790; *English Chronicle*, 31 July–3 August, 3–5 August 1790; *The Times*, 5 August 1790; *Ipswich Journal*, 7 August 1790; John Stevenson, *Popular Disturbances in England 1700–1870* (London and New York, 1979), p. 40.
38 *Whitehall Evening Post*, 21–23 April 1747.
39 TNA, Adm 1/3677/67–8.
40 TNA, Adm 1/3675/75; Adm 1/1439 (Allen) 13 March 1742; Hutchinson, *Press Gang*, pp. 223–4; *London Evening Post*, 6–9 March 1742.
41 *General Advertiser*, 15 April 1778.
42 William Spavens, *The Narrative of William Spavens, a Chatham Pensioner by Himself*, ed. N.A.M. Rodger (1796; London, 1998), p. 20.
43 *The Times*, 1 August 1794; Edward Gillett and Kenneth A. MacMahon, *A History of Hull* (Hull, 1989), pp. 233–4.
44 *All Alive and Merry, or London Daily Post*, 20 October 1741; *Norwich Gazette*, 19–24 October 1741; *Ipswich Journal* 24, 31 October 1741; *London Evening Post*, 17–20 October 1741.
45 TNA, Adm 1/3675/374.
46 TNA, Adm 3677/188–194.
47 *Lloyd's Evening Post*, 8–11 November 1776; *London Evening Post*, 9–12 November 1776; *Berrow's Worcester Journal*, 14 November 1776; *General Evening Post*, 9–12 November 1776; *Ipswich Jor*, 16 November 1776.
48 *Aris's Birmingham Gazette*, 2 November 1778.
49 *Gentleman's Magazine*, 50 (February 1780), pp. 72–4.

50  Francis Fleming, *The Life and Extraordinary Adventures ... of Timothy Ginnadrake*, 3 vols (Bath, 1771), vol. 2, pp. 8–9.
51  Tobias Smollett, *The Adventures of Roderick Random*, 2 vols (Dublin, 1748), vol. 1, p. 205; William Makepeace Thackeray, 'Denis Duval', in *Cornhill Magazine*, 9 (1864), 659.
52  TNA, Adm 1/1206 (Sandford Tatham) enclosures with letter 21 September 1803; Adm 1/1834 (Thomas Gordon) 1 February 1759.
53  TNA, Adm 1/1834 (Thomas Gordon) 17 June 1759.
54  TNA, Adm 1/1903 (William Hamilton) enclosure with letter 25 January 1776.
55  TNA, Adm 1/579, report by Rear-Admiral Pringle, February–March 1795.
56  TNA, Adm 36/11328, muster of Thetis tender, 1793–94.
57  TNA, Adm 1/2396 (Peter Rothe), 4 February 1793.
58  TNA, Adm 1/2141 (McKenzie) M 36, 37.
59  TNA, HO 42/24/550.
60  *Newcastle Courant*, 23 February 1793.
61  TNA, HO 42/35/165; *Newcastle Courant*, 23 March 1793.
62  TNA, HO 28/9/61–65; *Newcastle Chronicle*, 2 February 1793.
63  *Newcastle Courant*, 30 March 1793.
64  TNA, HO 42/25/164–5.
65  Lloyd, *The British Seaman*, appendix II, pp. 265–7.
66  See Elizabeth Gaskell, *Sylvia's Lovers*, ed. A.W. Ward (London, 1906), xxiv–xxvi.
67  TNA, Adm 1/3690, 4 February 1804, enclosure from Captain Richard Poulden.
68  TNA, Adm 1/508 (Phillips) 27 August 1804 and enclosures.
69  TNA, Adm 1/1509 (Brenton) 3 February, 6 June, 10 October, 14, 28 November 1793.
70  TNA, Adm 1/1802 (Robert Fanshaw), 9 April, 23 May, 3, 7 June 1803.
71  TNA, Adm 1/1802 (Fanshawe) April–June 1803.
72  TNA, Adm 1/2489 (Saumarez) 30 January 1793; HO 28/29/169–95.
73  TNA, HO 28/29/194–5.

*Chapter 4: Spotlight on Two Ports: Bristol and Liverpool*

1  Jonathan Press, *The Merchant Seamen of Bristol, 1747–1789* (Bristol, 1976), p. 1; Walter Minchinton, 'The Port of Bristol in the Eighteenth Century', in Patrick McGrath (ed.), *Bristol in the Eighteenth Century* (Newton Abbot, 1972), pp. 129–31.
2  M.J. Power, 'The Growth of Liverpool', in John Belchem (ed.), *Popular Politics, Riot and Labour: Essays in Liverpool History 1790–1940* (Liverpool, 1992), pp. 21–3.
3  Stephen Behrendt, 'The Annual Volume and Regional Distribution of the British Slave Trade 1780–1807', *Journal of African History*, 38 (1997), table 1, 189. See also David Richardson, 'The Eighteenth-century British Slave Trade: Estimates of its Volume and Coastal Distribution in Africa', *Research in Economic History*, 12 (1989), pp. 151–95.
4  Richard Brooke, *Liverpool as it Was during the Last Quarter of the Eighteenth Century, 1775 to 1800* (Liverpool, 1853), p. 505.
5  Power, 'Growth of Liverpool', p. 28; Brooke, *Liverpool as it Was*, p. 504. The estimates of seamen in Liverpudlian commerce may well be conservative. Gordon Jackson suggests

that over 6000 were working in the foreign trades alone by 1780. See Gordon Jackson, 'Ports 1700–1840', in Peter Clark (ed.), *The Cambridge Urban History of Britain*, 3 vols (Cambridge, 2000), vol. 2, p. 727.

6  TNA, Adm 1/2284 (John Peddie) 12 January, 12 November 1740. See also *Newcastle Courant*, 17 November 1740.
7  TNA, Adm 1/1440 (Amherst) December 1745, cited in Hutchinson, *Press Gang*, p. 196; TNA, HCA 15/48, cited by Davis, *Rise of the Shipping Industry*, p. 322.
8  TNA, Adm 1/3675/45–6, 74.
9  TNA, Adm 1/3675/45–6, 67–74, 88–90, 183.
10  TNA, Adm 1/3675/236–40.
11  See *English Reports* (168), pp. 77 et seq.; *Sussex Weekly Advertiser*, 2 December 1776.
12  TNA, Adm 1/3677/104.
13  TNA, Adm 1/1833 (Samuel Graves) April–May 1756; Adm 1/3677/149; Adm 1/2678/383.
14  TNA, Adm 1/1834 (Thomas Gordon), 27 January 1759.
15  TNA, Adm 1/1834 (Thomas Gordon) 1 February 1759.
16  TNA, Adm 1/1834 (Thos Gordon), c. 6 April 1759.
17  TNA, Adm 1/1834 (Thos Gordon) 10 May 1759.
18  TNA, Adm 1/1834 (Thos Gordon) 21 May 1759. This affray made the news: *London Evening Post*, 12–15 May 1759; *Felix Farley's Bristol Journal*, 12, 26 May 1759; *Bath Journal*, 14, 21 May 1759. For Hammick, see Adm 1/1834 (Thos Gordon) 1 May 1759.
19  TNA, Adm 1/1834 (Thos Gordon), 17 June 1759.
20  TNA, Adm 1/1834 (Thos Gordon) 29 August 1759.
21  TNA, Adm 1/1835 (Thos Gordon) 7 January 1760.
22  Wm L. Clements Lib., Shelburne Ms, 139, no. 64.
23  TNA, Adm 1/1786 (John Fortescue) 28 January 1759.
24  TNA, Adm 1/1786 (John Fortescue) 20 April 1759.
25  TNA, Adm 1/1786 (John Fortescue) 18 May 1759.
26  Spavens, *Narrative*, p. 22.
27  Ibid., p. 22; *Williamson's Liverpool Advertiser*, 3 August 1759; Gomer Williams, *History of the Liverpool Privateers* (London, 1897, reprint 1966), p. 159.
28  TNA, Adm 1/1786 (John Fortescue) early August 1759.
29  TNA, Adm 1/1786 (John Fortescue) 17 August 1759.
30  TNA, Adm 1/1787 (John Fortescue) 6 September 1761. See the accompanying list.
31  TNA, Adm 1/1787 (John Fortescue) 6 September 1761.
32  TNA, Adm 1/1787 (John Fortescue) 12 September 1761.
33  TNA, Adm 1/1787 (John Fortescue) 12 December 1761.
34  TNA, Adm 1/1787 (John Fortescue) 19 February 1762.
35  TNA, Adm 1/1787 (John Fortescue) 20 April 1762.
36  TNA, Adm 1/1787 (John Fortescue) 5 March 1762.
37  TNA, Adm 1/1787 (John Fortescue) 27 December 1761.
38  TNA, Adm 1/1788 (John Fortescue) 2 May, 5 August 1762.
39  Benjamin Silliman, *A Journal of the Travels in England, Holland and Scotland*, 3 vols (Boston, 1820), vol. 1, p. 70.
40  TNA, Adm 1/1788 (John Fortescue) 2 May 1762.

41 Gomer Williams, *Liverpool Privateers*, pp. 157–8.
42 TNA, Adm 1/1788 (John Fortescue) 12 September 1762.
43 TNA, Adm 1/1788 (John Fortescue) 2 May 1762. The actual number of seamen registered at the port in the 1780s was 6610, so clearly Fortescue is talking of the turnover of seamen. For the figures see Gordon Jackson, 'Ports 1700–1840', p. 727.
44 TNA, Adm 1/1788 (Fortescue) 18 April 1762.
45 For these figures, see Lloyd, *British Seaman*, appendix II, pp. 265–7. They are derived from the National Maritime Museum, Adm/BP/1, 10 April 1779, Navy Office.
46 TNA, Adm 1/2672 and 2673. The Liverpool figures seem accurate. The running accounts in the letters of Captain James Worth reveal from mid-December 1778 to mid-February 1780 a return of 775 men, of whom 639 or 82 per cent were impressed.
47 *Annual Register*, 23 (1776), p. 44.
48 *Hampshire Chronicle*, 11 September 1775.
49 For a detailed account of this riot, see Brooke, *Liverpool as it Was*, pp. 326–47.
50 *Hampshire Chronicle*, 11 September 1775.
51 TNA, HO 55/8/1.
52 On the anti-war contingent in Liverpool, see Bradley, *Religion, Revolution and English Radicalism*, pp. 275–89, 327–8.
53 *General Evening Post*, 11–13 March 1777. On the press room, provided rent free by the corporation, see TNA, Adm 1/2673 (James Worth) 6 November 1778.
54 TNA, Adm 1/2672 (Worth) 15 April, 7 July 1777.
55 TNA, Adm 1/2672 (Worth) 15 April 1777.
56 TNA, Adm 3/84, entry 13 February 1778, asking for an enquiry into the frequent desertions of volunteers from the tenders in Liverpool.
57 On the latter, see TNA, Adm 1/2675 (Worth) 30 January 1780.
58 TNA, Adm 1/2675 (Worth) 20 Sept 1780.
59 On the Union tender, for example, eleven of the sixteen crew complement deserted within the first month of service in 1777, and a further three deserted within six months. Five seamen were also discharged in the first nine months as unserviceable. In other words, the crew of this tender, stationed in the Mersey, was highly unstable. Six of the press gang under Lieutenant Charles Colvill were also discharged within three months of duty. See TNA, Adm 36/9358.
60 J. A. Picton, *Memorials of Liverpool* (London, 1875), p. 213.
61 Booth, *Liverpool as it Was*, p. 465. For the letters of marque, TNA, HCA 26/33–34. For the slave traders, see David Eltis, David Richardson *et al.*, *The Trans-Atlantic Slave Trade: A Database on CD-ROM* (Cambridge, 1999).
62 Rawlinson is not listed in the Transatlantic Slave Database as investing in slaves in the 1770s, although he was in business with one of the most prominent slavers, John Chorley.
63 TNA, Adm 1/2673 (Worth) 8 July 1778.
64 TNA, Adm 1/2673 (Worth) 19, 26 July 1778.
65 TNA, Adm 1/2673 (Worth) 19 July 1778.
66 TNA, Adm 1/2673 (Worth) 26 August 1778.
67 TNA, Adm 1/2673 (Worth) 6 November 1778.
68 *London Evening Post*, 3–6 July 1779; *Shrewsbury Chronicle*, 27 July 1779.

69  TNA, Adm 7/300 nos. 19, 189.
70  TNA, Adm 1/1786 (John Fortescue) 20 August 1759; Adm 1/1788 (John Fortescue) 2 May, 5 August 1762.
71  TNA, Adm 1/2673 (Worth) 27 March, 20 April 1778.
72  Wm L. Clements Lib., Shelburne Ms. 139, no 62. Liverpool delivered 447, London 1505. Bristol only delivered 127.
73  Picton, *Liverpool*, pp. 240–1.
74  TNA, Adm 1/1618 (Smith Child) 29 April, 29 May 1793.
75  TNA, Adm 1/579, inspection of the ports by Rear-Admiral Pringle, February–March 1795.
76  TNA, HO 42/27/499–503.
77  TNA, HO 42/27/504
78  TNA, HO 42/27/499–500.
79  TNA, Adm 1/1618 (Smith Child) 27 October 1793; HO 42/47/499–502; *Morning Chronicle*, 2 November 1793; *E Johnson's British Gazette and Sunday Monitor*, 3 November 1793; *London Packet or New Lloyd's Evening Post*, 1–4 November 1793; *York Courant*, 28 October 1793.
80  TNA, HO 42/27/501
81  TNA, Adm 1/1618 (Smith Child) 16 November 1793.
82  TNA, Adm 1/579, Pringle's inspection of select ports, February–March 1795.
83  Gomer Williams, *Privateers*, p. 194; *Ipswich Journal*, 25 January 1777.
84  TNA, Adm 1/1788 (Fortescue) 19 February 1762.
85  TNA, Adm 1/581/86–9.
86  Benjamin Silliman, *Journal*, pp. 71–2.
87  PRO Northern Ireland, T 3541/5/3 ff. 140–1. I owe this reference to David A. Wilson of the University of Toronto.
88  TNA, Adm 1/2220 (John N.P. Nott), 3 November 1770; Adm 1/3679/342–4, 306–7.
89  TNA, Adm 1/2220 (Nott) 22 December 1770.
90  On the Kingswood colliers, see Robert Malcolmson, '"A Set of Ungovernable People": The Kingswood Colliers in the Eighteenth Century', in John Brewer and John Styles (eds), *An Ungovernable People: The English and their Law in the Seventeenth and Eighteenth Centuries* (London, 1980), pp. 85–127.
91  TNA, Adm 1/1834 (Gordon) 17 June 1759.
92  TNA, Adm 1/1905 (Hamilton) 12 July 1779.
93  TNA, Adm 1/1905 (Hamilton) 18 Nov 1779
94  TNA, Adm 1/1905 (Hamilton) 12 July 1779.
95  TNA, Adm 1/1906 (Hamilton) 12 May 1781.
96  TNA, HO 42/71/96–7.
97  TNA, Adm 1/1910 (Thomas Hawker) 28 April 1793; Adm 1/ 1912 (Hawker) 2 March 1795.
98  TNA, Adm 1/581/117–127.
99  TNA, Adm 1/581/117–27.
100 TNA, Adm 3/85, letter of Capt. Hamilton, 17 July 1778; Adm 1/1906 (Hamilton) 12 May 1781; *Bonner and Middleton's Bristol Journal*, 6 June 1778; *Bristol Gazette*, 4 June 1778; Marshall, *Bristol and the American War of Independence*, p. 15.

101 TNA, Adm 1/1534, B291a, October 1805; James Dugan, *The Great Mutiny* (New York, 1965), p. 59; *London Evening Post*, 5–7 November 1776; *Bonner and Middleton's Bristol Journal*, 14 May 1803.
102 TNA, Adm 1/1903 (Hamilton), 25 April 1777. See also Adm 1/1905 (Hamilton), 25 June 1779.
103 James E. Bradley, *Popular Politics and the American Revolution in England* (Macon, GA, 1986), pp. 22–3, 65. For the continuation of conflict over America, see Marshall, *Bristol and the American War of Independence*, pp. 17–23.
104 John Latimer, *The Annals of Bristol in the Eighteenth Century* (Bristol, 1893; reprint Bath, 1970), p. 440.
105 See Lloyd, *British Seaman*, appendix II; see also *Ipswich Journal*, 3 July 1779, where it would seem that Bristol moved quickly to impress, for the early returns suggest that it did better than Liverpool, and even temporarily surpassed London.
106 TNA, Adm 1/1905 (Hamilton) 25 June 1779.
107 *Bath Journal*, 19 July 1779; *London Evening Post*, 17–20 July 1779; Marshall, *Bristol and American Independence*, pp. 15–16.
108 *Annual Register* 23 (1780), 223.
109 TNA, Adm 1/1906 (Hamilton) 5 February, 21 December 1780; see also Latimer, *Annals of Bristol*, p. 440.
110 *Bath Journal*, 15 February 1779; *Morning Chronicle*, 16 February 1779; *Ipswich Journal*, 20 February 1779; TNA, Adm 1/1905 (Hamilton) 12 February 1779; Marshall, *Bristol*, p. 15; *Aris's Birmingham Gazette*, 2 November 1778; Adm 1/1903 (Hamilton) 12 July 1777.
111 TNA, Adm 1/2326 Captain Prowse to Sir Evan Nepean, 28 March 1803. See also *Bristol Gazette*, 31 March 1803; *Bonner and Middleton's Bristol Journal*, 2 April 1803; *The Times*, 30 March 1803; *Sussex Weekly Advertiser*, 4 April 1803; *Reading Mercury*, 4 April 1803.
112 TNA, Adm 1/581/117–27. For protests about the impressment of coastal traffic, see Adm 1/1834 (Gordon) 2 July 1759, Adm 1/1910 (Hawker) 28 April 1793, Adm 1/1534 (George Barker), B 277, 302.
113 TNA, Adm 1/1537 (Barker) 24 April, 9 May 1806, cited in Hutchinson, *Press Gang*, pp. 94, 162.
114 TNA, Adm 1/1903 (Wm Hamilton) 25 April 1777, 1/1905, 25 June 1779.
115 *British Press or Morning London Advertiser*, 18 May 1803; *Bonner and Middleton's Bristol Journal*, 14 May 1803.
116 In the early phases of the American war it reached 41 per cent, but this seems exceptional. See TNA, Adm 1/1903 (Hamilton), January 1777. For Newcastle figures, November 1776–May 1778, see TNA, Adm 1/1498 (John Bover), 15 May 1778.
117 TNA, Adm 1/1906 (Hamilton) 27 August 1781.

*Chapter 5: Manning the Navy in the Mid-century Atlantic*

1 TNA, Adm 1/2007 (Knowles), f. 150.
2 TNA, Adm 1/2100 (Wm Montagu) 14 August 1745.
3 TNA, Adm 1/2100 (Wm Montagu) 14 August 1745.

## NOTES TO PAGES 82–85

4   TNA, Adm 1/3817, letter from William Shirley, 1 June 1745.
5   *Authentic papers concerning a late remarkable transaction* (London, 1746).
6   TNA, Adm 1/2100 (Wm Montagu), 14 August 1745.
7   TNA, Adm 1/2100 (Wm Montagu), 26 November 1745.
8   TNA, Adm 36/2008. The muster book of the *Mercury* has not survived for 1744. This number is derived from the muster of September 1745, when the *Mercury* had returned from the Caribbean.
9   TNA, Adm 1/2652 (John Williams) 19 January 1740. There were at least 55 anti-impressment affrays reported by recruiting officers from the inception of the war to October 1744.
10  [Edward Vernon], *Original Letters to an Honest Sailor* (London, 1746), p. 4.
11  Cyril Hartmann, *The Angry Admiral* (London, 1953), pp. 124–5. These are the figures offered for the 6th regiment from Cork under Lt. Col. Haldane. Hughes thinks the overall figure may have reached nearly 90 per cent. See also John Robert McNeill, *The Atlantic Empires of France and Spain* (Chapel Hill and London, 1985), pp. 102–3.
12  Duncan Crewe, *Yellow Jack and the Worm. British Naval Administration in the West Indies, 1739–48* (Liverpool, 1993), pp. 73–4, 78, tables 5–6.
13  Smollett, *Roderick Random*, chs 33 and 34.
14  For requests for supernumeraries in 1739, see TNA, Adm 1/232/172–3. For a similar request in 1756, see TNA, Adm 1/234/590–1.
15  Crewe, *Yellow Jack*, p. 123. Richard Pares, 'The Manning of the Navy in the West Indies, 1702–63', *Transactions of the Royal Historical Society*, 4th series, 20 (1937), p. 42. For examples of impressment from the logbooks, see TNA, Adm 51/691, part V, entries for 24 and 27 March 1741 on HMS *Princess Louisa*, and TNA, Adm 51/232 part II, entries for 29 February, 31 August, 5 September 1744, 1 January 1745 on HMS *Deal Castle*.
16  TNA, Adm 1/233/5/30.
17  Gareth Rees, 'Copper Sheathing: An Example of Technological Diffusion in the English Merchant Fleet', *Journal of Transport History*, 2 (1972), 85–94.
18  Crewe, *Yellow Jack*, pp. 73–4, 83, tables 5 and 8. See also TNA, Adm 36/1730, the muster book of HMS *Lenox*, which registered a 21.8 per cent desertion rate in 1744–48, far higher than that recorded by Crewe for the period January–December 1747. For home desertions, see Rodger, *Wooden World*, p. 144.
19  TNA, Adm 1/2007 (Knowles) 16 August 1744. See also TNA, Adm 1/5285, the trial of Thomas Kavanagh for desertion on board HMS *Suffolk*.
20  TNA, Adm 1/233/4/159.
21  Pares, 'Manning', p. 40.
22  TNA, Adm 1/232, 5 September 1742, cited in Pares, 'Manning', p. 39.
23  TNA, CO 137/57/163–5.
24  TNA, CO 137/57/1/198, 210, 249–69; *The tryal of Sir Chaloner Ogle, Knt., Read Admiral of the Blue, before the chief justice of Jamaica, for an assault on the person of his Excellency, Mr Trelawney, the governor* (London, 1743).
25  6 Anne, c. 37 cl. 9 exempted mariners 'who shall serve on board or be retained to serve on board any privateer'.
26  TNA, Adm 1/2006 (Knowles), Memorial of Charles Knowles; Adm 1/2654 (Peter Warren) 24 May 1744; Crewe, *Yellow Jack*, p. 135; Pares, 'Manning', pp. 48–9.

27 Pares, 'Manning', pp. 48–9; TNA, Adm 1/2006 (Knowles), Memorial of Charles Knowles.
28 TNA, Adm 1/2007 (Knowles) 15 October 1744.
29 TNA, Adm 1/1829 (Samuel Goddard) 1 October, 15 November 1743.
30 Douglas Edward Leach, *Roots of Conflict: British Armed Forces and Colonial Americans, 1677–1763* (Chapel Hill and London, 1986), pp. 146–48.
31 6 Anne, c. 37; on the origins of the act, see Dora Mae Clark, 'The Impressment of Seamen in the American Colonies', in *Essays in Colonial History Presented in Charles McLean Andrews by his Students* (New Haven, 1931), pp. 205–10.
32 Clark, 'Impressment of Seamen', pp. 208–9.
33 Leach, *Roots of Conflict*, pp. 146, 148–9.
34 Ibid., pp. 150–51.
35 Ibid., pp. 152–3.
36 Cited in John Lax and William Pencak, 'The Knowles Riot and the Crisis of the 1740s in Massachusetts', *Perspectives in American History*, 10 (1976), p. 180.
37 19 Geo. II, c. 30. The act only applied to the West Indies; Clark, 'Impressment of Seamen', pp. 208–9.
38 Clark, 'Impressment of Seamen', p. 214.
39 Lax and Pencak, 'The Knowles Riot', p. 183.
40 TNA, Adm 1/3818/285–94.
41 Lax and Pencak, 'The Knowles Riot', pp. 186–7; TNA, Adm 1/3818/285–94.
42 Ibid., 193–201.
43 Hiller B. Zobel, *The Boston Massacre* (New York, 1970), pp. 124–31.
44 Ibid., pp. 113–14. Jesse Lemisch, *Jack Tar vs. John Bull: The Role of New York's Seamen in Precipitating the Revolution* (London and New York, 1997), p. 34.
45 Lemisch, *Jack Tar vs. John Bull*, pp. 13–14; Zobel, *Boston Massacre*, pp. 115–19.
46 Leach, *Roots of Conflict*, pp. 156–7.
47 Lax and Pencak, 'The Knowles Riot', pp. 204–5.
48 Alan Rogers, *Empire and Liberty: American Resistance to British Authority, 1755–1763* (Berkeley and Los Angeles, 1974), pp. 146–48.
49 TNA, Adm 1/242/540–1.
50 TNA, Adm 1/242/29–30; for sweeping the streets of stragglers, see Pares, 'Manning', p. 56.
51 TNA, Adm 1/233/4/168–9.
52 W. Jeffrey Bolster, *Black Jacks* (Cambridge, MA, 1997), pp. 18, 20.
53 TNA, Adm 1/3817, Trelawny to Corbet, 21 December 1743.
54 Charles Roberts, *Observations on the Windward Passage, or the Passage between Jamaica and St. Domingo* (London, 1795), pp. 4–5.
55 TNA, CO 137/57/2/274. For contemporary recognitions of good pilots in the Bahamas, see Adm 1/237/42. In 1762, the second best was reckoned to be 'Johnno, a Free Negro Man'.
56 Rodger, *Wooden World*, p. 272; Andrew Jackson O'Shaughnessy, *An Empire Divided: The American Revolution and the British Caribbean* (Philadelphia, 2000), p. 180; Simon Schama, *Rough Crossings: Britain, the Slaves and the American Revolution* (New York, 2005), p. 93.
57 Clarence J. Munford, *The Black Ordeal of Slavery and Slave Trading in the French West Indies 1625–1715*, 3 vols (Lewiston, 1991), vol. 3, p. 753.

58  Richard Pares, *War and Trade in the West Indies, 1739–1763* (Oxford, 1936), p. 254.
59  Philip D. Morgan, *Slave Counterpoint* (Chapel Hill and London, 1998), p. 238. In 1784, concerned that an increasing number of slaves worked the rivers and tidewater, the Virginia legislature enacted that only a third of a crew should consist of slaves (p. 240). For the fear that runaway slaves would seek berths in wartime, see Billy G. Smith and Richard Wojtowicz (eds), *Blacks Who Stole Themselves* (Philadelphia, 1989), nos. 7, 18, 19, 21, 27, 32, 41, 51.
60  TNA, CO 137/57/2/139v. For further evidence of blacks on privateers, see TNA, Adm 1/232/270.
61  Elsa V. Goveia, *Slave Society in the British Leeward Islands at the End of the Eighteenth Century* (Westport, CT, 1965), p. 256.
62  We know this because some later applied for compensation for loss of property in London. See Stephen Braidwood, *Black Poor and White Philanthropists 1789–1791* (Liverpool, 1994), pp. 24, 28–9.
63  Rodger, *Wooden World*, pp. 159–60.
64  TNA, Adm 1/309/383, 21 November 1775; Adm 1/306, 20 July 1757.
65  *Letter-Books and Order-Book of George, Lord Rodney, Admiral of the White Squadron 1780–1782*, 2 vols (New York, New York Historical Society, 1932), vol. 2, pp. 108–9, 597.
66  TNA, Adm 1/2007 (Knowles) 12 June 1744.
67  TNA, Adm 1/231/253, 7 October 1740. On the price of adult male slaves, see David Richardson, 'The Slave Trade, Sugar, and British Economic Growth, 1748–1776', in Stanley Engerman (ed.), *British Capitalism and Caribbean Slavery* (Cambridge, 1987), p. 108.
68  On privateers taking slaves, see Howard M. Chapin, *Privateering in King George's War 1739–1748* (Providence, RI, 1928), pp. 125, 127, 132–3, 147, 154, 200, 216, 229, 238. See also TNA, Adm 1/3818/311–13, which cites evidence of Bahamian privateers taking slaves, especially off the coast of Hispaniola.
69  Peter Linebaugh and Marcus Rediker, *The Many-Headed Hydra* (Boston, MA, 2000), p. 311; on the ship as a micro-system of hybridity, see Paul Gilroy, *The Black Atlantic: Modernity and Double Consciousness* (Cambridge, MA, 1993), p. 12.
70  The figure is derived from Normal Leys, Kenya (2nd edn, London, 1925) p. 367 and was first noted, in a very qualified manner, by James Walvin, *Black and White: The Negro and English Society 1555–1945* (London, 1973), pp. 51–2. The qualifications were subsequently ignored. See Kathleen Wilson, *The Island Race. Englishness, Empire and Gender in the Eighteenth Century* (London and New York, 2003), p. 44; Gilroy, *Black Atlantic*, p. 13.
71  See TNA, Adm 36/15474, HMS *Asias* (1794) and Adm 36/14701, HMS *Vengeance* (1802); see also Tom Malcomson, 'Order and Disorder in the Royal Navy during the War of 1812', PhD Thesis, York University, Toronto, 2007, table 10. For the Leeward Islands, see Byrn, *Crime and Punishment*, p. 76.
72  Michael Lewis, *A Social History of the Navy 1793–1815* (London, 1960), p. 129; Dudley Pope, *Life in Nelson's Navy* (Annapolis, Maryland, 1981), p. 109.
73  Ira Dye, 'Physical and Social Profiles of Early American Seafarers, 1812–1815', in Colin Howell and Richard Twomey (eds), *Jack Tar in History*, p. 225.

74 Olaudah Equiano, *The Interesting Narrative and Other Writings*, ed. Vincent Carretta (London and New York, 1995), pp. 79–94.
75 TNA, Adm 36/2775, muster book for HMS *Plymouth*, 1747.
76 TNA, Adm 36/466 and Adm 36/1730.
77 On the possibility of blacks being enslaved for vagrancy in Antigua, see J. Luffman, *A Brief Account of the Island of Antigua* (London, 1789), pp. 130–1.
78 Pares, 'Manning', pp. 32–33n.
79 TNA, Adm 1/2006, 21 September 1740.
80 Mavis Campbell, *The Maroons of Jamaica 1655–1796* (Granby, MA, 1988), p. 151.
81 TNA, Adm 51/232, part II, entry for 17 January 1744.
82 TNA, Adm 1/234/96; PRO, Adm 1/2041 (Lisle) 23 November 1743.
83 *An essay concerning slavery, and the danger Jamaica is expos'd to from too great number of slaves* (London, 1746).
84 For those in Jamaica, TNA, Adm 1/233/4/166–7. The fine was £.50 for carrying off sailors or soldiers by an act in 1745. An earlier act, in 1725, had levied fines of £.200, and £100 for hiding deserters or runaway servants.
85 TNA, Adm 1/233/5/233–4, 240–1.
86 TNA, Adm 1/233/5/256–7.
87 Jane Landers, *Black Society in Spanish Florida* (Urbana and Chicago, 1999), pp. 41–5.
88 For an example of this, see the entry for 2 November 1746 in the muster book of HMS *Lenox*, TNA, Adm 36/1730. For an instance of a privateer handing over recalcitrant seamen to a man of war, see the case of the *Stephen and Elizabeth* in Chapin, *Privateering*, p. 132.
89 TNA, Adm 1/2007/141–8.
90 TNA, Adm 1/5283, court martial of Lieutenant Joseph Willis, 14 March 1743; Adm 1/5284/507–48.
91 TNA, Adm 1/5285, court martial of Edward Stow, quartermaster of HMS *Eltham*, 7 November 1745.
92 TNA, Adm 1/5285, court martial of Humphrey Lion and William Hillman of HMS *Dorsetshire*, 9 December 1745.
93 Rodger, *Wooden World*, pp. 128–9; Carl E. Swanson, *Predators and Prizes* (Columbia, SC, 1991), pp. 216–19.
94 Swanson, *Predators*, p. 219.
95 TNA, Adm 1/3818/311–313A. For Bermudan privateering raids on the coast of Hispaniola in search of slaves, see Chapin, *Privateering*, p. 125.
96 Swanson, *Predators*, p. 118.
97 Pares, 'Manning', p. 46.
98 Edward Long, *The History of Jamaica*, 3 vols (London, 1774), vol. 1, p. 331.
99 TNA, CO 137/57/1/179.
100 Nathaniel Uring, *A History of the Voyages and Travels of Capt. Nathaniel Uring* (London, 1726), p. 355.
101 TNA, Adm 36/2775, entries for December 1743–February 1744.
102 TNA, CO 137/57/2/236.
103 TNA, CO 137/57/2/275v.
104 TNA, Adm 1/306 (Henry Osborn), 4 August, 15 December, 1748.

105 TNA, Adm 1/3818/424–5.
106 TNA, CO 152/45/136–8. On Norman's as a rendezvous for contraband goods, see TNA, Adm 1/578, letter of Thomas Frankland, 28 April 1757.
107 TNA, Adm 1/2041 (Lisle) 24 October 1743. Among the trials was that of the crew of the *Old Noll* privateer, which had mutinied off Baltimore in Ireland in October 1747. Ten received 300 lashes each; eight were hanged. *London Evening Post*, 3–6 September 1748.
108 *General Evening Post*, 3–5 November 1748. See also Nicholas Rogers, 'Confronting the Crime Wave: The Debate over Social Reform and Regulation, 1749–1753', in Lee Davison et. al. (eds), *Stilling the Grumbling Hive. The Response in Social and Economic Problems in England, 1689–1750* (New York, 1992), pp. 77–98.
109 John Brown, *An Estimate of the Manners and Principles of the Times* (London, 5th edn, 1757), pp. 88–9.
110 Linebaugh and Rediker, *The Many-Headed Hydra*.
111 TNA, Adm 1/2007/150, 162.
112 TNA, SP 36/52/137–9; Lax and Pencak, 'The Knowles Riot', p. 165, although Lax and Pencak make the further point that the riot 'was indeed actively supported by all of Boston'.
113 Thomas Thistlewood, *In Miserable Slavery. Thomas Thistlewood in Jamaica 1750–1786*, ed. Douglas Hall (London, 1989), pp. 97–104; TNA, CO 137/71/228, 236–7.
114 Daniel Horsmanden, *The New York Conspiracy of 1741*, ed. Thomas J. Davis (Boston, 1971), pp. 117, 151, 159, 177–87, 260–61.
115 Thomas J. Davis, *A Rumor of Revolt: The 'Great Negro Plot' in Colonial New York* (New York, 1985), pp. 5–6, 60, 131–7; Horsmanden, *New York Conspiracy*, pp. 13–16, 48, 73, 446–8, 450.
116 Daniel Defoe, *A General History of the Pyrates*, ed. Manuel Schonborn (London, 1972), pp. 222–8, 280, 513, 517, 528, 533–38, 688; TNA, CO 137/57/2/157.
117 Dorothy Porter (ed.), *Early Negro Writing 1760–1837* (Boston, 1971), p. 524: Vincent Carretta (ed.), *Unchained Voices* (Lexington, Kentucky, 1996), p. 22.
118 Linebaugh and Rediker, *Many-Headed Hydra*; see also 'The Many-Headed Hydra: Sailors, Slaves and the Atlantic Working Class in the Eighteenth Century', *Journal of Historical Sociology*, 3 (Sept. 1990), pp. 225–51.
119 Bernard Bailyn, *The Peopling of North America* (New York, 1986), pp. 112–21.
120 Philip D. Morgan, 'Encounters between British and "Indigenous" Peoples, *c*.1500–*c*.1800', in Martin Daunton and Rick Halpern (eds), *Empire and Others: British Encounters with Indigenous Peoples, 1600–1850* (London, 1999), p. 62. See also Peter Way, 'The Cutting Edge of Culture: British Soldiers Encounter Native Americans in the French and Indian War', Ibid., pp. 123–48.
121 See *London Daily Post*, 17 March 1740

*Chapter 6: The Navy and the Nation 1793–1820*

1 Colley, *Britons*, p. 365.
2 For an example of toasting Lord Wellington as a hero of the Peninsula, see the account of a thanksgiving dinner at Liverpool, 17 December 1813, in the *Liverpool Mercury*,

24 December 1813. For a proposal to set up an equestrian statue of Wellington in Manchester, *Leeds Mercury*, 20 November 1813.

3  Harriet Arbuthnot, *The Journal of Mrs Arbuthnot 1820–1832*, ed. Francis Bamford and the Duke of Wellington, 2 vols (London 1950), vol. 1, p. 24.

4  Elizabeth Longford, *Wellington: Pillar of State* (London, 1972), pp. 66–7.

5  *Journal of Mrs Arbuthnot*, vol. 1, p. 36; Longford, *Wellington*, p. 68.

6  Allan Cunningham, *Life of David Wilkie*, 3 vols (London, 1843), vol. 2, p. 46.

7  Iorwerth Prothero, *Artisans and Politics in Early Nineteenth-Century London* (London, 1978), p. 148.

8  See accounts in the *Champion*, 16 July, 7 October 1820; *Cobbett's Weekly Register*, 5 August 1820.

9  *Life of Wilkie*, vol. 2, p. 69.

10  *Examiner*, May 1822, cited by Nicholas Tromans, *David Wilkie: Painter of Everyday Life* (London, 2002), pp. 89–90.

11  Peter Kemp, *The British Seaman. A Social History of the Lower Deck* (London, 1970), p. 91.

12  *A Garland of New Songs* (Newcastle, 1785?), p. 7.

13  TNA, Adm 1/1509 (Jahleel Brenton) 6 June 1793.

14  TNA, HO 42/24/550.

15  *Newcastle Courant*, 23 February 1793.

16  TNA, HO 42/24/538–9.

17  *Newcastle Courant*, 2 February 1793.

18  TNA, HO 42/22/447–8.

19  *Newcastle Courant*, 30 March 1793; see also 2 February 1793 for evidence of circulation.

20  Nicholas Rogers, 'Burning Tom Paine: Loyalism and Counter-Revolution in Britain, 1792–3', *Histoire sociale/Social History*, 32 (1999), pp. 166–7.

21  TNA, HO 42/24/613–4.

22  TNA, HO 42/22/387.

23  TNA, HO 42/23/2; 42/24/574, 613–4.

24  British Library, Add Ms. 16927 f.41; TNA, Adm 1/1509 (Jahleel Brenton) 13, 15 February 1793. For more on this frontier see Rogers, 'Burning Tom Paine', pp. 142–4. Not all seamen were illiterate, as is commonly assumed. On HMS *Garland* in 1797, for example, over 50 per cent of the 126 man crew could sign their names. See TNA, Adm 1/5125, petition of crew of HMS *Garland*.

25  TNA, HO 42/24/321–2.

26  Conrad Gill, *The Naval Mutinies of 1797* (Manchester, 1913), pp. 6–12.

27  Sir William L. Clowes, *The Royal Navy from the Earliest Times to the Present*, 7 vols (London, 1897–1903), vol. 4, p. 169.

28  For a brief summary of the mutinies, see N.A.M. Rodger, 'Mutiny or Subversion? Spithead and the Nore', in Thomas Bartlett *et al.* (eds), *1798: A Bicentenary Perspective* (Dublin, 2003), pp. 550–4.

29  Anthony G. Brown, 'The Nore Mutiny – Sedition or Ships' Biscuits? A Reappraisal', *Mariner's Mirror*, 92 (2006), p. 66.

30  Gill, *Naval Mutinies of 1797*, p. 300.

31  TNA, Adm 1/5125, petitions, 1793–7.

32 TNA, Adm 1/727, C 370, No. 4.
33 TNA, Adm 1/5345, court martial 9 April 1798 cited by Roger Wells, *Insurrection: The British Experience 1795–1803* (Gloucester, 1986), p. 83
34 TNA, Adm 1/5339, court martial against Guthry, Ashley and others, 20–23 June 1797, cited in Wells, *Insurrection*, p. 95.
35 Anthony Brown, 'The Nore Mutiny', p. 67.
36 Dugan, *The Great Mutiny*, p. 336.
37 TNA, PC 1/38/A122; Adm 1/727/C393; Adm 1/5340; cited in Wells, *Insurrection*, pp. 97–8.
38 TNA, Adm 1/5486/17/19.
39 *Sussex Weekly Advertiser*, 19 June 1797.
40 *Morning Chronicle*, 22 April 1797.
41 See, for example, *Manchester Mercury*, 9 October, 6 November 1798.
42 *Northampton Mercury*, 28 October 1797; *Shrewsbury Chronicle*, 19 October 1798.
43 *Oracle*, 14 October 1797, cited in Timothy Jenks, *Naval Engagements: Patriotism, Cultural Politics, and the Royal Navy, 1793–1815* (Oxford, 2006), p. 113.
44 *Worcester Herald*, 21 October 1797.
45 *True Briton*, 20 December 1797; *Morning Chronicle*, 17 October 1797.
46 *Gentleman's Magazine*, 94 (1803), p. 804, best exemplified at Aboukir Bay.
47 Gill, *Naval Mutinies of 1797*, pp. 281–2.
48 TNA, Adm 1/727 C370, and Adm 1/5125, cited in Hutchinson, *Press Gang*, p. 17; Gill, *Naval Mutinies of 1797*, pp. 281–4. Cf. N.A.M. Rodger, 'Mutiny or Subversion? Spithead and the Nore', in *1798*, p. 553 and his *Command of the Ocean*, p. 447, where Rodger asserts that impressment was not a grievance of the mutineers.
49 TNA, Adm 1/727 C370.
50 *Cobbett's Political Register*, 20–27 August 1803, col. 272.
51 TNA, Adm 1/2406, R131.
52 TNA, Adm 1/1634 C292.
53 TNA, Adm 1/581/19.
54 TNA, Adm 1/1633, C2.
55 TNA, Adm 1/581/ 53, 71.
56 A.K. Hamilton Jenkin, *Cornwall and its People* (Newton Abbot, 1970; repr. 1988), pp. 93–7.
57 TNA, Adm 1/581/298.
58 TNA, Adm 1/581, ff. 83–4, 230, 265–71, 305. See also Hamilton Jenkin, *Cornwall*, pp. 24–9 and Alan G. Jamieson, 'Devon and Smuggling 1680–1850', in Michael Duffy *et al.* (eds), *The New Maritime History of Devon*, 2 vols (London, 1992), vol. 1, p. 248.
59 TNA, Adm 1/581/73–4.
60 TNA, Adm 1/581/117–27.
61 TNA, Adm 1/581/207–12.
62 *Cobbett's Weekly Register*, 26 July 1803, col. 135–9.
63 *Bonner and Middleton's Bristol Journal*, 24 September 1803.
64 Frank Klingberg and Sigurd Hustvedt (eds), *The Warning Drum* (Berkeley and LA, 1944), pp. 72, 106, 161.
65 Horatio Nelson, *The Dispatches and Letters of Vice-Admiral Lord Viscount Nelson*, ed. Sir Nicholas Harris Nicolas, 7 vols (London, 1845), vol. 4, p. 432.

66 TNA, Adm 1/1528 B219; HO 42/72/52–4.
67 B. Brownrigg, *Life and Letters of Sir John Moore* (Oxford, 1923), pp. 145–6, cited in Peter A. Lloyd, *The French Are Coming: The Invasion Scare of 1803–5* (Tunbridge Wells, 1991), pp. 107–8.
68 TNA, HO 42/71/137–8.
69 G.E. Mainwaring and Bonamy Dobree, *The Floating Republic* (London, 1955), p. 8.
70 The floggings on the *Victory* in the second half of 1804 averaged one per day; on HMS *Sandwich*, 1780–81, 26 flogging were reported in 18 months, roughly three every two months. See Douglas Hay and Nicholas Rogers, *Eighteenth-Century English Society: Shuttles and Swords* (Oxford, 1997), p. 150; TNA, Adm 51/840, parts 6 and 7, logbooks of HMS *Sandwich*, 1780–81.
71 'Starting' was an informal beating with a double-knotted rope. N.A.M. Rodger, 'The Naval World of Jack Aubrey', in A. E. Cunningham (ed.), *Patrick O'Brian: Critical Appreciations and a Bibliography* (Boston Spa, Wetherby, 1994), pp. 61–2.
72 Pay was 22s 6d per lunar month, 1653–1797, then 28s a month, then in 1806 32s a month, all net of fixed deductions.
73 National Maritime Museum, Milne to Navy agent in Bermuda, 26 April 1814, David Milne Letter Book, MLN/36/8; Rodger, *Command of the Ocean*, p. 500.
74 Rodger, *Command of the Ocean*, p. 522; on casualties, see Dudley Pope, *Life in Nelson's Navy* (Annapolis, MD, 1981), p. 263.
75 William Robinson, *Jack Nastyface, Memoirs of a Seaman* (1836; London, reprint, 1973), pp. 25–88.
76 Eden, *State of the Poor*, vol. 2, p. 167 and vol. 3, p. 837.
77 Colley, *Britons*, ch. 7.
78 *Sussex Weekly Advertiser*, 8 October 1798; *Manchester Mercury*, 9 October 1798; *Leicester Journal*, 8 October 1798.
79 *Sun*, 11 October 1798.
80 *Sussex Weekly Advertiser*, 8 October 1798.
81 Joshua White, *Memoirs of the Professional Life of the Right Honourable Horatio Lord Viscount Nelson* (London, 1806), pp. 337–9.
82 Nelson to Earl Spencer, 7 September 1798, in *Nelson's Letters*, ed. G. Rawson (London, 1971), pp. 200–01.
83 *Gentleman's Magazine*, 84 (1801), 207; 96 (1804), 972.
84 T.J. Howell, *A Complete Collection of State Trials*, 33 vols (London 1809–26), vol. 28, p. 346; Gerald Jordan and Nicholas Rogers, 'Admirals as Heroes: Patriotism and Liberty in Hanoverian England', *Journal of British Studies*, 28 (July 1989), p. 218.
85 Evelyn Berckman, *Nelson's Dear Lord* (London, 1962), p. 240.
86 Silliman, *A Journal of Travels*, vol. 1, p. 335.
87 *Gentleman's Magazine*, 85 (1799), 344. These were the words of his father in a published letter to the Reverend Brian Allot. Nelson's lowly origins were in fact exaggerated. His social background was not atypical for naval officers, although only 19 per cent from clerical families reached flag rank. See Michael Lewis, *Social History of the Navy*, ch. 1.
88 *Leeds Mercury*, 16 November 1805.
89 Cited in G. J. Marcus, *A Naval History of England: The Age of Nelson* (London, 1971), p. 139;

H.W. Richmond (ed.), *Private Papers of George, Second Earl Spencer, 1794–1801*, 4 vols (Pub. Navy Records Society, London, 1913–24), vol. 2, p. 473.

90  *Newcastle Courant*, 13 October 1798.
91  It is difficult to determine just how many families had a direct involvement in war, but one in five does not seem too high. Of roughly two million adult males aged 15–40 in 1815–16, some 350,000 (17.5 per cent) were demobilized at the end of the war, about one in six. This calculation does not allow for deaths, desertions or for the uncles, brothers, fathers and son who would have been involved. The size of the cohort is drawn from the 1821 census, *British Parliamentary Papers* (1822), vol. 15, p. 583. The figures on recruitment and demobilization are derived from Douglas Hay, 'War, Dearth and Theft in the Eighteenth Century', *Past and Present*, 95 (1982), 138–40.
92  E.W.H. Moorhouse, *Letters of the English Seamen* (London, 1910), p. 303.
93  John Nicol, *Life and Adventures*, pp. 188–9.
94  *The Times*, 8 January 1806, cited by Timothy Jenks, 'Contesting the Hero: The Funeral of Admiral Lord Nelson', *Journal of British Studies*, 39 (October 2000), 437.
95  *Star*, 9 December 1805.
96  For a close reading of the funeral see Jenks, 'Contesting the Hero', pp. 422–53, and his *Naval Engagements*, pp. 232–38.
97  Nicolas (ed.), *Dispatches of Nelson*, vol. 1, p. 98.
98  *Cobbett's Weekly Register*, 15 November 1805, col. 741.
99  On this issue, see William Windham's letter to Earl Spencer, 4 October 1798, in *Spencer Papers*, vol. 3, p. 7.
100  *Sun*, 29 July 1815; TNA, HO 42/145/105–7, 137–8, 152. In wartime foreigners could constitute 75 per cent of crews on British ships; in peacetime only 25 per cent.
101  TNA, HO 42/145/105.
102  TNA, HO 42/146/79–80, 151,192, 196–200; *The Times*, 21 October 1815.
103  *The Times*, 31 October 1815; TNA, HO 42/146/192.
104  Norman McCord, 'The Seaman's Strike of 1815 in North-East England', *Econ Historical Review*, second series, 21 (1968), pp. 127–43 for a discussion of the main issues of the strike. See also, Robert Colls, *The Pitmen of the Northern Coalfield* (Manchester, 1967), pp. 233–6.
105  TNA, HO 42/146/206–9, 246–50.
106  TNA, HO 42/146/109–110.
107  TNA, HO 42/146/208–9.
108  TNA, HO 42/146/207.
109  *The Times*, 19 October 1815.
110  TNA, HO 42/ 146/215
111  *Sun*, 5 October 1815; *The Times*, 19 October 1815.
112  TNA, HO 42/146/257–8
113  On these proposals, see *Naval Chronicle*, 35 (July–December 1815), pp. 473–5; 36 (January–June 1816), pp. 214–15. On the bill, see *The Times*, 17 November 1814.
114  TNA, HO 42/145/158, for the seamen's address to the Regent, August 1815.
115  *The Times*, 18 October 1815.
116  TNA, HO 42/146/ 217–18; *Naval Chronicle*, 35 (January–June 1816), pp. 115–23; *Sun*, 3 October 1815.

117 Normal McCord, 'Tyneside Discontents and Peterloo', *Northern History*, 2 (1969), 91–111; D.J. Rowe, 'The Decline of the Tyneside Keelmen in the Nineteenth Century', *Northern History*, 4 (1971), 111–31.
118 G.H. Haswell, *The Maister: A Century of Tyneside Life* (London, 1896), p. 132, cited in Barrow, *Trafalgar Geordies*, pp. 84–5.
119 Linda Colley, 'Whose Nation? Class and National Consciousness in Britain 1750–1830', *Northern History*, 4 (1971), pp. 111–31.
120 TNA, HO 42/190/127–8.

## Epilogue

1 Jackson, 'Ports 1700–1840', p. 719.
2 Lionel Charlton, *The History of Whitby, and of Whitby Abbey* (York, 1779), p. 361.
3 TNA, Adm 1/2660 (Edw Wheeler) 3 June 1755.
4 *Newcastle Chronicle*, 23 February 1771; TNA, Adm 1/2660 (Edw. Wheeler) 3 June 1755.
5 TNA, HO 28/9/71; Gaskell, *Sylvia's Lovers*, intro A.W. Ward, xxiii–xxiv.
6 TNA, Adm 1/579/86–9; *Newcastle Courant*, 9 March 1793.
7 Gaskell, *Sylvia's Lovers*, intro A.W. Ward, xxiv; TNA, HO 28/9/72v.
8 TNA, Adm 1/579 (Pringle) February–March 1795.
9 TNA, Adm 1/3090 (Richard Poulden), 4 February 1804; Adm 1/3689 21 June 1803, 7 July 1803; Adm 1/2326 Poulden to Nepean, 23 June 1803; *The Times*, 31 May, 21 June 1803.
10 TNA, Adm 1/1236, 24 March 1803.
11 TNA, Adm 1/2141, 23 October 1803.
12 TNA, Adm 1/3090 (Poulden) 4 February 1804; Adm 1/580 (Phillip), 24 April 1804.
13 TNA, Adm 1/581/86–9.
14 Thomas Perronet Thompson, 'Impressment and Flogging', *Westminster Review*, 20 (April 1834), pp. 489–94.
15 Elizabeth Gaskell, *Sylvia's Lovers*, ed. Nancy Henry (London, 1997), p. 36.
16 Ibid., pp. 8, 38; Butler, *An Essay on the Legality of Impressing Seamen*, p. 6.
17 Ibid., p. 37
18 Terry Eagleton, '*Sylvia's Lovers* and Legality', *Essays in Criticism*, 26 (1976), pp. 17–27, quote p. 19.
19 Gaskell, *Sylvia's Lovers*, pp. 28, 234.
20 TNA, Adm 1/1500 (Wm Bennett) 1780; Gaskell, *Sylvia's Lovers*, intro. A.W. Ward, xxiii–xxiv; *The Times*, 22 Oct 1803; Norman McCord, 'The Impress Service in North-East England in the Napoleonic War', *Mariner's Mirror*, 54 (1968), pp. 165–6.
21 Eagleton, '*Sylvia's Lovers*', p. 26.
22 Jenny Uglow, *Elizabeth Gaskell. A Habit of Stories* (London, 1993), pp. 509–10.
23 Gaskell, *Sylvia's Lovers*, p. 8.
24 *Elizabeth Gaskell, The Critical Heritage* ed. Angus Easson (London and New York, 1991), pp. 440, 447–8.
25 5 and 6 Will IV, c. 24, section 1; 16 and 17 Vict. c. 69, section 10; see J.S. Bromley, 'Away from Impressment: The Idea of a Royal Naval Reserve, 1696–1859', in A.C.Duke and

C.A. Tamse (eds), *Britain and the Netherlands, VI, War and Society* (The Hague, 1977), p. 175.

26   See account of the debate in *The Times*, 16 April 1835, and the protest from Greenock.

27   *The Red Republican*, 2 November 1850. 'The sovereign people will refuse to tolerate flogging, impressments, and the many other evils that afflict and degrade both sailors and soldiers.'

28   Thomas Hodgkin, 'Abolition of Impressment', *Edinburgh Review*, 41 (October 1824), pp. 154–81; J. R. McCulloch, *The Principles of Political Economy* (4th edn, Edinburgh, 1849), pp. 385–6.

29   Hodgkin, 'Abolition of Impressment', pp. 172–4. Hodgkin calculated over £300,000 pa for the impress service and the tenders and £400,000 for the marines.

30   Thomas Urquhart, *A letter to William Wilberforce ... on the subject of impressments* (London, 1816).

31   Julian Thompson, *The War at Sea 1914–1918* (London, 2005), p. 23.

32   Hodgkin, 'Abolition of Impressment', p. 165.

33   Army conscription overwhelmingly dominates the literature on national service, 1914–1918, but there are a few bits of information about naval conscription in R.J.Q. Adams and Philip P. Poirier, *The Conscription Controversy in Great Britain, 1900–1918* (London, 1987).

34   John Winton, *Hurrah for the Life of a Sailor* (London, 1977), pp. 28, 112.

35   J.S. Bromley, 'Away from Impressment', pp. 183–4.

36   Lewis, *Social History of the Navy*, p. 36, table II.

37   TNA, PRO 90/69, Holdernesse to Mitchell, 17 July 1757, cited by Jeremy Black, 'Naval Power and British Foreign Policy in the Age of Pitt the Elder', in Jeremy Black and Philip Woodfine (eds), *The British Navy and the Use of Naval Power in the Eighteenth Century* (Trowbridge, 1988), pp. 101–2.

38   Rogers, 'Liberty Road', pp. 117–18.

39   This is the figure cited by 'Marinero' in the *Public Advertiser*, 17 June 1777.

40   Rogers, 'Opposition to Impressment', pp. 70–1.

41   *Lloyd's Ev Post*, 26-28 Aug, 19 September, 31 October 1776; *Ipswich Jor.*, 9 November 1776. See also McCord, 'The Seaman's strike', pp. 127–43.

42   See, for example, TNA, Adm 1/3681/112.

43   William L. Clements Lib., Townshend papers, 297/3/2, 21, 23; BL, Add Ms, 32907, ff. 427–8, 32916, ff. 43, 33053, ff. 282–3; Cheshunt College Archives, Cambridge, F 1/25, 1161. I am indebted to Dr Jeff Chamberlain and Susan Foote for these last references.

44   Jacob Nagle, *The Nagle Journal: The Diary of the Life of Jacob Nagle, Sailor, from the Year 1775 to 1841*, ed. John C Dann (New York, 1988), pp. 182–3.

45   Ibid., p. 185.

46   Ibid., p. 90.

47   Samuel Bamford, *Early Days* (London, 1849), p. 246.

48   Ibid., p. 250.

49   David Hume, *Essays and Treatises on Several Subjects*, 2 vols (London, 1784), vol. 1, p. 396.

# Index

Abercrombie, Sir Ralph, 74
Aberdeen, 122
Adams, John, 89
Adams, Samuel, 90
Affleck, Captain Thomas, 28, 32
Aitkin, John, aka John the Painter, 2
Alms, Captain James, 26
Antigua, 81–2, 85, 95
Appledore, 13–14
Aubrey, Jack, 3

Baird, Captain Patrick, 31
Bailyn, Bernard, 100
Bamford, Samuel, 137–8
Barking, 40
Barnstable, 14
Baugh, Daniel, 5
Beaver, Captain Phillip, 116
Berkeley, Admiral George, 114–15
Biddeford, 14
Blundell, Henry, 72
Boston, Massachusetts, 68, 86–9
Bover, Captain John, 31
Bristol, 5, 7, 8, 14, 19, 25, 32, 41, 48, 52, 59–80, 112, 115
Brenton, Captain Jaheel, 57
Brighton, 26, 34
Broadfoot, Alexander, 20, 24, 61
Bull, Frederick, 1
Burke, Edmund, 77
Bury St. Edmunds, 50–1
Butler, Charles, 12, 130

Carmarthen, 46
Caroline of Brunswick, 104–5

Caldwell, John, 74
Caton, James, 77–8
Child, Captain Smith, 42, 72–3
Clinton, George, Governor of New York, 98
Clutton, 76
Cobbett, William, 115
Colley, Linda, 103, 105, 111, 118, 125
Collingwood, Admiral Cuthbert, Lord, 11–12
Colpoys, Admiral Sir John, 108
Cork, 42
Cruickshank, George, 105

Davers, Admiral Thomas, 83–4, 95
Deal, 30
Dennison, Thomas, 61
Despard, Colonel Edward, 116, 119
Dover, 32, 63
Dublin, 40
Duncan, Admiral Adam, 110, 121
Dunmore, John Murray, 4th Earl, 92
Dunning, John, 21, 77
Durbin, Sir John, 77

Eden, Sir Frederick, 3
Edinburgh, 11, 12, 31, 73
Equiano, Olaudah, 94
Eyemouth, 32

Falkland Islands, 2, 21, 22, 38, 46, 55, 74, 127
Fergusson, Captain John, 18–19
Fortescue, Captain John, 61–7
Foster, Michael, Sergeant at law, 19–21, 24, 61, 74, 79
Frankland, Admiral Sir Thomas, 94
Furet, François, 37

Gardner, Admiral Sir Alan, 108
Gaskell, Elizabeth, 129–31, 134
Gill, Conrad, 111
Gillray, James, 51
Glynn, John, 21
Gordon, Captain Thomas, 32, 52, 61–3, 75, 80
Graham, Sir James, 132–3
Graves, Captain Samuel, 61
Gravesend, 21, 23, 63, 82
Greenock, 23, 45, 46, 47, 57, 72, 106
Guernsey, 57–8

Hallifax, Sir Thomas, 24
Hamilton, Lady Emma, 119
Hamilton, Captain Thomas, 25, 75–6, 80
Hamilton, Sir William, 119
Hammon, Briton, 100
Hardy, Admiral Sir Charles, 90
Hawker, Captain Thomas, 76
Hebrides, 57
Hodgkin, Thomas, 132, 133
Hodgson, Ralph, 98
Holderness, Robert D'Arcy, 4th Earl, 135
Hood, Commodore Samuel, 89
Hosier, Admiral Francis, 83
Howe, Admiral Richard, Lord, 22, 108
Hull, 5, 7, 56, 122, 128
Hume, David, 138
Hunt, Leigh, 105
Huntington, Selina Shirley, Lady, 136
Hurry, William, 31, 34
Hutchinson, Captain Howard, 23
Hutchinson, J.R., 38
Hutchinson, Thomas, 88–9

impressment
    age impressed, 11–12
    definition, 3–4, 8–9, 20–1
    defence of, 12, 19–21
    domestic dislocations, 2–3, 10
    development of impress service, 7
    eligibility, 8–9, 11–12
    exemptions, 8, 21
    legal action against, 17–35
    proportion of recruits impressed, 4–6
    protections, 30–1, 33
    and Caribbean, 4, 83–6, 90–1, 95
    and debt, 32–3
    and hazing, 53, 106
    and Kingswood colliers, 75–6, 80
    and Levellers, 18
    and libertarianism, 18, 22
    and local government, 22–4
    and London opposition, 23–5, 28
    and Magna Carta, 18, 87, 107
    and maritime trades, 8–9, 40–1, 46
    and mobilization, 42–5
    and mutinies on tenders, 52–3, 68–9
    and North America, 86–90
    and paternalism, 34
    and privateers, 69–70, 85, 96–7
    and race, 14–15, 91–5
    and register, 19, 134
    and sea fencibles, 112–18
    and slavery, 14, 19, 82, 133
    and women, 1–3, 32, 41, 46, 47, 50–4, 64, 73–4, 112, 127–8, 131
    and vagrancy, 10–11, 33–4,
    and violence, 14, 17, 27, 46–53, 61–9, 72–3, 78–9, 127–8
Ipswich, 47

Jamaica, 83, 90, 91, 95, 97–8, 99
Jervis, Admiral Sir John, Earl St. Vincent, 121
Jones, Mary, 1–2

Keith, Admiral Sir George, 112
Kemp, Peter, 105
King's Lynn, 23, 28, 31
Kirke, Captain James, 24
Knowler, Captain Charles, 23
Knowles, Captain (later Commodore) Charles, 81–2, 85, 88–9, 93, 95, 97

Lefebvre, Georges, 37
Leith, 73, 122
Le Roy Ladurie, Emmanuel, 37
Lewis, Michael, 5

# INDEX

Liverpool, 5, 7, 8, 11, 31, 32, 42, 52, 55, 59–80, 106
Lloyd, Owen, 98
London, 1–3, 9–10, 17, 22–4, 27–8, 46, 48–9, 50, 54–6, 122, 136
Loudon, John Campbell, 4th Earl, 90
Louisbourg, 87
Lovett, William, 8

Matthew, Thomas, Governor of Antigua, 85, 95
McCulloch, J.R., 132
Merchant Venturers, Society of, 67, 76, 79
Meredith, Sir William, 1–2, 68
Montagu, Captain William, 81–2, 99
Montgomery, Hamilton, 17
Morgan, Philip D., 100
Mosquito Shore, 97–8, 100
Murray, Willliam, Lord Mansfield, 20, 21

Nagle, Jacob, 136–7
Napier, Captain Charles, 31, 32,
naval mutiny of 1797, 2, 15, 107–10, 124
Nelson, Admiral Horatio, Lord, 16, 93–4, 110, 116–17, 118–22
Newcastle-upon-Tyne, 2, 6, 7, 8, 11, 31, 33, 41, 72
New York, 90, 99–100
Nicol, John, 12, 120
Nootka Sound, 21, 52
Norris, Admiral Sir John, 30
North, Frederick, Lord, 39
Northey, Sir Edward, 86
Norwich, 46

Ogle, Sir Chaloner, 84–5
Oglethorpe, James 12

Paine, Thomas, 107, 109, 122
Parker, Sir Peter, 90, 92
Parker, Richard, 108, 122
Peddie, Captain John, 60
Perth, 33
Peterloo, 104, 126
Phillip, Admiral Hugh, 113–14

Pill, Somerset, 76–7, 79, 115
Pitt, William, the younger, 118
Poole, 29, 41, 56, 115
Poulden, Captain Richard, 128–9
Plymouth, 5, 7, 32, 107
Portsmouth, 7, 14
Prowse, Captain William, 78

Rawlinson, Henry, M.P., 69
Richmond, Charles Lennox, 3rd Duke, 4
Rodger, N.A.M., 4, 5, 13–14, 38
Rodney, Admiral George Brydges, 92, 93, 117
Robinson, William, aka Jack Nastyface, 12, 13
Rochester, 30
Rooke, George, JP, 26
Roscoe, William, 71
Rowley, Admiral William, 90
Rowlandson, Thomas, 94, 120

Sainsbury, Sir Thomas, 22
Sandwich, 30
Saumarez, Sir James, 58
Sawbridge, John, 25
Scott, Walter, 105
Seaford, 5
seamen
    coastal, 76, 79, 113, 115, 123, 137
    Greenland whalers, 7, 18–19, 30, 47–8, 55–6, 137
    mercantile, 6–7, 122–5
    numbers borne, 6, 40
    and blue jackets, 134
    and by-employments, 9
    and desertion, 84, 96
    and disease, 83
    and piracy, 97–9
Sedden, Samuel, 28
Shambrooke, James, 26
Sharp, Granville, 11, 21, 22
Shetland islands, 57–8
Shirley, Thomas, Governor of Massachusetts, 87–9
Shoreham, 40

Sidmouth, Henry Addington, Lord, 104, 122–4
Smollett, Tobias, 51–2, 83
Snell, Hannah, 41
Somersett, James, 19
Stono Rebellion, South Carolina, 101
Syliva's Lovers, 129–32

Tarleton, Clayton, 71–2
Thackeray, William Makepeace, 51
Thompson, Thomas Perronet, 129
Thurlow, Edward, Lord Chancellor, 22, 34–5
Tilly, Charles, 38
Townshend, Charles, 3rd Viscount, 136
Traflagar, 117, 120, 125
Trelawny, Edward, Governor of Jamaica, 84–5, 95, 97
Tubbs, John, 20
Tyne and Wear, 3, 7, 8, 24, 26, 31, 40, 41, 45, 52–4, 73, 104, 106, 117, 120, 123–4, 127

United Irishmen, 107, 109–10, 116
Urquhart, Thomas, 133

Vernon, Admiral Edward, 5, 82–3, 84, 93, 100–1

Wager, Sir Charles, 83
Walpole, Sir Robert, 19
Warren, Sir Peter, 85, 87
Waterloo, 103–5, 122
Wedderburn, Alexander, 21, 33
Wellington, Arthur Wellesley, Lord, 103–4
Whitby, 55–6, 106, 127–131
Whitehaven, 5, 42, 60
Wilkie, David, 103–4
Wilkes, John, 1
Worth, Captain James, 68–71

Yarmouth, 7, 23, 34, 114, 122
Young, Admiral James, 92